Naked Barbies,
Warrior Joes,
and Other Forms
of Visible Gender

Naked Barbies,

Warrior Joes,

and Other Forms

of Visible Gender

Jeannie Banks Thomas

University of Illinois Press

Urbana and Chicago

Library of Congress Cataloging-in-Publication Data
Thomas, Jeannie B.
Naked Barbies, warrior Joes, and other forms of visible
gender / Jeannie Banks Thomas.
p. cm.
Includes bibliographical references and index.
ISBN 0-252-02854-6 (cloth : alk. paper)
ISBN 0-252-07135-2 (pbk. : alk. paper)
1. Folklore—United States. 2. Material culture—United
States. 3. Popular culture—United States. 4. Barbie dolls.
5. G.I. Joe figures. 6. United States—Social life and cus-
toms. I. Title.
GR105.T46   2003
398'.0973—dc21   2002155080

For Rio,
who understands
the value of play

Contents

Acknowledgments

I am grateful to Utah State University for the sabbatical that enabled me to complete my research and begin writing this book. The Women and Gender Research Institute at USU provided crucial financial support that allowed me to present much of this research at academic conferences. The members of the International Society of Contemporary Legend Research, especially the Rowdy Grrlz and the San Antonio Tracks Crew, were particularly helpful in their responses to my presentations on this material. Diane Goldstein deserves acknowledgment for generously sharing her compassionate wisdom, and Carl Lindahl knew just when to supply me with conjunto music and beer. Jack Santino also earned my gratitude by providing many astute revision suggestions.

Kind colleagues in the Department of English and Folklore Program aided and abetted my research on Barbie, and my sincere thanks goes to them. Colleagues Melody Graulich, Jan Roush, Barre Toelken, and Jennifer Drake in Utah and Indiana merit thanks for reading various sections. Evelyn Funda demonstrated impressive dedication in her quest to keep me supplied with advertisements for yard geese clothing. Thanks also to Polly Stewart, Sharon Sherman, and Jan and Judy Brunvand, who kept the Barbie articles, funny photographs, and even posters coming.

Nancy Banks and Brian McConnell proved to be true cemetery buddies; I am grateful for their delightful and witty company during my European visits. I am especially indebted to Nancy for her indispensable French translations. Marc Jerilo provided fascinating, behind-the-scenes information and adventure at Père Lachaise. I thank Marty Davis at Crown Hill Cemetery in Indianapolis for her good-humored assistance, which was above and beyond the call of duty. Janferie Stone made material from the University of

California–Berkeley Folklore Archives more accessible to me. Marge Eggers did not know me but graciously helped me find Paco anyway, and a big thanks to Paco for the great "Rancho Heartbreak" t-shirt, which I wear with pride. I am grateful to all those, such as Paco, who kindly consented to interviews for this book. Thanks as well to Chris for his interest in the subject. Finally, my students' stories about cemetery statues, yard art, and Barbies inspired this book. I thank them for helping start me on what proved to be a fascinating journey. I hope this book returns something of that favor.

My ever-patient parents John and Dorothy were accommodating of my strange research interests, as always. Winnie Barnhart gave me the bounty of her garden, her yard art, and her love. Finally, heartfelt thanks to Madison and Rio, who were especially enthusiastic.

Naked Barbies,
Warrior Joes,
and Other Forms
of Visible Gender

Introduction: Cemetery Statues, Yard Art, and Barbies: Making Sense of Pervasive and Sculptural Gendered Forms

This book was born out of the marriage of story and form, a partnership I work to maintain throughout its pages. My attention was first drawn to everyday, gendered sculptural forms by the stories that my undergraduate folklore students told about them when we discussed children's folklore, yard art, and legends. Their narratives included humorous recollections of play with Barbie dolls, accounts of dressed concrete geese in front yards, and stories about the supposed supernatural activities of cemetery statues.[1]

Initially, I made no connection among these types of narratives, but I enjoyed them. Over time, however, I began to notice that they emerged frequently in class discussions, and they generated a high level of interest and audience response. Then I realized that these different but equally engaging accounts had something significant in common: They all focused on the most visible, gendered sculptural forms on the American "culturescape," both inside and outside the home.[2]

As I began comparing the narratives it became apparent that both the stories and the objects to which they referred are instructive concerning views of gender in contemporary America. It was also clear that little had been written concerning either the gendered nature of these common forms or the folklore about them. As I researched the history of these figures, documented the folklore about them, and identified the gender patterns associated with them, it became evident that the forms are pervasive enough to constitute a major way for Americans to construct and see gender in everyday life.

These objects appeared repeatedly in the stories I was hearing because they are the most noticeable, sculptural gendered forms in the everyday world. This book, then, treats the three most visible types of forms and their related folklore. Specifically, each chapter explores a kind of gendered material culture, including:

—cemetery statuary and gravemarker images of females
     and males;
—yard art figures of females and males;
—and Barbie and G.I. Joe dolls.

The fact that the material culture is the focus of a significant amount of folklore indicates that these forms are meaningful enough so people not only register them visually but also talk about them. I analyze this talk, this folklore, because it helps in the process of understanding the ways in which gendered material culture is viewed and interpreted.

Each chapter could stand on its own in interpreting the specific form that is its emphasis. I consider the three types of gendered figures in relation to each other not only because they share some commonalities but also because, together, they elucidate a larger picture of culture than each is capable of doing alone. When conjoined, they reveal how Americans have viewed and created gendered forms in everyday life since the early nineteenth century. Juxtaposing the forms illuminates an overarching and historically consistent way of constructing gender in American culture that remains influential to this day.

Some of the objects I discuss emerge from the folk level of culture. By "folk level" I mean that part of culture that is informally learned—that which is traditional, customary, or learned in nonformal and noninstitutional settings.[3] Not all the items in this book are folk forms. Some, such as

Barbie and G.I. Joe, are mass-produced. Others, such as the cemetery statuary, are rooted in elite culture. My approach is that of a folklorist looking at how people use, personalize, "folklorize," and make meaningful a range of forms, including mass-produced ones. Not only is this work unique in its focus on culturally prominent, gendered, three-dimensional types of material culture, but it also adds to the literature concerning folklore and material culture by examining mass-produced material culture in relation to the folk narratives and folk behaviors it generates.

In researching this book I worked with a variety of cultural forms and visited numerous cemeteries in both North America and Europe. The research led me to an elderly Japanese American man's sculpture garden and, on a hot summer's day, propelled me down a barbwire fence laced with shoes. Through the research I also managed an invitation from an eight-year-old Hispanic girl to sit on the floor of her room and talk about and play with some of her approximately sixty Barbies, most of them naked. We were not only outnumbered but also dwarfed by their big hair and little plastic accessories.

To sum it up by borrowing a phrase from James Deetz's classic work *In Small Things Forgotten,* "[These are] Americans engaged in commonplace activities; all in their fashion were communicating with us" (1996, 4). Deetz's presentation of several different case studies of various types of material culture was influential in structuring this book around three discrete but related kinds of material culture. His groundbreaking work relies primarily on form and written documents to discern meaning, which allows him "to say something about the past that could not have been said using only one set of data" (1996, 32). My study emphasizes contemporary objects that are gendered, a focus that allows me to add current folklore to the mix in order to help decipher the meanings communicated through these images.

The title of this book refers specifically to Barbie (figure 1) and G.I. Joe. The title also works, however, as a metaphor for two cultural and historical patterns that all three of the studies reveal. First, the bodies of culturally visible female figures are often emphasized or sexualized through nudity or partial nudity, and, second, the depictions of male bodies are not only clothed but also armored in the trappings of action and aggression. Each chapter discusses how the figures embody these two cultural currents.

Each of the following chapters includes a section addressing the patterns revealed through form. Then the objects are placed in a larger historical context, and the antecedents of the gendered image and the cultural attitudes it reflects are considered. Finally, each chapter concludes with an analysis of the form in relation to the folklore and folk customs it prompts.

Figure 1. Drawer of naked Barbies belonging to eight-year-old girl.

Chapter 1 addresses the gendered imagery found in the statuary and gravemarkers of cemeteries. Statues of females are more eroticized than those of males, which are more likely to be individualized. I discuss why male sexuality is downplayed to the point where most images show males to be emasculated and what that means in light of verbal lore that focuses on male genitalia.

Most of the statues I consider are from the nineteenth century or influenced by art trends of that time. Several scholars have traced the increasing historical emphasis on individualism in gravemarker imagery, but it does not reflect an increase of individualism in general. Instead, it is a selective, gender-differentiated individualism in which men are presented as individuals (with careers and hobbies) and women are used as beautiful but stock symbols. Despite the social and political advances of women in the latter half of the twentieth century, their images on gravemarkers are still much less likely to be individualized than are men's. A nineteenth-century trend thus continued throughout the entire twentieth century.

Particularly apparent in both legends and the forms themselves is the manner in which statues of women (whether angels, Virgin Marys, or eroticized mourners) are consistently used to gender intimacy as feminine. I point to some of the problems that can occur when the female is primarily associated with intimacy. Finally, I describe the influence of elite art traditions, paying particular attention to two nineteenth-century conventions: the use of the female nude to represent ideal beauty and the construction of what gender scholar Michael Kimmel calls the "self-made man."

Chapter 2 analyzes gender and yard art. In the first section, I identify the common patterns in the yard art that I saw and argue that gender is a significant component in each category, even though it need not be. Yard art presents traditional, conservative, and stereotypical male and female roles that are, to some extent, based in fine-art traditions. I also discuss why the ethnic yard art statuary I saw was more likely to be of males than females.

In the second section of the chapter, I trace the evolution of lawns and the types of images used on lawns to show how this particular history has influenced yard art. Despite the seemingly plastic newness of much contemporary yard decoration, many motifs are hundreds of years old. Much yard art could be argued to be in poor taste, but some pieces of elite art—such as the statuary artists of the Renaissance era created for the wealthy—are evidence of taste that is equally poor (or worse). Some scholars have seen America's lawns as reflective of democratic values, an assertion I question in light of the history of lawns.

In the final section of chapter 2, I employ folklorist Jack Santino's definition of assemblage to discuss folk behaviors associated with yard art. Santino explains that an assemblage is a type of public display, a genre of sculpture done with found objects (1992a, 158). Homeowners create yard assemblages out of stock and stereotypical yard statuary, which are idiosyncratic expressions of their views and interests. I include excerpts from several interviews with yard artists, including an elderly white woman known for her holiday assemblages, two women who sew and sell gendered costumes for concrete and plastic lawn geese, the owner of a garden gnome, a Japanese American who creates his own yard sculpture, women who have placed statues of the Virgin Mary in their yards, a female sculptor who created functional yard decor, a cowboy who used his mailbox art to solve a vandalism problem, and a man and a woman whose large-scale "fence of shoes" recalls both folk traditions and fine-art ones such as that exemplified by Christo. I also discuss the customs associated with yard art. Pranks and theft involving lawn statuary are considered, for example, with a particular focus on the activities of France's Gnome Liberation Front.

In relation to the words and creations of these yard artists and the actions (such as gnome theft) of those who view yard art, I argue that yard art is a material manifestation of social relationships. It clears a space for children in an adult world and creates a physical place for the playful life of the mind. In addition, it allows for caretaking and nurturing behaviors ("comfort art") and can both reinforce and deviate slightly from gendered norms. In a consideration of the issues of taste and class, all art should be studied not only as form and product but also as a behavioral process.

Chapter 3 employs the same attention to pattern, history, and folklore to analyze the uses and meanings of the Barbie doll and some of her consorts, such as Ken and G.I. Joe. The section addressing the patterns exemplified by Barbie's form discusses the connections between Barbie, Ken, and fine-art nudes. Barbie's adult female body makes her appear as a sort of Everywoman, and because most women's bodies do not look like Barbie's, that quality often generates controversy. Currently, Barbie's biggest public relations problem is her overly perfect physique. Balancing that is her greatest strength—the idiosyncratic uses people make of her, which are apparent from paying attention to the folk level of culture. Like cemetery statuary and yard art, Barbie has stock and stereotypical characteristics. She is, however, the most individualized of the female forms examined in this book. The folklore I analyze indicates that she is more creatively presented and played with, in general, than her male counterparts, Ken and G.I. Joe. Of the three types of material culture under discussion, Barbie also presents the least conservative rendering of gender. Paradoxically, she generates the most controversy, in part because of her gender and greater cultural visibility.

When Barbie is considered in historical context, it is apparent that many controversies that surround her are neither new nor particular to her. Like cemetery statuary and yard art, doll production is grounded in the nineteenth century. Barbie is influential as a girls' toy and has shaped boys' toys as well, although she is not usually recognized for doing so. In the second half of the twentieth century Barbie inspired the creation of dolls, such as G.I. Joe, for boys.

As attention to Barbie folklore (personal experience narratives about her) and folk behaviors (play) demonstrates, if media advertising invades homes and shapes consumers by pushing products such as Barbie, consumers respond by reshaping mass-produced goods—again like Barbie. In addition, I analyze the electronic folklore ("e-lore") that circulates about Barbie. Play narratives from the world of childhood and parodic e-lore about Barbie both reveal that adult "cyber-lore," even though it often critiques Barbie's form, is parallel to much children's play with Barbie. Frequently, adults' electronic wordplay and children's play behaviors place Barbie into what both groups deem "real-life" situations.

In the last section of the chapter, and in the final chapter of the book, I consider the manner in which electronic folklore addresses Barbie's "body beautiful" but ignores G.I. Joe's "body violent." All of these narratives and play behaviors indicate the enduring attraction of the human body as a symbolic field. They also indicate the existence of an ongoing need to manipulate and play with this form in order to make sense of gender or revise gendered lives.

The final chapter of this book brings together all the forms, and their folklore and histories, for a comparative and cumulative discussion of meanings generated by these types of culturally visible, gendered images. Although I initially did not relate the three forms to each other, some individuals did through assemblages and the venues in which they placed them. For example, Barbies as well as yard statuary—even pink flamingos—are left on graves (figure 2). People do so because they want a concrete manifestation of their relationship with the deceased. Material culture also has aesthetic appeal and the capacity to communicate information, such as personal interests or hobbies, about an individual.

The same stock roles for figures of both males and females are apparent in all types of spaces I studied, whether public (e.g., cemeteries) or private (e.g., homes). Beautiful, classically attired figures of women appear publicly and semipublicly, for example, as both cemetery statuary and yard art (figues 3, 4). In homes, the same form materializes as Greek Goddess Barbie (figure 5). In a parallel fashion, the male as warrior is found in cemetery statuary, children's action figures, and yard art (figures 6, 7, 8). Attention to these objects, along with their placement and use, reveals commonalities and ubiquity. When examined as a group, the three types of gendered material indicate that the most pervasive gendered and sculptural figures are presented in a fashion approximately two hundred years behind current discourse on gender and equality.

Overall, this book is intended to illuminate the meanings of these types of gendered material culture and the folklore that accompanies them. It also provides a venue for the voices of those who create, use, or re-create the forms and makes histories that have shaped such images more apparent. All of that is significant because these products of history and culture have the potential to inform and influence views of gender on an everyday basis.

Figure 2. Yard art flamingo on gravemarker, Salt Lake City, Utah.

Figure 3. Classical-style woman in cemetery, Lexington, Kentucky.

Figure 4. Classical-style woman in yard art, Pigeon Forge, Tennessee.

Figure 5. Classical-style Barbie.

Figure 6. Soldier in cemetery, Cincinnati, Ohio.

Figure 7. Soldier doll.

Figure 8. Soldier in yard art near Bloomington, Indiana.

1

Cemetery Statues: Vengeful Virgins, Naked Mourners, and Dead White Guys

Just as by cutting away, O Lady, one extracts
from the hard alpine stone
a living figure which alone
grows the more, the more the stone diminishes.
—Michelangelo, trans. Alexander

If I traveled through hot, liquid-thick midwestern summer air, bumped down gravel or dirt roads, and passed endless acres of still, tasseled cornstalks, I would find *them,* my Indiana college students told me. *They* were sites where the spirits of the past would not relinquish the world of the present. And, true enough, I did not have to look far to locate legendary landscapes that held impressions of the supernatural. I journeyed upon many a poorly maintained and marked road that ran rhythmically up and down the green Indiana hills. I passed lake after lake created by mining—"stripper pits, good for swimming," the students told me. I drove through the dappled light created by acres of shade from hardwood trees. I trekked the dark woods along the White River and scrambled up dirt embankments in order to find a mysterious train tunnel haunted by strange lights and the apparition of a man looking for his head. In the mud and rain I traversed gravel roads in night's deepest blackness to find a viaduct, where, if I stood in front of my car lights, I would see my shadow along with that of an extra being—a demonic figure who, drawn by my car lights and my desire as a "legend-tripper" to see and believe, would join me at the site.

There were many other places where the preternatural was supposed to intersect with the earthly. On the front porch of a yellow house just across the state line was a well-executed abstract sculpture that included an animal skull, a sure sign of Satanists according to adolescent oral tradition. Not far from the Satanists' house was the "Haunted Breakfast House," a deserted home where, any time of day or night, the kitchen table was set and a paranormal breakfast smell was evident: eggs and bacon frying even though none were ever to be found in the house. Or, if all that did not pique my interest, I could visit the family farm of one of my blue-eyed, blonde students and experience a rare haunting of the porcine kind. The spirit of a prized pig was often felt in one of their barns.

Folklorist Bill Ellis argues that going to a location associated with a legend in the hope of experiencing or participating in that legend descends from long-practiced European traditions of visiting sacred sites and holy wells (1996, 440). The journeys of contemporary teenagers are but a recent manifestation of a venerable folk practice. Legend-tripping, as folklorists call it, and the narratives that detail experiences on the trip are common among today's teenagers, so I was not surprised when, one day in my folklore class, Tamar, a slight, intelligent woman in her twenties, narrated a legend and a subsequent legend trip.

Forty-plus college students were sitting in that humid classroom when she told her story. As Tamar built her narrative the students turned toward her. Noticeably, they stopped staring out the window, ceased looking through the open door at the person at the drinking fountain, and rallied enough from their Ballyhoo Bar hangovers to listen carefully:

Okay, the statue is located in a cemetery on Dover Hill Road in Dover Hill [Indiana]. I had originally heard that it was a statue of the Virgin Mary, and she had her hands outstretched, and you could go and put a quarter in her hand, and she would—if she took the quarter, then you were going to die or something bad was going to happen to you. Later I heard you could also put the quarter on the stone that she was sitting on. And that instead of taking the quarter, she might either cry or her eyes might glow and that her eyes were made of jewels . . . but that the church had painted her eyes over because of all the legends, and everybody coming out there and looking at her; they painted her eyes. Well . . . I have gone to see her recently, and her hands aren't outstretched, so I don't know how you would put a quarter in her hand, that would be kinda hard, but you'd have to wedge it I guess. . . . I don't even know if it's the Virgin Mary; it is a young lady, and she's like kneeling down, but she's been pushed off of the original headstone that she was sitting on . . . so she sits like beside of the headstone now. . . . Her eyes have been painted but they're, the paint is peeling off, and you can see that it's just reg—she doesn't have any stones or jewels for eyes; it's just the statue with the peeling paint. . . . But I do know that my husband, one of his best friends, his brother was with a group of friends, and he did this—touched the statue and the statue supposedly cried, and within a few weeks, he did die in the, the lake in, in Martin County where this is at. . . . He drowned.

This is about where she ended the legend, but I asked if perhaps there were nonsupernatural explanations for his death. "Could he, perhaps," I wondered, "have been drinking?"

"Oh, yes," she replied, "he was drunk when he drowned."

In a later interview, when I had asked Tamar to repeat for the tape recorder the legend she had told in class, she added, "He . . . was with a bunch of friends and he was swimming and he was intoxicated, and they think that that had a lot to do with the reason why he couldn't continue. But apparently he just got tired, and he just drowned."

> Jeannie: Uh huh [yes]. So after that happened, did they start linking him with the statue? Did that happen?
>
> Tamar: Yes, that's what . . . and all his friends were like, "Oh, this happened and so—." But the legend was before his death, but this more or less confirmed it. . . . My husband and I were with a group of friends after—we took a picture of the statue . . . and we told them what we had done that day and everything. And we told them about how it had been pushed off 'cause this was a recent thing—where it, where it has been vandalized, and they said, "Oh, well just look at the obituaries, and you'll see who it was that . . . pushed her off."

One of the things that intrigued me about Tamar's story was the manner in which she, a bright and analytical young woman who was a good student, ignored an earthly causation (drunkenness) in favor of a supernatural one (the preternatural powers of the statue) when she told the legend. Also of interest was the way she carried the class along with her into the realm of the supernatural. I enjoyed the imagery in the legend and began to speculate about why the Virgin required quarters. "Did she need the money in order to do her laundry at a coin-operated laundromat? Was she craving sweets or sodas from a vending machine? What?" When I voiced

these questions to the class we returned to reality, laughing but still respect-
ing the power of Tamar's story.

Tamar's narrative reminded me of a legend told nearly a year earlier by
two other students, Dan and Zach. Although different from Tamar's, it
shared her focus on a cemetery statue with supernatural abilities. According to Dan's brief account, "In the Vermilion Cemetery [in Vermilion
County, Illinois] is a large statue of an angel with outstretched arms. Legend has it that if a person would happen to fall asleep, for some crazy reason, in the arms of the angel, when you wake your shoes will be off. Just like
people being buried . . . they don't put shoes on them." Zach had heard the
same legend, which he collected from a friend: "There's this angel in that
cemetery, you know, by Vermilion [Illinois]. They say that if you sit in its
arms at midnight, that it will take your soul away. That's it; I don't know
what that does to you."

Just as my students in the Midwest had heard and told these types of
cemetery legends, so, too, had my students in the West. One of the most
popular legends told by my Utah students centered on a cemetery statue
known locally as the weeping woman (figure 9).[1] As of the spring of 2000,
I had located thirty-six versions of the weeping woman legend in the Fife
Folklore Archives at Utah State University in Logan. Representative versions include the following:

Version One: The story goes like this. . . . There once was a lady who had 4 boys[;]
all of these boys were trouble makers. . . . The mother was stricken with a[n] ill-
ness and died soon after. She was buried in the Logan[, Utah,] cemetery and a
weeping lady resembling her was place[d] on the grave stone to remind the boys
[of] all the hell they put their mother through.

It is said that if you go to the cemetery at night and remind her of her boys[,]
she weeps with sadness. There are quite a number of people who will swear on it.

Version Two: In [the] Logan Cemetery[,] there is a stone statue of a lady wearing a
shawl. On a dark night, when the moon is full, if you stand before the statue and
tell it what a lousy mother it was, the statue will cry.

Version Three: There once was a lady who lived in Logan. She was the mother of
seven children. As her husband said she was always sad and weeping over children; she gave them everything but life. She loved her seven children so much
that she took their lives to save them from the evil of the world.

She killed each one in a different way. When she died her husband bought her
a gravestone to match her self-image. It is the size of the woman herself. The statue
is weeping so it will remind him of the way his wife was. The story lives on, all you
need to do is go to the Logan cemetery at 12:00 at night, and if you touch under
her left eye, you can feel the tears from her eye.

Figure 9. Weeping woman statue, Logan, Utah.

As I listened to and researched legends about cemetery statues I noticed that they focused more on statues of females than males. The few legends I heard about statues of males often centered on soldiers.[2] For example, I heard some versions of the following legend, which I also found in the Fife Folklore Archives: "It is believed that if any daring and brave persons would drive to the Ogden City Cemetary [*sic*] and follow the road to a statue of a soldier [figure 10] and drive around the statue three times at midnight, the statue would come to life. Those who have tried tell of the soldier getting into their car, scratching and clawing at their faces, and deliberately trying to harm or kill them."

Figure 10. Soldier statue in cemetery, Ogden, Utah.

In order to better understand these cemetery legends, I began looking at the material culture associated with them. I traveled to numerous cemeteries and searched for patterns in statuary of males and females. Ultimately, this interest took me to Europe in search of statues that were the predecessors of the American subjects of legends. As I walked through cemeteries, certain patterns became obvious, and other, more unexpected, patterns emerged, all of which provided entrée into understanding worldview, gender, and cultural change.[3]

Pattern and Gender in Cemetery Statues

I found material reason in cemeteries for the prevalence of female protagonists in legends. The legends mirror what is most noticeable in a cemetery: statues of women. Not only are they fairly common but they are also, significantly, often more visible and dramatic than the markers around them. Statues of women are more noteworthy than those of males because the women are frequently portrayed as young, Anglo, beautiful, erotic, and even naked (figure 11). Cemetery statues of males are rendered in a different fashion. Garbed in business suits, they are not beautiful, naked, sensual, or eye-catching (figure 12). Many are crafted and placed to indicate the prestige of the person whose grave they mark. Because they are not dramatic, however, and are considerably less sexy than statues of women, they are less memorable and receive less attention.

The sensual statues of females do not usually represent women buried at the gravesites but rather symbolize mourning in general. They often mark the grave of a man or a family, and, as surrogate mourners, they indicate

Figure 11. Nude female figure, Père Lachaise, Paris.

Figure 12. Male statue, Crown Hill Cemetery, Indianapolis, Indiana.

the common historical place of women as key figures in the grieving process. That role was evident as early as approximately 740 B.C.E. in Greek culture. Christine Havelock (1982, 50–51) reports that women in antiquity primarily performed laments for the dead and could be hired as mourners.

If the statues do not show a woman as a beautiful, young, and often sexualized surrogate mourner or angel, they portray an idealized maternal mourner such as Mary. The statue that is the locus of the weeping woman legends is a surrogate mourner. More visually arresting than statues of males, statues of females are the subjects of a majority of the cemetery legends I heard. The oral tradition has unintentionally documented a gendered pattern found in the material culture of the cemetery.

Just as I did with statues of females, I started going to cemeteries specifically to examine statues of males and see what patterns might emerge. They are commonly portraits of the actual man buried at the site, so they are individualized and specific; they may also reference an occupation or a hobby. Their subjects are more likely to be old, staid, Anglo, and clothed rather than young, erotic, and semi-nude. Soldiers like the one in the Ogden, Utah, legend are often the subjects of memorializing statues. Although men's gravesites are decorated with sexualized renderings of women, a parallel pattern does not exist for women's. Images of handsome, sensuous, nude, or partially nude men posed in fetching, prostrate, arresting, and vulnerable postures are not erected to mark women's graves.

Yet another intriguing but not immediately obvious pattern in statuary depicting males became apparent in February 1998 when I was visiting cemeteries in the area of Bloomington, Indiana, with colleagues Jennifer Drake, Nan McEntire, Katie Enders, and Rosetta Haynes; novelist Helena Maria Viramontes; and Warren Roberts, the renowned material culture scholar. I owe a debt of gratitude to this group for helping me notice what I would eventually discern as a striking motif in the way males are depicted in cemetery statues. Warren inadvertently drew my attention to the pattern by taking me to visit a statue of the cartoon hero Joe Palooka that stands in the tiny town of Oolitic, Indiana (figure 13). Helena tactfully but humorously remarked that she felt rather sorry for Joe because the sculptor had stripped him of masculinity, a reference to a significant lack of detail below Joe's belt. Joe apparently had no genitals.

Since that February day I have examined the crotches of statues of males in cemeteries across the United States and abroad and found little of note, literally. Of course, a few exceptions do exist. I photographed one twentieth-century male nude statue that marks a grave in Louisville, Kentucky, and in Cincinnati, Ohio, I noticed a statue's faint nod to physical accuracy in the form of a testicular bulge. I also visited one of the most infamous cemetery renderings of male genitalia, the monument at Oscar Wilde's grave in Père Lachaise Cemetery in Paris, France (figure 14). As Judi Culbertson and Tom Randall explain,

In death, as in life, Oscar Wilde's privates were a cause for public concern. . . . It took Jacob Epstein three years to sculpt his monument, which represents the poet as a winged messenger, done in an Egyptian art deco style. When Epstein arrived to put the finishing touches on the statue, he found it shrouded and guarded by a gendarme; the cemetery conservateur had found it "indecent" and had it banned. Officials refused to bow to public intellectual pressure until an acceptable alternation was made—a plaque serving as a fig leaf. The tomb was unveiled in 1914, but by 1922 students in nocturnal raids, had hacked away the fig leaf as well as a substantial portion of what lay beneath. (A richer story is that two Englishwomen, offended at Wilde's being publicly portrayed as so well-endowed, committed the emasculation themselves. The conservateur, after finding the parts at the monument's base, is supposed to have used them as paperweights.) (1986, 79–81)

Figure 13. Joe Palooka statue, Oolitic, Indiana.

Figure 14. Oscar Wilde's grave, Père Lachaise, Paris.

Given the much-heralded sexual liberalism of France and that nation's leading role in neoclassical sculpture (Smith 1996, 103–4), I expected to see many more eroticized male statues than just Oscar Wilde's and its notorious genitals. Michel Dansel calls Père Lachaise "a bastion of roguery, humor, and sexuality" and "the largest, most historical, most religious, most romantic, most airy, most bizarre, and most erotic of promenades which overlook Paris" (quoted in Ragon 1983, 97). In many ways, however, the overall depiction of men in Père Lachaise is comparable to what I saw in the United States and Great Britain. The more sexualized statues of females are obviously the artistic rule, even in libertine Père Lachaise.

The gendered practices manifested in cemetery statuary include the use of the eroticized female body as a symbol of mourning and only rarely as an actual individual. Like statues of females, statues of males can be symbolic (those of soldiers, for example, serve as memorials), but they also frequently depict a specific individual. Women are more likely to be presented as symbols, and men are more likely to be individuals. Moreover, women are more often rendered in a sexualized fashion than are men.

The Cemetery and Its Images in Historical Context

The nineteenth-century gendered monuments that are the stuff of contemporary legends reflect larger cultural patterns. Because nineteenth-century statues emerged from Western Europe and its customs, I will focus on that region, although a chronology of gravemarkers should begin with Greece and Rome, the civilizations that influenced European art.

Citizens of both ancient Greece and Rome initially buried their dead in their homes and cities. Eventually, however, they separated the dead from the living (Sloane 1991, 17). Early Christians, who retained the same taboos against burying the dead among the living, used areas outside towns (Ariès 1981, 30). Romans, Jews, and Christians also used abandoned quarries, catacombs, for burial places (Ragon 1983, 59). Persecution forced early Christians to mingle with the dead; their first churches were in the catacombs. In the young Christian church, a community of both the living and the dead was formed, a practice that became more pronounced in the church's later history when the dead were customarily interred in churches (Ragon 1983, 59). By the late sixth century, new church canons allowed bishops, abbots, priests, and chosen lay members to be buried in churchyards—and then in churches. The custom was due primarily to the church's growing emphasis on the Resurrection and the fact that some Christians equated proper burial with salvation (Ariès 1981, 31; Sloane 1991, 17).

The appeal of burial inside a church included social distinction, protection for the corpse, and the spiritual benefits of closeness to altars, relics, and images of saints. Intramural burial grew during the later Middle Ages, but a great majority of people, especially children and poorer adults, were still buried in churchyards (Houlbrooke 1998, 331). A significant attraction of being interred in either a church or a churchyard was the fact that the living came in contact with the gravemarker, and the deceased's chances of having intercessory masses said increased. After the Reformation, which repudiated purgatory and masses said for those in purgatory, the need for burial inside a church was no longer so great (Houlbrooke 1998, 333–34).

A churchyard burial ground was also a place of trade and social interaction. The custom developed from the notion that it was a refuge: "People became accustomed to meeting within this asylum, as had the Romans in the Forum or the Mediterraneans on the Plaza Major or the Corso, in order to carry on business, to dance and gamble, or simply for the pleasure of being together. . . . Within the Cemetery of the Innocents [in Paris] public scribes offered their services" (Ariès 1981, 23).

Until the nineteenth century the situation was somewhat similar in America. Churchyards and graveyards were used for markets, fairs, meetings, walks, and the pasturing of animals (Sloane 1991, 20). Churchyard burial, however, was not as dominant in America as it was in Europe. The earliest American burials were in unorganized, isolated graves. Later, family graveyards, churchyard plots, and potters' fields came into wider use (Sloane 1991, 13).

In Europe around the fourteenth century it became common to dig up bones in older graves and make room for new graves. The places where the "clean bones" were stored were known as charnels, and separate buildings or sometimes vaults under a church were set aside for bone storage (Houlbrooke 1998, 332). The charnel houses at the Cemetery of the Innocents hosted a variety of commerce, including "haberdashers, linen-sellers, fruit-sellers, vendors of cookies, macaroons, and gingerbread" (Cerf and Babinet 1994, 23).

Some cemeteries became hazardous because they were overcrowded. The Cemetery of the Innocents, a burial ground since at least 1168, is a famous example of that problem: "In 1780 Parisians living in the apartment buildings next to the ancient and venerable *Cimetière des Innocents* were shocked by a rumbling in their basements. Soon many were overwhelmed by the stench rising from below, and several became seriously ill from mephitic gas. . . . The overcrowded graveyard had broken down the basement walls and sent over two thousand partially decomposed bodies into the basements" (Sloane 1991, 28).

Ultimately, the disaster led to the establishment of the Parisian Catacombs (Ragon 1981, 61). From 1785 to 1871 eleven or twelve centuries of the dead buried in the Innocents and other churchyards in Paris were relocated to the abandoned quarries that ran underneath the city, which had provided the stone for many buildings in Paris (Ragon 1981, 61). The bones were often sorted by type and placed in a kind of folk art macabre. Skulls were arranged in cornices or crosses, for example. Bones, crossed tibias, and skulls were piled six-and-one-half feet high and were sometimes a hundred feet across (Ragon 1981, 64). The Catacombs have been visited by the living since 1800. Visitors have included those who came to pray for the dead, guests attending wild parties given by the Comte d'Artois in 1787, Nazis, members of the Resistance during World War II, tourists, and contemporary "catophiles" who visit even the forbidden and dangerous parts of the Catacombs because of fascination with the place (McManners 1981, 317).

Both churchyard pits and the Catacombs reflect cultural comfort with a communal, anonymous burial, even one in which bodies did not remain intact. Such interments did not afford much differentiation based on gender. The average observer cannot discern the gender of the original owners of the bones in the Catacombs. Moreover, the Catacombs' decorative imagery, folk art macabre, is based in abstract designs or religious symbols, not in artistic representations of the human form—which became important in later centuries when the bones of the dead ceased to be displayed publicly. By the nineteenth century, many Europeans became more uncomfortable with the kind of anonymity and collectivity found in the Catacombs. A transformation in attitudes toward the dead occurred, as did a corresponding change in burial customs. The harbinger of that shift was France's Père Lachaise Cemetery, which was established in 1804.

During the Revolutionary era, cemeteries were viewed as harbors for disease, the "superstitions" of Christianity, and the privileges of wealth (Kselman 1993, 166). After the Revolution and the Terror, graveyards were still a source of public health concerns, but negative attitudes toward Christianity and its "superstitions" began to decline (Kselman 1993, 167). In response to public health worries, reformers called for cemeteries to be situated outside cities so city-dwellers would be more protected from noxious cemetery odors, known as miasmas, then believed to carry death and disease.

In this period the macabre imagery that had appeared on gravemarkers since the medieval period, especially the skeletons of the Baroque era, was rejected (Kselman 1993, 168). In addition, the era literally transfigured and more overtly gendered the body as it was revealed in cemeteries. The visions of the body (the actual skeletons themselves or the artistic images of them on gravemarkers) were transformed. They ceased to communicate the material realities of death and instead were artistically encased in flesh that conveyed individual status or idealized and symbolic notions of death, mourning, and the afterlife. Gender became a critical element of design in this romanticized process.

The historical change in the presentation of bodies in cemeteries is exemplified by contrasting the treatment of the remains of two French artists, both buried in Paris: Rabelais and Chopin. The bones of the French writer were mixed in with the bones of others in a genderless, anonymous mass grave, and the general public could view many of these skeletal remains (figure 15). Chopin's bones, however, were hidden from public view in a conspicuous burial site marked by the statue of a beautiful but anonymous grieving woman: a surrogate mourner (figure 16). Rabelais died in the sixteenth century, and his remains ended up in the Catacombs. Chopin, who died in the nineteenth century, was buried in Père Lachaise Cemetery.

During the 1800s reformers wanted cemetery visitors to ponder "heroic deeds and natural sublimity" instead of the literal remains of the dead (Kselman 1993, 168). By the end of the century, English landscape design was incorporated and proffered a view of nature as a regenerative force. The idea took material form in cemeteries such as Père Lachaise, which was the first "rural cemetery." In 1804 the Decree of 23 Prairial (named after the date of its proclamation, according to the Revolutionary calendar) aided in the establishment of Père Lachaise by prohibiting burial in churches and

Figure 15. Skeletal remains interred in the Catacombs, Paris.

Figure 16. Surrogate mourner marking Chopin's grave, Père Lachaise, Paris.

towns.[4] The decree held that bodies must be juxtaposed and not superimposed. As a result, private graves became the rule instead of being reserved for those who could afford them. Economics later brought back common graves for the poor, but in the mass graves of this later era bodies were separated from each other through the use of coffins. Gone were the days of winding sheets (Ariès 1981, 516).

Père Lachaise eventually became renowned for its remarkable monuments and for some of the customs that took place at the gravesites of its more famous inhabitants. It also houses what is argued to be the largest collection of nineteenth-century statuary in the world in addition to twelve thousand trees and three to four hundred cats (Robinson 1996, n. p.; Ragon 1981, 97). During the nineteenth and twentieth centuries it continued to attract the famous for burial—ranging from Marcel Proust to Jim Morrison. Like many other graves in Père Lachaise, Proust's, Chopin's, and Morrison's generate folklore and folk behavior, the most obvious of which is a stream of those on folk pilgrimages to leave flowers or mementos—which in Morrison's case tend toward love notes, hotel keys, wine bottles, and cigarette packs. Legend has it that lovers leave letters for each other at Chopin's grave (Ragon 1981, 101).

On a July 2000 visit to Morrison's grave I talked to a police officer stationed there, she told me, to cut down on vandalism and graffiti. The site is much cleaner than it used to be, but there is still a great deal of Jim-related graffiti on other graves in the cemetery. Speculative folklore also persists about whether Morrison is actually buried at the site. Such folklore in combination with the large number of notables buried there has made Père Lachaise a major tourist draw.

Despite the fact that it represents the move away from anonymous mass burial, Père Lachaise also picks up where the Catacombs left off. Behind the haunting *Aux morts* (To the dead) monument sculpted by Paul Albert Bartholme lies an ossuary of the bones of Parisians from cemeteries all over the city, a smaller kind of modern-day Catacombs. Although the monument is well known, it is not general knowledge that it is also an ossuary, and its doors usually remain closed and locked to the public. When it became overcrowded recently, the bones were removed for cremation and return, according to Marc Jerilo, an employee who assisted with this process. Like in the Catacombs, there is still a sense of the communal in the Père Lachaise ossuary; its divergence from the Catacombs, however, is instructive. In the Père Lachaise ossuary, efforts are made to store bones and ashes in separate boxes. Earlier, engravers were even paid several francs per letter to hand-chisel the names that went with the bones on the outer panel of each storage compartment. That process became too expensive and now names are tracked via computer lists, but both practices seek to preserve the personal identities of those interred there. As the first rural cemetery, Père Lachaise represents a rupture with the old styles of churchyard burials, but a walk through the portals at the *Aux morts* monument and into the ossuary shows that it retains some traces of the earlier tradition, transmogrified to reflect contemporary concern with the individual.

After Père Lachaise, the second rural cemetery was founded in America in 1831: Mount Auburn in Massachusetts. As in France, America's rural cemetery movement was prompted by concerns about hygiene. England, especially London, also had problems with overcrowded and noxious cemeteries. Charles Dickens wrote that "rot and mildew and dead citizens formed the uppermost scent" in the city (quoted in Culbertson and Randall 1991, 179). In order to deal with this problem, Kensal Green Cemetery was licensed by an Act of Parliament in 1832 (Culbertson and Randall 1991, 179). London's more famous Highgate Cemetery opened soon after in 1839 (Culbertson and Randall 1991, 197).

Originally known for its beautiful grounds and famous inhabitants, including Karl Marx, Mary Ann Evans (George Eliot), and Christina Rossetti, during the latter half of the twentieth century Highgate became noteworthy for the grandiose scale of its decay. Richard Altick describes it as "what would result if the accumulated monuments of Westminster Abbey were transferred, in their full marmoreal extravagance to the Amazonian rain forest" (quoted in Ellis 2000, 216). By the 1970s Highgate generated many legends and much gossip; it was said to be a haven for vampires, satanic activities, and other assorted general depravities. American cemeteries that grew out of the rural cemetery movement were generally quiet and not home to so much lurid folklore, but their statuary did give rise to legends like those related at the beginning of this chapter.

The nineteenth century was the golden age of cemetery statuary. Both the burial customs and the statues reflect an even greater emphasis on the individual. As early as the age of the Greeks, however, there were some signs of individuality on classical gravemarkers. Greek burial sites along roadways were indicated by funerary columns, vases, stelae, or statues that could be human or symbolic, such as a lion, sphinx, or bull (Ragon 1983, 48). The art of the sarcophagus rose with Rome, and Romans also carved portraits on gravemarkers and created lifelike funerary statuary (Ragon 1983, 49, 85).

According to Michel Ragon, a "timid desire" to affirm one's identity was established with the flat graves and stone markers of the medieval era (1983, 84). Weeping figures were carved as early as the twelfth century (Ragon 1983,

87). The emphasis on the individual became even more pronounced when gravestone inscriptions became common. They, in turn, were followed by outlines engraved on tombstones, a practice that lasted into the seventeenth century (Ragon 1983, 84–85). After outlines came *gisants* (recumbent figures in lifelike poses), which appeared in Europe during the twelfth century. Fourteenth-century sculptors deemphasized gisants' deathlike appearances in favor of sleeplike ones. In some parts of Europe, such as eastern France and western Germany, the *transi* (perished one) or *charogne* (carrion)—depictions of the partly decomposed cadaver, sometimes complete with worms—appeared (Ariès 1974, 39–40). The seventeenth century saw the widespread use of skeletons or bones on gravemarkers (Ariès 1974, 40). Allegorical figures also appeared in the seventeenth century and became more common in the eighteenth (Ragon 1983, 86).

Thomas Kselman observes that burial practices in nineteenth-century France indicate that even the poor tried to assign some identity to individual places of burial (1993, 188). In addition, he notes, they used burial as a means of seeking more equitable treatment; interment was one venue in which the poor could achieve "individual autonomy and equal treatment with the wealthy" (188). He characterizes French cemeteries as mediating between the democratic and egalitarian impulses inherited from the Revolution and the class-bound nature of nineteenth-century French society (187). He also maintains that ostentatious monuments of the day reflected the "intense" Parisian interest in status (185).

Sloane maintains that the "new monuments represented a shift from an eighteenth-century religious orientation to a more ecumenical, individualistic atmosphere, imbued with nature and hope. . . . The change was startling. . . . The new monuments were created by a generation of American and European sculptors imitating the grand art of the salons" (1991, 77, 79). Works by American sculptors such as Horatio Grenough, Thomas Crawford, Henry Dexter, and E. A. Brackett appeared in cemeteries. The railroad made precut, standardized family monuments available across the country, and these replaced locally carved markers (Sloane 1991, 79). Markers were also imported from Europe.

In her study of the eighteenth-century gravemarkers in Georgia and South Carolina that presaged some types of nineteenth-century markers, Diana Williams Combs describes the ascension of individual portraits on gravemarkers as being influenced by the fine arts of Great Britain (1986, 3). She argues that portraiture, the major contribution of the eighteenth century to American gravestone art, was prompted by the increased popularity of portrait busts during the first half of the eighteenth century in En-

gland (1986, 131). She notes that the "majority of the commissions under-
taken by the leading sculptors, Michael Rybrack and Peter Scheemakers,
were for funerary monuments" (1986, 131).

Combs contends that the motif of the mourning woman goes back at
least to Greek reliefs and grave stelae of the fifth and fourth centuries B.C.E.
(1986, 94). It is also found in such eighteenth-century pattern books as architect George Richardson's *Iconology* (1779), in which a draped female
figure represents "Melancholy" (1986, 94–95). Mourning cards of the Victorian era employed stock images such as the inverted torch, the weeping
willow, the shrouded urn, the kneeling female, and surrogate mourners
(Curl 1972, 13).

Ragon views nineteenth-century statuary as reflective of an "unquestion-
able democratic conquest. From the monument for the king to the monument for all, the development of the funerary site corresponds to other mass
phenomena. The right to a burial vault parallels the right to housing. The
urban cemetery-museum grew up with the claim to political rights" (1983,
84). Taking gender into consideration, I would note that this is a "democratic conquest" that allots more political rights to men.[5]

Other American forms of material culture traced over the past several
hundred years—such as homes, dishes, and personal possessions—also
indicate the rise of individualism, as Henry Glassie (1975) and James Deetz
have demonstrated (1996, 161–62, 85–86, 184–85). Nineteenth-century
gendered statues and images, however, indicate that it is a particular type
of individualism in which some people count more than others. Renderings of men frequently embody specific individuals. Female figures, however, are part of the language of symbols, for example, the dove, the rose,
and the lamb. They often mark the power and status of the man or his family buried at the site. A consideration of nineteenth-century cemetery statuary reveals the rise of a selective, gender-differentiated individualism. Simply put, white males had greater access to individualism than women and
ethnic minorities.[6]

An important exception should be noted, however. Along with such
symbols of childhood as a lamb or an empty baby chair, statues of specific
female children did appear, as did statues of male children. Ellen Marie
Snyder says that the statues reinforced the Victorian perception of the sepa-
rateness of adult and childhood spheres. Through the statuary, children
were linked to home, purity, and goodness of nature, as opposed to their
adult counterparts, "particularly men, for whom signs of the world of business or even the battlefield are reserved" (1989, 14). The statues are also
emblematic of the particular tragedy of a child's death.

The factory system of the Victorian period marked the first major use of female labor, and many women left their homes to work in cities. It was, however, still "the men who were perceived as the main players" in industry (Snyder 1989, 12), and images of women as workers did not appear on gravemarkers. There were, however, portrayals of the specific child buried at the site—a pattern parallel to the statues of adult males. Moreover, the images of children were not sexualized (Snyder 1989, 20). Statuary of all sorts, whether of children, men, or women, begin to decline with the advent of the twentieth century, but that did not signal a waning of attitudes—such as emphasis on the individual—that the statues typified.

Advances in technology propelled the individual to even greater heights in twentieth-century America. New technologies in sandblasting (Edison 1985, 185–86), along with the computer and lasers, made carvings on markers more inexpensive, complex, and idiosyncratic. Concern for individualism began to go beyond portraits and indications of occupation, evident in the nineteenth century, to expressions of personality via images of a deceased's interests, hobbies, and loves in life.

Even in the late-twentieth and early-twenty-first centuries, which have been affected by feminism and the women's movement, the very individualistic carvings on gravemarkers follow the gender-differentiated pattern that emerged from the nineteenth century. Although women are in the workforce in great numbers, for example, few gravemarkers are expressive of female occupations, something that is not the case for males. Some individualized images of women are inscribed on gravemarkers, and also some indication of their hobbies and what they loved, but, overall, I have not observed as many of those images as I have their male counterparts. Indications of a love of a particular sport are common on men's markers (figure 17) but much less so on women's.

Some markers shared by a husband and wife appear egalitarian and depict the interests of both, whether love of a pet, place, or hobby. Many of the women's hobbies indicated on these, however, fall into the realm of traditionally constructed female roles. For instance, one shared marker shows a man racing a horse and chariot (a winter pastime in the region) while above his wife's name is a picture of a pleasant, grandmotherly woman seated in a chair, two children on her lap. Another shared gravestone features cowboy paraphernalia above the husband's name and a rose above the wife's. Yet another depicts a Frito-Lay truck above the husband's name and a rose over the wife's. I saw several shared markers that had only one image, almost invariably above the male's name.

More single graves of men had headstones with imagery than single

Figure 17. Statue of male golfer, Bedford, Indiana.

graves of women. On several, for example, I saw mountain scenes with fishermen or riderless horses. Horseback riding and fishing are two activities that women enjoy as well, but I did not see them depicted on women's gravemarkers. In general, markers for women do not have an abundance of imagery, although I did find a twentieth-century statue that portrays the woman buried at the site. The rendering, however, is not far removed from the surrogate mourners of the earlier century. She is limned in a way that emphasizes her beauty and her body (figure 18). The marker also mentions that the woman was a model, cheerleader, and mother, roles associated with a traditional female domain, the body, and beauty.

Even though much has been made of the number of women in the workforce and the impact of feminism, women's gains and the changes in gender roles and expectations have made little mark in cemeteries. It is rare to encounter a woman's gravemarker that references her career. More likely are the graves of women born earlier in the twentieth century, and their markers may reflect traditional roles. Perhaps a significant change will occur when more gravestones are erected for women born during and after the women's movement. Ideas about gender are part of the cultural attitudes that can be traced through nineteenth-century statuary and twentieth-century images on gravemarkers. As striking and lucid as that pattern is, it is surprising that so little scholarly attention has been paid to it.

Gendered Cemetery Statuary in Its Folkloric Context

After hearing Tamar's legend about the cemetery statue, I realized that its details heighten the statue's association with the extraordinary and improbable.[7] For example, Tamar's supernatural explanation of the boy's death is unlikely. She said that when she first heard about the boy who drowned she was told that touching the statue had caused his death. She did not learn the whole story until after she met her husband. The omission of the intoxication aspect and an improbable emphasis on a statue's culpability in this tragic event are significant.

Why stress the paranormal at the expense of the obvious and rational? The answer lies in what is pleasing from a cultural perspective. At times it is more appealing to think that mysterious supernatural forces are more responsible for death than faulty human actions. In some contexts, telling a legend about the statue and death can be a way of not dealing with the possible, very real, consequences of engaging in binge-style drinking while swimming in a lake. Moreover, even though it may be "scary," sharing a legend in which beyond-the-grave forces are at work may also be comforting

Figure 18. Contemporary statue in Louisville, Kentucky.

at a deep level; the presence of these kinds of powers reinforces the idea that there is some sort of existence after death.

This emphasis on the extraordinary and strange at the expense of the probable figures in other legends about statues purported to be the Virgin Mary. I found several Virgin Mary statue legends in the Indiana State University Folklore Archives that delineate offerings such as soda pop being left for the statues. The legends raise several questions. Why is the Virgin the surrogate mourner, why is she depicted as reaching out to the legend-trippers, why does leaving an offering of sorts seem appropriate, and why is she portrayed as dangerous or sinister? The answers lie in the ways in which the Virgin has been constructed throughout the ages.

The history of belief and custom that surrounds statues in general, and images of the Virgin in particular, includes leaving offerings. It is also long and on-going.[8] In medieval miracle stories, as in some contemporary legends, statues of the Virgin are described as frequently coming to life. In many she weeps, as she does in Tamar's legend (Warner 1983, 293). These statues function like religious relics; they also make addressing the divine much easier and more tangible for mortals. According to Marina Warner, the Middle Ages created the Virgin "in the image of a human, approachable, supremely adorable woman, she stood by humanity like a mother but loved it like a mistress" (1983, 155). Warner's comments exhibit a common cultural tendency to describe intimacy as female through referencing both maternal and sensual love.

The renderings of both the statues and the legends share the use of sexuality and traditional gender roles as a primary means of referring to the female—a vestige of the way women have frequently been viewed and categorized throughout history. Associating statues with sex may hearken back to pagan practices in which statuelike structures—the menhirs of Brittany, for example—were associated with sexuality and fertility (Burl 1985, 44, 64). Narratives from prechristian times link statues and the erotic; the Pygmalion myth is one such story. Similar beliefs were manifest in much later eras. Women wishing to become pregnant, for example, rub the groin of the statue of Victor Noir in Père Lachaise.

In contemporary times, local folklore links statues on many college campuses to sexuality. Humorously, some are said to do something dramatic if an actual virgin walks by, whether firing a musket, drawing a sword, or tipping a hat. Of course, the statues are never seen to engage in such activities, because the campus supposedly lacks virgins (Bronner 1995, 179).[9] On the Utah State University campus a statue of the large letter A (for Aggie, the school's nickname) is the site of romance. In order to be a "true Aggie," someone who is already an Aggie must kiss the initiate at midnight while both are on the statue. Students refer to this as "getting kissed on the A." A more complicated variant of the folk custom also exists. In order to be a "true blue Aggie," it is necessary to have sex with a true Aggie, again on the statue. The university's mascot is a bull, "Big Blue," and there is also a statue of a bull, "Meet the Challenge," on campus. Opposing sports teams sometimes take the liberty of painting the bull's testicles their school colors, and, supposedly, a local fraternity is in charge of cleaning them when this happens. The bull sported a condom for several weeks in November 2000, a prank that blatantly associated the statue with sex. Moreover, students intent upon earning the title of "ultimate Aggie" must, while naked, climb astride the bull and be photographed to document the accomplishment. All of this folklore seems appropriate to college campuses, where relationships and sex are the focus of much interest and energy. It also seems probable that the historic linkage of statues with fertility, sex, and the erotic is making a contemporary appearance in these venues.

Besides the erotic, legends and statues also speak to the angelic. The history and lore associated with angels can illuminate the possible meanings of the legends about statues of cemetery angels, such as the stories Dan and Zach told. It makes sense to see statues of the Virgin in the company of statues of angels in a cemetery. Like Mary, the angel can function as a link between God and humans and inspire humans and intervene on their behalf. Mary and angels have been marked since the fourth century with halos to signify their special metaphysical status. Prechristian cultures also used halos in their imageries to depict supernatural or superintellectual power (Guiley 1996, 81).

The types of angel imagery in cemeteries and in other contemporary art forms originated largely during and after the Renaissance. Boticelli, Raphael, Fra Angelico, Titian, Tintoretto, Veronese, Perugino, Murillo, Rembrandt, Rubens, and El Greco are among the artists who contributed to the depiction of angels as idealized, mystical, winged human forms (Guiley 1996, 21). Earlier Greek myth provided many winged figures. Nike, for example, was associated with victory. Like many nineteenth-century statues of surrogate mourners and some of angels (figure 19), she is portrayed as having prominent breasts—one of which is frequently exposed from a flowing tunic—or sometimes as fully nude. She carries medallions and palm branches, symbols Christians borrowed to depict angels. Her image appears in statuary, funerary, ceremonial, and triumphal art as well as on coins (Guiley 1996, 197). Greek renderings of figures such as Nike also influenced neoclassical cemetery sculpture.

Figure 19. Angel marker, Père Lachaise, Paris.

Some cemetery statuary might reference guardian angels. Traditionally, a guardian angel watches over a person from birth to death, providing guidance and protection in the form of putting good thoughts into people's minds, praying for people, protecting them from danger, revealing the will of God, receiving and protecting the soul at the moment of death, and encouraging them to praise God (Spirago 1921, 150–52). The concept has prechristian roots; similar spirits existed in Babylonian, Greek, and Roman cultures (Guiley 1996, 77).

The cemetery angel in Dan and Zach's legend shares some characteristics with a guardian angel; her arms, for example, are outstretched as if reaching out to comfort or protect a mortal. This idea of an angel providing solace and security is heightened by the fact that the statue's embrace is said to be so inviting that it causes mortals to climb into her arms and fall asleep—just as a trusting child might sleep in the arms of a parent—even though in a place that is public, fearsome, and potentially dangerous: the cemetery.

Cemetery legends about the Virgin Mary and angels can narrate a more unsettling or threatening side of divine characters. Touching the Virgin can cause death, and falling asleep in the arms of the angel can cause one's soul to disappear. Those components of angel legends could be reminiscent of the Angel of Death, who is charged with taking souls to either heaven or hell (Cavendish 1970, 7; Davidson 1967, 194). That angel is able to manifest in a pleasing form in order to lure and calm the living into giving up their souls. The lovely female angel of legend, whose arms entice humans to sleep, could be the Angel of Death. According to Dan and Zach's legend, sitting in the angel's arms can also take away a person's soul, which is suggestive of death. That detail could reflect belief that an angel can receive a soul at the moment of death and act as a "celestial escort," guiding the soul to the afterworld (Guiley 1996, 78). The notion is frequently seen in cemetery statues that depict angels guiding humans heavenward.

The angel in the legend could be viewed as slightly sinister because it is not clear how direct a role it plays in taking a person's soul. In addition to the Angel of Death, who works at God's behest, there is also a possibility that this is a fallen angel who is engaging in evil activities. There are pagan antecedents for these blacker angels, figures such as the dark-winged Furies that Rosemary Guiley describes as personifying the vengeful aspect of Demeter (1996, 20). Demeter and the Furies are yet another depiction (like the Virgin and the angel in legends) of a comforting, intimate, even motherly figure who also has a threatening side.

Those who listen to legends can be left wondering whether this woman is a guardian angel, the Angel of Death, or a fallen angel.[10] Moreover, is her embrace that of a mother, a lover, or something darker? It is not apparent what manner of angel she is, nor is it known where the person's soul or shoes go. Answers to questions the legend could raise are left, in a bit of masterful narrative ambiguity, to the imagination of the listener. The angel legend succinctly touches upon powerful human issues such as death and its relationship to the divine or supernatural.

In the variant Zach collected, the link between the person embraced by the statue and death is even more obvious. The soul is also taken away at the folkloric witching hour of midnight, a time of transition: "If you sit in it's [sic] arms at midnight . . . it will take your soul away." Although his informant is unsure as to "what that does to you," many would interpret the removal of the soul from the body as death. Paradoxically, death is a commonplace, but the experience of it is not considered mundane. It is a state of radical otherness. It exists before we do, and as such it is a state of alterity. As Emmanuel Levinas says, "The approach of death indicates that we are in relation with something that is absolutely other" (1996, 43).

Both legend versions at least suggest that the embrace of the angel allows passage from the ordinary to the extraordinary, but one of the fascinating things about the legend, as legend-trippers to the site must notice but then blithely ignore, is the difficulty, if not the impossibility, of actually climbing into the angel's arms. Her arms are not "outstretched," and it would be very difficult to sit in them. Even sitting on the angel's lap would pose a challenge. Her posture makes sense from a sculptural point of view; if her arms were extended, they would be more likely to break. Certainly, legend-trippers to the site notice the position of the statue, but the notion of the statue somehow reaching out to them overrides the reality. This detail in the legend versions must be important, otherwise it would be dropped. Perhaps it is retained in the legend because of its dramatic implications. It symbolizes the otherworldly embracing the living and is also reminiscent of the traditional motif of the dead reaching out to touch the living (Motif E542 in Thompson 1955–58).

Both versions suggest a parallel between experiencing the embrace of the statue and experiencing death itself—a connection reinforced in the symbolism of the angel as a "quasi-human personage who helps us make the transition into incomprehensible eternity" (Brown 1994, 25). A subtle intimate or sexual subtext may also be at work. First an embrace is described, and in one version the informant mentions falling asleep while being held by a female angel, a posture reminiscent of lovers or of a mother and child. Yet it is a most dangerous embrace and can cause death. If the sexual overtones are emphasized, perhaps the legend carries traces of the older notion that sex is linked to death (Wilson 1994, 55).

The states of radical otherness such as death are among the mysteries directly or indirectly addressed on legend trips. For many, an encounter with otherness in legend focuses on statues of females rather than males because of their prevalence in representing death and mourning. Photographer David Robinson has movingly documented statues of female surrogate mourners in *Saving Graces,* a collection of photographs from European cemeteries (1995). His book contains image after image of statues of female surrogate mourners, but these women do not exhibit the common physical attributes of their flesh-and-blood counterparts. There are no red and puffy eyes, runny noses, or even clothes. This is mourning become erotic. The Graces are sexualized witnesses to death and idealized depictions of mourning. They are part of the larger tradition of using the female form to symbolize such abstract principles as liberty or victory; statues of males, however, more often refer to specific men, such as generals.

Simone de Beauvoir argues that the role of observer or sexualized witness is a frequent one for women, as is the position of the other (1971, xvi).[11] Following de Beauvoir, the statues of females, linked as they are to death and otherness, reinforce a cultural association of women with otherness. Women, de Beauvoir contends, are often seen as sexual beings, and Robinson's photographs reveal that sensuality can still be pronounced even when depicted in a role as somber as surrogate mourner. That role is passive, however. The mourner is desirable but not desiring.

The statues demonstrate the association of the female with the intimate and sexual—even the statue of the Illinois angel has some of these alluring and sensual characteristics. Although the angel's sensuality is not as pronounced as some other statues of females, it is still evident. I also observed several beautiful and erotic angel statues in other cemeteries. These three-dimensional images of women are part of a larger cultural process, the gendering of intimacy. Frequently in graphic arts and in narrative, the female is presented as an intimate and loving figure, such as a mother (e.g., the portraits of the Madonna and Child) or a lover, such as the portrait of Nell Gwynne, Charles the Second's mistress (Berger 1977, 52–56).

Men are too rarely represented in tenderly intimate roles in folk and elite traditions. They can be connected with sexuality, but it is often to demonstrate virility and sexual prowess (Duncan 1982, 293). As Linda Nochlin observes, "In the nineteenth century, and still today, the very idea—much less an available public imagery—of the male body as a source of gentle, inviting satisfaction for women's erotic needs, demands and daydreams is almost unheard of" (1972, 14).[12]

I find many of the Graces to be very beautiful and engaging. Yet these statues with perfect bodies and without individual personalities recall cultural ways of seeing female sexuality. They evoke the way that the female has been viewed as an eroticized other. That perspective, Berger argues, can be found in elite art. "Her body is arranged the way it is, to display it to the man looking at the picture. This picture is made to appeal to his sexuality. It has nothing to do with her sexuality. . . . Women are there to feed an appetite, not to have any of their own" (1977, 55).[13] It is unfortunate that female bodies and female sexuality have throughout history often been used to define the sphere of the female and conscribe her power. Gender and sexuality have limited women to certain roles and have often been emphasized to the detriment of labor or intellect. The artists who shaped the Graces' bodies were molded by individual cultural backgrounds and attitudes toward women. The Graces' beauty does not divorce them from history, nor should it blind contemporary viewers to the gender inequities that shaped the lives of the Graces' flesh-and-blood counterparts.

Although Robinson's European Graces are arresting, similar, although perhaps not as dramatic, patterns exist in America and England. In both American and European cemeteries there are also statues of women whose physical appearance is not sensual. For example, the statue to which Tamar refers is aesthetically a far cry from Robinson's "Saving Graces." One of my folklore students noted that she looked more like the rock musician Ozzy Osbourne than the Virgin Mary. In fact, she probably is a surrogate mourner rather than the Virgin. Whatever her identity, it is apparent that statues of the Virgin are not as sensualized as are those of surrogate mourners, and some of the surrogate mourners are also not particularly eroticized. On the surface they seem to constitute a different subspecies than the sexualized mourners. There are, however, significant areas of connection. Both the Graces and Mary are women, both act as surrogate mourners, and there is a strong sexual subtext to their rendering, whether in stone or narrative. One of the Graces' most noticeable qualities is eroticism. Sexuality, albeit a different aspect of it, defines Mary as well. She is, after all, the *Virgin* Mary.

The statue of the weeping woman in the Logan, Utah, cemetery is of a surrogate mourner. Seeing such a cemetery statue can give pause, and the fact of the statue's silence heightens the mystery. Ordinary people sometimes tell legends about the supernatural when they encounter these silent, humanlike figures associated with death. The oral texts they create are voluntarily reactions to encounters with art.

The legends individualize the statues more than their sculptors did and do not indicate any understanding of the statue as a symbol. More often, in the case of the surrogate mourners, the legends posit that the statue represents

Surrogate Mourners are individualized More by legends than sculptors pictured

Surrogate Mourner More sexalized than "Virgin Mary" or "Angel" the woman presumed buried at the site and detail particulars of the statue's "life" (which is seen to represent an actual decedent's). Many versions are rich in individuating and dramatic details. According to one version:

> There was a lady who lived in Logan [Utah] around 1900. She had five children all under eight years old. Her husband had been committed to the State Mental Hospital in Provo [Utah] following some bizarre cat killings in Logan. He escaped from the hospital, returned to Logan and killed the five children and the babysitter while the mother was at work. She returned home from work and saw her murdered children. She died from depression and lack of will to live a week later. If you visit her grave today you will see a monument of a woman kneeling over five small graves crying. Kent told me if you go to the grave at night you can hear the woman crying and [see] tears running down her face. I have never seen or heard her crying but there are brown streaks on her face from her hollowed out eyes. Cats are said to roam around the graves at night too.

This variant is loaded with specifics: the date, the ages of the children, the cat killings, the institutionalized husband, and the working mother who died of depression at the deaths of her children. Just as with the legends of the cemetery angel in Illinois, however, the narrators ignore some of the actual details of the site. In this case, a wife, her husband, and two children—not five as the legend says—are buried there.

The woman as mother is a major element in this legend corpus. She appears as a mother who cries because of the deaths of her children, because of their bad behavior, because legend-trippers accuse her of being a bad mother, or because she is a murdering mother. The only version that indicates that she had a job outside of the home is the one wherein all her children are killed while she is away at work. Regardless of specific details, the guilt and anguish of a mother, who is often flawed, is a theme that runs through many legend versions. When compared to the Virgin and angel legends, all three types of legends share major elements, including emphasis on traditional roles for the female (mother, lover, mourner). They also portray the woman either as a victim or as threatening.

The monuments of surrogates such as the weeping woman that mark family plots, and the legends told about these statues, bring attention to the women buried at the sites—if a woman is interred there, as is the case for the weeping woman gravesite. The legends told about the anonymous surrogate mourners could individualize the woman buried at the site, although the stories are usually inaccurate. The legends give the statue a life story, whereas the sculptor had given her only stock characteristics and anonymity. The problem with the legends is that they do not present the life stories of the actual women buried at the sites. Those stories are generally not told, and the women continue to remain anonymous and unknown despite the legend-tellers' belief that they are repeating a specific story.

In summary, the legends are different from the nineteenth-century forms that prompted them. Because these legends were in circulation during the late twentieth century, that period's ever-greater emphasis on the individual could be responsible for the increased individualization of the legends. The fact that women have received recognition and equality may affect legend-telling's focus on the stories of individuals. However, the legends also contain, and therefore carry into the present, some very old story lines and conservative ways of seeing women that tie them to traditional female roles and the domestic realm. In that sense the legends share a lot with cemetery depictions of women, especially images I saw on contemporary shared spousal markers.

Those images and legends present deeper pictures of individuals, but the individuals are constrained by traditional, even stereotypical, gender roles and expectations. Many of today's legend-tellers were born after the women's movement of the 1960s, yet they still pass along stereotypical views of women through legends, visions also made material via grave-markers. I have not yet encountered, whether in the material culture of cemeteries or in the details of legends, imagery that reflects the varied nature of women's current labors and lives. Perhaps the change in gender roles and how they are viewed has yet to be internalized collectively enough to effect a significant change on everyday forms of cultural expression such as cemetery material culture and legends.

Some elements of the statuary of males are common to those of females, primarily that, to be the focus of a legend, the statues are usually among the most visible markers in a cemetery. A marker that is noticeable or unusual is more likely to become the subject of legend, and all of the markers associated with the legends I have discussed are prominent in the cemeteries that house them. They are also depictions of human beings, which may suggest to legend-trippers that the statues have some sort of "life story" to tell. The construction of that story emerges as a legend.

Another common factor is that statues of either gender can be symbolic of a larger group. A soldier represents those who lost their lives in war, for example. Because the soldier and the surrogate mourner both symbolize mourning at the loss of loved ones, it may seem illogical that the legends draw both figures as threatening. In legends, for example, the soldier is aggressive, frightening, and even threatening. According to an Indiana cemetery legend a student told me, the statue of a soldier actually leaps off its pedestal at night and chases the other statues in the cemetery, intimidating them with his gun. The weeping woman and the Virgin are also rendered in a similar frightening and intimidating fashion. They can cry tears of blood and cause death. The dominant theme of the legends is death and the fears that surround it, all of which dwarf the original intentions of those who created and placed the statues. Ultimately, legend-trippers are concerned with narrating death's uncanny, unnerving, frightening, and even aggressive nature, and the stories about the statues reflect these qualities.

The ubiquity of soldier statues in cemeteries makes sense to me, but I was curious as to why male nudity is so rare. Specifically, the lack of erotic male statuary raises three questions. First, why is the major root of masculinity so downplayed in the statuary? And I do mean minimized. Upon hearing about these statues, for example, colleagues who know of my Barbie research have commented, "Oh, so the statues are just like Ken." To that I have had to respond, "Well, no, actually they are more like Barbie; Ken at least got a bump." Second, in light of the historical presence of male nudes in both sculpture and painting, why don't nude or semi-nude males appear in nineteenth-century neoclassically inspired cemetery statuary (for example, see Clark 1976, 26)? And, third, this lack of male genitals does not seem to dovetail with the folklore and folk behaviors that foreground them as a source of pride, pleasure, power, and identity. In light of the importance of male genitalia and the folklore about them, why doesn't there appear to be more congruity between the verbal lore and the material culture (in this case, cemetery statues)?

Art history explains the visual tradition of genital sketchiness. Abigail Solomon-Godeau has discussed the "diminutive scale of the genitalia on the male nude in its classical, Renaissance or post-Renaissance incarnations" (1997, 36). She quotes Norman Bryson, who describes the custom as comforting for male viewers because "diminishing the genitalia" assures that viewers will experience "no anxiety concerning discrepancy" when looking at the male nude (1997, 179). She notes that the classical nude provided a model for later nudes. In the art of the classical period, a "dainty penis" was the rule for male gods, heros, or athletes. Satyrs, however, were believed to have "spectacular" genitals but not as an index of masculinity. Rather, the convention of the times equated large genitals with an animalistic nature (Solomon-Godeau 1997, 181–82). Such traditions, she reasons, may have emerged in the classical era because of cultural practices such as the veneration of youth, especially adolescent males, as the ideal of beauty. The traditions may also be due to the "scientific" views of the period. As expounded by Aristotle, science held that a small penis was more fertile than a large one because "the distance for the seed to travel was shorter, and therefore had less time to cool" (1997, 182). The fine artists of later eras were trained in this tradition of rendering nudes. They also frequently created cemetery statues, so it is probable that statues of males emerged from the elite art tradition that deemphasized male genitalia.

Now to my second question about the lack of nude or semi-nude, eroticized statues of males in cemeteries. What makes the scarcity of male nudes particularly puzzling is the dominance of male nudes in the European fine-art tradition until the beginning of the nineteenth century (Smith 1996, 25). Their prevalence extends back into the classical era. Greek sculptures of female nudes did not appear until the sixth century (Clark 1976, 231). Even though periods like the Italian Renaissance or the first half of the eighteenth century produced a significant number of female nudes, the male nude was still the historical norm (Solomon-Godeau 1997, 22). Solomon-Godeau argues that male nudes can generally be placed in one of two categories, which she terms "hard" and "phallic" (a reference to the Lacanian sense of the phallus as a signifier of the ideal) or "soft" and "feminized" (1997, 23). "Hard" male nudes are heroic, active, or dominating, whereas "soft" male nudes are adolescent, ephebic, sensual, erotic, or passive (Solomon-Godeau 1997, 22).

In the early 1800s, especially in French culture, Solomon-Godeau observes that emphasis on sexual difference increased, which contributed to the rise of female nudes. The clothes of the era exhibited that shift. The male abjuration of "previously masculine prerogatives such as lavish and richly decorative clothing, wigs, make-up, [and] high heels" was part of a movement wherein "the domain of exhibitionism and display" was defined as female. Clothes emphasized sexual difference, and women's clothing revealed part or even all of the breast and arm. Like the drapery on statues of women, the light fabric used for gowns revealed women's bodies (1997, 218–19).

During this time, Solomon-Godeau notes, the sensualized male body, such as the ephebe, was replaced in art with the eroticized female body.[14] By 1870 art critics were applying the term *nude* almost exclusively to renderings of female bodies (Smith 1996, 135). Artists approached the female nude as a "decorative entity": "While a decorative treatment was considered appropriate and natural for female figures, male nudes were seen to demand historical conceptualization, a view that resulted in the condemnation of many a decorative male as effeminate" (Smith 1996, 119–20).

Alison Smith, an art historian, maintains nude male models were the norm in art schools before the 1830s (1996, 25). The traditional view was that artists, in rendering them, could "demonstrate their proficiency in mastering anatomy, proportion and muscular structure" (1996, 136). A gradual influx of women into the schools as both students and models occurred during the later part of the century. By the 1860s the use of female models for nudes was growing more common (Smith 1996, 136), and their presence sometimes gave rise to accusations of salaciousness and scandal. Artists employed several strategies to get beyond such controversies. In presenting female nudes in mythological scenes, for example, artists attempted to mute the narrative and moral dimensions of their work and tried to paint the women in a light that made them an "embodiment of universal beauty, a paradigmatic metaphor for the artist's power to create perfect form" (Smith 1996, 119). Female nudes were also placed in pastoral scenes, an association with nature and all that was "passive, timeless and remote" (Smith 1996, 91).

Male nudes were fashioned in the manner Solomon-Godeau describes as "hard." They were heroic, dignified, and strong (Smith 1996, 133). The male models who posed for nude renderings were valued for their "musculature, stamina and physique; many were pugilists or soldiers" (Smith 1996, 25). Female models, frequently members of the working class, were often regarded with suspicion and stereotyped as prostitutes or as being sexually promiscuous (Smith 1996, 119–20). Thus both the female models and the statues for which they posed were often sexualized.

This rise of a female nude associated with softness, display, and decoration, combined with a cultural shift described by Michael Kimmel, may help explain the paucity of male nudes in cemeteries. The sculptures of men in American cemeteries from the nineteenth century to the twentieth may have been influenced by a change in masculine identity brought about by the Industrial Revolution. According to Kimmel, at the beginning of the nineteenth century American manhood was rooted in landownership or in the self-possession of independent artisans, shopkeepers, or farmers. After the Industrial Revolution, "American men began to link their sense of themselves as men to their position in the volatile marketplace, to their economic success. The Self-Made Man of American mythology was born anxious and insecure, uncoupled from the more stable anchors of landownership and workplace autonomy" (1996, 9). As the self-made man moved into the early decades of the twentieth century, Kimmel asserts, "[H]e turned to leisure activities like sports" because they could boost his sense of manhood, provide a chance to be with other men, and create an opportunity to teach his sons to become self-made men (1996, 9–10).

It is probable that the self-made man is evident in many nineteenth-century monuments, a pattern that continues in gravemarker imagery. Cemetery statues and markers that depict males also pick up on some of the interests of the self-made man, such as a fascination with sports. This cultural shift in masculine identity coincided with the decline of male nudes in art. Given these two factors, it makes historical sense that statues of males in cemeteries appear as they do.

When I asked several male friends and acquaintances why they thought the statues had no apparent genitals, one, who worked in a largely male environment at the time, responded that cemetery statues—whether of men or women—are primarily made for men to look at. He pointed out that a key tenet in the folk behavior of supposed heterosexual American males when with other males is not to focus on the penis. American men, for example, do not generally "look down" when standing at urinals. Most do not want to be seen looking at other penises, whether at urinals, or cemeteries, or anywhere else.

Recalling that artists schooled in the tradition of fine art created much cemetery statuary, it is again instructive to review art history. In the nineteenth century:

> The image of man was always intended for the consumption of men. This is not to deny the existence of women spectators or even the rare female critic, but rather, to insist on the overwhelmingly masculine character of the artistic sphere in its widest sense. Thus, the beautiful painted or sculpted male body, in principle geared to a universal spectator, was in practice addressed to a rather specific one; an adult white male subject usually, but not exclusively, a member of the dominant class. As a result, the male nude, whether of antique or European manufacture, was in almost all instances produced, received, commissioned, sold, discussed, celebrated or criticized within entirely male formations. The effective exclusion of women artists from this highly specialized cultural arena further guaranteed that visions of ideal masculinity would be articulated only by men. (Solomon-Godeau 1996, 199–200)

Culture thus teaches men about the conventions associated with the male form and the manner in which it is supposed to be viewed. A process similar to the aversion of the male gaze that my informant describes in folk culture was part of elite art circles during the 1800s. In a discussion of nineteenth-century art and art criticism Smith notes, "In representing the male nude most artists negotiated the problem of nakedness by overlooking the phallus altogether, instead implying virility by means of displacement, through the use of heavy muscles, tools, or weapons. Nevertheless, for many observers, the male nude was both distasteful and obsolete" (1996, 140). Because most of the audience for these male nudes was composed of men, Kimmel's argument concerning the homosocial nature of male interaction is applicable:

In large part, it's other men who are important to American men; American men define their masculinity, not as much in relation to women, but in relation to each other. Masculinity is largely a homosocial enactment. . . . Such a bold claim does not mean that women are incidental to men's efforts to prove their manhood. Far from it . . . men often go to elaborate lengths and take extraordinary risks to prove their manhood in the eyes of women. Women are not incidental to masculinity, but they are not always its central feature, either. At times, it is not women as corporeal beings but the "idea" of women, or femininity—and most especially a perception of effeminacy by other men—that animates men's actions. Femininity, separate from actual women, can become a negative pole against which men define themselves. Women themselves often serve as a kind of currency that men use to improve their ranking with other men. The historical record underscores this homosociality. . . . From father and boyhood friends to teachers, coworkers, and bosses, the evaluative eyes of other men are always upon us, watching, judging. (1996, 7)

This presentation of the male as the self-made man was attractive to artists because it associated manliness, dignity, and power with visual trappings of a career, such as a business suit. The image of the career man allowed communication of some of the same ideas about power and the male body that Solomon-Godeau's "hard" male nudes had signified. Véronique Nahoum-Grappe discusses the manner in which nineteenth-century males clothed and presented their bodies to indicate seriousness:

Men renounced the "nonutilitarian" and "conspicuous": makeup, jewelry, long hair, brightly colored clothing, and so on. In Europe "important" men now dressed in sober, neutral garb: when they appeared in public it was in black, grey, or white. The male's social presence was thus euphemized under the aesthetic mask of the "serious." Any transgression of this code entailed a loss of credibility and effectiveness. . . . Any infraction of this aesthetic . . . became a suspect sign of femininity, that mélange of weakness and perversion, impotence and incompetence, inconstancy and inconsistency. . . . The effeminate was increasingly stigmatized as male and female appearances diverged. (1993, 91–92)

In the case of the career man, unlike the male nude, fewer potential taboo associations of effeminacy, homosexuality, or sensuality could correspond with this type of limning of a male body. It was both free from stigma and a way to communicate male power.

Verbal lore about male genitalia is incongruent with the actual depiction of male anatomy (or lack thereof) in statuary. In a discussion of male sexuality, Kimmel provides examples of some of the folklore about male genitalia (see also Cameron 1992):

If men's sexuality is "phallocentric"—revolving around the glorification and gratification of the penis—then it is not surprising that men often develop elaborate relationships with their genitals. Some men name their penises—"Willie" "John Thomas," or "Peter"—or give them cute nicknames taken from mass-produced goods like "Whopper" and "Big Mac." Men may come to believe that their penises have little personalities . . . threatening to refuse to behave the way they are supposed to behave. If men do not personify the penis, they objectify it; if it is not a little person, then it is supposed to act like a machine, an instrument, a "tool." A man projects "the coldness and hardness of metal" onto his flesh writes the French philosopher Emmanuel Reynaud.

Few women name their genitals; fewer still think of their genitals as machines. Can you imagine if they called their clitoris "Shirley" or their labia "Sally Ann"? In fact, women rarely refer to their genitals by their proper names at all, generally describing vulva, labia, and clitoris with the generic "vagina" or even the more euphemistic "down there" or "private parts." And it would be rare indeed to see a woman having a conversation with her labia. (2000a, 224)

Verbal lore and cemetery material culture may actually have more in common than I initially thought. The apparent disparity between the two has to do more with the difference between literal depictions and references to the penis and symbolic substitutions for it or the potency it can be seen to represent culturally. According to Kimmel, important characteristics of the self-made man include having power, respect, and standing—which can be symbolized and signified in a number of ways beyond a demonstration, literal or otherwise, of "cohones" or "testicular fortitude." As art historians indicate, in recent history the male nude has many risqué associations. Busts or statues of dressed men in cemeteries, however, often signify that their subjects had money, power, or respect—or all three—without running any of the risks that revealing more of the male anatomy could incur. The acknowledgment of courage or achievement is sometimes verbally marked with the phrase "he really has balls," which, of course, is a linguistic and symbolic reference to male power (Murphy 2001, 92–93). The expression reveals nothing about the actual physique or genitals of the male in question. The contemporary, aggressive male custom of grabbing one's crotch is a gestural parallel to all the verbal lore concerning male genitals. The gesture is usually performed to intimidate or claim some type of power but does not reveal anything of substance. Men do not drop their pants before employing the gesture. It is a reference to the idealized phallus in the Lacanian sense.

Actual display of the body, however, especially the erotic body, can make one vulnerable. Susan Bordo explains how the film *The Full Monty* (1997), which is about a group of unemployed, male, English metalworkers who decide to take up stripping, meditates on this concern:

> They had been sheltered by their guyhood, as they learn while putting the show together. One gets a penis pump. Another borrows his wife's face cream. They run, they wrap their bellies in plastic, they do jumping jacks, they get artificial tans. The most overweight among them (temporarily) pulls out of the show. Before these guys hadn't lived their lives under physical scrutiny, but in male action mode, in which men are judged by their accomplishments. Now, anticipating being on display to a roomful of spectators, they suddenly realize how it feels to be judged as women routinely are, sized up by another pair of eyes. "I pray that they'll be a bit more understanding about us" than they've been with women, David (the fat one) murmurs. (1999, 174)

One way to avoid the vulnerability of exposure is to armor the body in powerful musculature, which is what Bordo often sees in contemporary displays of erotic masculinity: "Nowadays, men—the Chippendales, for example, and men in ads as well—*do* strip for erotic display. But when they do so, they tend to present their bodies aggressively and so rarely seem truly exposed. . . . And what can a viewer's eyes do but admire the bulging bundles and gleaming muscles of the Chippendales and their ilk? Their bodies are a kind of armor" (1999, 30).

Parallels to the practice of emphasizing the power and achievements of a man through manipulation of symbols such as gestures, clothes, or even a well-muscled body appear in other types of verbal folklore, too. The gendered patterns that surround the folklore of place names provide a linguistic example. In general, a place, if named after a man, will be named after a specific individual and, again in general, not a sexualized part of male anatomy. Colorado, for example, has a place named Pike's Peak instead of a place named Penis Peak. Men usually (although not necessarily always) see having their names connected to an actual place as an indication of status and distinction. The substance and materiality (the actual place, mountain, river, or town) to which the name links the man help mark him as successful and someone to be remembered.

The place-name pattern for women is usually different. Female place names are more likely to be the first names of a saint or a woman with whom the man who named the place was intimate, perhaps his mother, daughter, or girlfriend. Places named after women are also more likely to be named after an eroticized part of the female body. The Grand Tetons (*téton* being French slang for breast) provide a well-known western American example, but the list goes on. Nippletop and Little Nippletop are in the Adirondacks, Nipple Mountain is in Colorado, Squaw Tit in Oregon, Mary's Nipple in

Utah, and there are many others (Nilsen 1991, 230). This folk practice parallels the cemetery statuary practice. Statues of females are more likely to be anonymous and sexualized than are those of males, and statues of males are more apt to be individualized and not eroticized than are those of females.

Some surrogate mourners are so vividly erotic that they seem to promise the unfolding of a Pygmalion story; that is, one waits for them to come to life. They do not, but they seem to offer some hope of doing so. They are improbable women in form and promise, and such sexualized depictions have not generally been used to transform gender relations more equitably or offer images of self-made, successful women. They represent the intimacy offered in a sensual, sexual relationship. The Virgin promises life and a connection with another, but her own life, from the immaculate conception to the miraculous birth of her child, is something of a puzzle. She is improbable, defined by sexuality and associated with the intimacy that can be found in a mother-child relationship, but she has not been revered as an equal in the godhead. Virgin Mary legends reference the intimacy of motherhood divorced from the intimacy of sexuality. Traditionally, angels are known neither for their intimate roles as mothers nor as sexual partners, yet cemetery angel legends could suggest either or both.

Perhaps one of the most simultaneously inviting and troubling aspects of the statues and legends is the way in which they use the female to embody close connections. Although these representations of intimacy can be seen as beautiful and comforting, three aspects of the gendering of intimacy are disturbing. First, when the intimacy depicted is of a sexual nature the woman is often presented in a passive role. Second, some legends connect the embrace of a female with death and thus recall a much older and negative depiction of woman, notably the equation made between Eve and death and physical corruption. Finally, it is possible that the pervasive association of the intimate with the female bears some responsibility for the lack of a deep history of images of men portrayed in tenderly intimate roles. The scarcity of this imagery may, in turn, have contributed to making these roles less culturally comfortable and less acceptable for men to assume.[15]

These women, according to legend, can often offer both an intimate, loving connection and the fearful horror of death. It is a disquieting pairing and a construction that heightens the strangeness in the legends and the otherness that can be culturally connected to women. Like Eve and Mary, these women of stone and story encompass sensuality, motherhood, and death—and with both positive and negative overtones. The angel, the mourners, the Virgins, and the self-made men are true monuments to the complex, engaging, contradictory, and estranging gender positions in which European and American cultures have often cast women and men.

2
Yard Art:
Geese in Bikinis,
Garden Gnomes,
and Peeing Boys

One day an archaeologist, excavating our town from beneath the sediment of ash and beer cans and fast-food wrappers, will be able to reconstruct something of our days and dreams by exhuming these lumps from our vanished lawns.

—Scott Russell Sanders

As a child, I spent many long, wind-howling winter days at my babysitter's house in a small town in the northern Rocky Mountains. Her honey-colored log home was a nice place to spend time year-round. In spring the ditch filled with water skippers and ran through the front yard; lilacs also bloomed there in May. The road in front of the house was a gravel lane, and horses always grazed in pastures that ran behind the backyard. It was a place where I reverently ate Velveeta macaroni and cheese, green beans, and Wonder Bread with margarine for lunch while *The Dating Game* babbled on the television in the background. This was all stuff I never had at my back-to-nature, grind-your-own-wheat, bake-your-own-bread home of the

1970s. It was also the place I discovered spring and flowers. I'll never forget the shock and wonder of encountering a purple flower, the first hyacinth I had ever seen, that came to bloom through March and snow. I did not know things like that happened in northwestern Wyoming.

The powerful, binding, and secret pact my babysitter had negotiated with the harsh forces of nature granted her dispensation for a huge garden—one much more successful than the plot that struggled up from the rocky soil at my parents' house. Her garden was about an acre in size and a home for monarch butterflies in the fall. It was half vegetable garden and half formal rose garden—and both could qualify as exotic given the harshness and brevity of the growing season in that corner of the West.

In the formal garden she had constructed a rose garden of concentric rings stacked in three levels, and it was here the deer were. I would duck the wind and stagger out to look at the plastic deer in wonder and hope during the winter and spring. As a young child, they made me think of Bambi, which was good even though I did not really like the story of Bambi because deer die in it and it frightened me. I liked the idea of it, however, because it involved deer and fawns, which I found quite beautiful. As an older child, they reminded me of the big-eared but graceful mule deer that lived in the mountains all around me. The deer in my babysitter's garden were a promise of what was good about that area and what made people stick out the winter winds.

Many years later and as a scholar, I find myself still thinking about plastic deer. My sense of what is aesthetically pleasing has changed much over time, but my interest in what yard art may mean, and why it is there, has not. Yard decoration, which Colleen Sheehy calls "one of our most pervasive forms of public art" (1998, 25), is a custom learned through the folk process. It is informally acquired; one doesn't usually consult how-to books or attend special schools to determine concrete goose placement. In this chapter I explore the history and folklore of yard art and its meanings. My purpose is to analyze the lawn ornamentation I have observed, with a particular emphasis on gender. I have seen and photographed the yard art of several states, but my focus is on the Midwest and West with some attention to the Upper South.[1]

In his book about American front yards, Fred E. H. Schroeder observes, "One reason that it takes a practiced eye to see the underlying vernacular pattern [in the presentation of grass-planted front lawns] is that there is such variety among the choice and establishment of specimen trees, flower beds, foundation plantings, low hedges, mock fencelets, chain-link fences and the decorative jetsam of concrete urns, plastic flamingoes, bird baths and fiberglass deer. In short, there is almost anarchical latitude for self-expression that evolves with the neighborhood" (1993, 141). Sheehy notes that American yards host a diverse "mélange of vernacular imagery" (1998, xii). There are, however, distinct patterns that underlie the apparent diversity.[2]

I have grouped the gendered yard art I saw and photographed into three categories: first, gendered animals such as geese in bikinis, bears in overalls, and frogs holding hands; second, "little people," which includes depictions of gnomes, dwarves, and children, for example, wooden cutouts of peeing boys; and, third, adults, which encompasses figures of adult men and women, including lawn jockeys, the Virgin Mary, classical statuary, and silhouettes or cutout depictions of various figures, from soldiers to women's backsides (otherwise known as granny fannies or yard butts). The three types of yard art can be found in perimeter decorations (mailboxes, fences, and gates) as well.

Pattern and Gender in Yard Art

My overview of the general patterns of yard decoration is constructed with gender in mind, although the categories I have identified are common in yard art. In addition to displays of holiday imagery, equipment, and discarded items such as shoes or bottles, they encompass the bulk of material I saw in yards. Because my focus is on gender, it is beyond the scope of this book to consider all types of yard art except in the way they relate to the parameters of the study (as in, for example, farm equipment sculpted into human figures).

Statues of animals constitute one of the most common decorations in American yards. I viewed pink flamingos; plastic or concrete deer; white concrete or plastic geese, often dressed in various outfits; concrete alligators; a variety of ducks; planters shaped like swans or lambs; statues of songbirds, parrots, eagles, chickens, resting lions, pigs, Holstein cattle, dogs, squirrels, skunks, rabbits, giraffe, zebra, bears, both clothed and naked, and, in fountains, fish, dolphins, or seahorses; butterflies; various frogs, including some sporting bikinis; animal images as part of ranch entrance gates; horses, some hitched to real wagons; wooden cutouts of sea monsters; and cartoon figure–whirligigs such as Sylvester the Cat, Tweety Bird, and the Road Runner. Some appear singly, on a lawn with other yard art, or they can be part of a yard menagerie.

Yard animals are not usually rendered with great anatomical accuracy, and gender need not be apparent. It is frequently visible in two ways, however, through placing the animal in a couple or family setting or through the way it is clothed. In the Midwest, geese are a visible and popular example of that practice. Those presented as couples are dressed as males and females; if presented singly, they are more likely to be garbed as females. I found more clothing for females than males advertised for concrete geese, and outfits for females are sexier than those for males (a bikini versus an Uncle Sam costume, for instance). The popularity of "Mother Goose" rhymes and images may have contributed to concrete geese being depicted as female. They are also known to engage in cross-species dressing, whether as bumblebees, reindeer, cats, mice, ladybugs, or cows, for example.

Yard art black bears, shirtless and wearing overalls, are another illustration of the use of human clothing to indicate gender. Women now wear overalls, once traditionally masculine clothing, but it is primarily men who wear overalls and no shirts, so the concrete bears appear more masculine than feminine. Bears are also culturally conjoined with maleness because they are big, powerful, and frightening.

Images of deer are common as well, but they, unlike geese, are not dressed in human clothing. Deer gender is indicated by physical attributes and whether the deer have been grouped in couples or as families. Couples or family groups are invariably composed of a buck, whose gender is communicated by antlers; a doe, whose gender is apparent by a lack of antlers; and a fawn, shown lying on the ground. Just as the buck's masculinity is obvious because of his antlers, so all the lion statues I saw in the Midwest and West are male, a fact signaled by manes. Sometimes one adult animal figure is given several offspring, for example, a white duck might have several ducklings. Because of enculturation, people are probably more likely to see that group as a mother and her babies than as a single father out for a stroll with his children. Gendered characteristics are not always part of animal yard art, however, and need not be. Yet the fact that gender is apparent suggests its importance as a cultural category and its usefulness in anthropomorphosis and connecting the human world and the natural world.

The second of the two most common types of gendered yard art I observed is a category I call "little people," which includes children as well as dwarves and gnomes. Portrayals of boys include concrete statues of black and white youths who fish, sit, eat large pieces of watermelon, and ride on donkey carts. There are also seated putti; boys in fountains, sometimes urinating; and wooden cutouts of toy soldiers that look like little boys, boys who play on tire swings, and the bare backsides of boys who appear to be urinating.

Girls are shown wearing close-fitting or frilly dresses, playing on swings, or holding watering cans; there are also wooden cutouts of Betty Boop–like

Bo Peeps. There are yard art boy and girl couples, for example, statues of a Dutch boy and girl kissing, and wooden cutouts of the backsides of peeing boys who stand next to wooden cutouts of little girls who seem to be hiding their eyes. Finally, dwarves are usually used in the company of a concrete Snow White, and gnomes wearing brightly colored hats grace yards singly or occasionally in male-female couples.

Images of boys are more common than those of girls, and more male gnomes and dwarves are evident than female ones. Children are grouped in male-female couples and shown engaged in activities associated with play or leisure. Ethnic representations of males are more frequent than ones of females. The gender roles assigned to yard art boys and girls are traditional, even conservative. Boys are dressed appropriately for outdoor play and engage in such sports as fishing. Girls are not shown fishing or participating in other sports, nor are they presented as tomboys or clothed appropriately for outdoor play. When shown at play outdoors, perhaps swinging, they often wear frilly dresses.

Images of little black boys are more likely than ones of little black girls. The only ethnic depiction of a girl I saw with regularity was the girl in the Dutch kissing couple (figure 20), and I encountered no racially mixed statues of kissing couples.[3] Both genders are somewhat sexualized in certain types of yard art. Some yard art girls lift and twist their form-fitting dresses, and the fountains and wooden cutouts of peeing boys remain popular.

Adult forms include black and white male lawn jockeys, Latino men with donkeys, Indians, sacred heart Jesuses, St. Francises, and cowboys. There are wooden cutouts of Uncle Sam; silhouettes of cowboys; hunters with rifles, bows, and arrows; and soldiers. Also apparent are statues of the Virgin Mary, angels, small white women eating watermelon, cowgirls, classically styled and draped women, saloon girls, scantily clad women, Venuses, and women constructed from parts of old farm equipment.[4] Moreover, there are wooden cutouts of women, seen from behind as they bend over, and some reveal undergarments. Again, statues of ethnic figures are much more likely to be male than female.

Male statuary includes figures of aggression, for example, hunters and soldiers poised and ready to fire. Religious images of both males and females can be found in yards and cemeteries. Yard angels, more likely to be of females than males, are styled in a fashion very similar to those in cemeteries, and classical images of women appear in both yards and cemeteries. In both locales women are commonly portrayed as either motherly or as subtly, or not so subtly, sexy.

Figure 20. Kissing Dutch children in Bernice's yard, Logan, Utah.

Decoration around the perimeters of yards often evinces the same general patterns seen in the yards themselves, including the use of equipment, adult figures, and images of animals (such as cow mailboxes). For example, ranch entrance gates are sometimes decorated with images of animals, animal skulls, abstract designs such as cattle brands, and renderings of human forms. One gate I photographed incorporated the figure of a man into its design, and another, constructed in the form of the ranch's brand, featured an image of two people roping a cow.

Material culture scholars who study fences usually analyze the different designs of fencing, for example, snake, chock-and-log, rip-gut, buck-and-pole, and jack-leg (Jordan, Kilpinen, and Gritzner 1997, 87–100). An occasional shoe does, however, show up on stretches of barbwire fencing, a folk custom used to mark a gate or particular spot. One fence I photographed in Colorado demonstrated the custom to excess. Some shoes on it were grouped on the basis of gender patterns, and gendered human and animal figures (such as Miss Piggy) dangled among the shoes. Nearly three hundred shoes hung on three-tenths of a mile's worth of barbwire. Like the public art found on lawns and in cemeteries, the fence's decoration emphasized sports, play, and gendered forms.

Yards in Historical Context

Gardens are the precursors to today's lawns and yards, and the word *garden* originally meant an enclosed space (Jackson 1980, 20–21). Asian cultures, notably China and Japan, have long and highly developed gardening traditions in which symbolism plays an important part. In sixteenth- and seventeenth-century Japanese gardens, for example, flowering blossoms were excluded from most gardens because of the influence of Zen Buddhism. They were replaced with evergreens and trees to represent eternal rather than transitory beauty (Thacker 1979, 66). The practice of Buddhism also shaped the philosophy that led to Japan's famed dry gardens, which are constructed from raked gravel enhanced by a few large stones. Because every part of creation is considered a part of Buddha, even the stones are said to convey the "universality of Buddha and the essence of reality" (Thacker 1979, 71). Asian gardens, excellent illustrations of the manner in which gardens reflect cultural values, influenced at least one yard artist profiled in this chapter.

Many European gardens are recognized for formal and orderly qualities informed by Egyptian and Persian gardens (Plumptre 1989, 27). Gardens throughout Islam, for example, the one constructed at the Taj Mahal in

1652, were well known for their architectural components (Thacker 1979, 27–28, 32). The Taj Mahal, a tomb, evinces the relationship that exists between gardens and burial places, a concept that also developed in the West from the nineteenth century onward.

The Greeks contributed much to the ornamentation of contemporary lawns and gardens. Their gardens contained statues of gods and heroes along with smaller features such as urns and vases (Plumptre 1989, 27), versions of which can still be seen in the most pedestrian yard art. Romans were fond of topiary gardens (Huxley 1998, 31), and the villa gardens of the wealthy combined horticultural and ornamental features such as a colonnade (copied from the Greeks), statues, water, and a wide variety of ornamental plants (Plumptre 1989, 28), all of which are still found in contemporary yards. Even though yard art statuary is now often considered kitsch, its distinguished pedigree extends to the elite art of ancient times.

There is not as much scholarly analysis of the cultural meanings of gardens and their ornaments as there is of gravemarkers and cemeteries. Gardens share much in terms of aesthetics, form, and statuary with cemeteries but do not leave durable artifactual remains, so tracing garden history can be difficult (Helphand 1999, 138). Some descriptions of gardens from the Middle Ages survive, however, and the cultural meanings of those can be discerned. Walled gardens in medieval cloisters were intended to symbolize the Virgin (Thacker 1979, 83). Such gardens were common, and whether secular or not they were influenced by the shape of the cloisters that enclosed them (Harvey 1981, 110). Space within walled gardens was often divided into squares (Thacker 1979, 82). One medieval document, a plan that shows the layout of an ideal monastery, details herb gardens, shrubbery, and a burial ground that is also used as an orchard, another example of the link between cemeteries and gardens (Harvey 1981, 25). In this early period it was customary to scatter roses in churches to symbolize the gift of the Holy Spirit, and Benedictine monasteries likely grew flowers in their gardens to deck altars on feast days (Harvey 1981, 26).

A new era of gardening dawned with the Renaissance. As Derek Clifford observes, "Nowadays gardening is thought of more often as a pastime than an art. But there was a time in the sixteenth century in Italy, in the seventeenth century in France, and in the eighteenth century in England, when it was considered a very important art, perhaps the most important of all, the one at which all others met. Painters, architects, sculptors, poets and philosophers gave their minds to the comprehension of its nature and the perfecting of its practice. Men who excelled at it became the confidants of statesmen and the friends of kings" (1967, 17).

Renaissance gardens were walled and, ordered in even rows and straight lines, influenced by Roman gardens. Visual surprise, one of their contributions that became important in succeeding eras, was achieved through siting that took advantage of glorious views (Thacker 1979, 95, 96). The stress on vistas that delight, even though they are executed on a much smaller scale, is still manifest in contemporary yards in the United States and Europe.

During the Renaissance, Leone Battista Alberti suggested that the walls of gardens should be enhanced by bas-reliefs, grottos, and pictures. Grand houses could show the "memorable Actions of great Men," and more modest homes might have pictures of "pleasant Landskips, of Havens, of Fishing, Hunting, Swimming, Country Sports, of flowery Fields, and thick Groves" (quoted in Thacker 1979, 96). Those practices prefigure elements of current yard ornamentation such as grottos and fountains. Precursors to some of the themes of contemporary yard art are evident in Renaissance reliefs. Images of fishing and hunting, along with fields of plastic flowers (especially flower whirligigs), are part of contemporary yard art assemblage. All are part of an emphasis on images of pleasant landscapes, often rural ones.

Wealthy Italian mercantile families such as the Medicis and other church leaders commissioned architects, engineers, and artists to create gardens. In 1584 Cardinal Ferdinand de' Medici purchased a villa in Rome and brought to it a collection of sculptures and reliefs that were incorporated into its garden. The classical emphasis of the garden at Villa Medici continues to be important in fine-art sculpture, cemetery statuary, and even yard art.

Renaissance gardens also featured statues of dwarves, rustics, servants, or peasants, and similar types of statues remain in today's yards. Dwarves and gnomes are popular, and rustic, rural life is often signaled through such statues as the "fishing boy." Sculptural representations of servitude such as lawn jockeys, or "faithful groomsmen" as they are sometimes known, exist on American lawns despite national ideals of democracy and equality.

"Joke fountains," which have sprinkled the unwary since at least the Middle Ages, became popular during the Renaissance. Monk Francesco Colonna's *Hypernaotomachia Poliphili* (1499) describes the dream of a protagonist named Poliphilus, along with the many gardens through which he passes. In one instance he is taken to a bath where two sculpted nymphs are cradling an "infant holding his little Instrument in both hands" and "pissing into the hot water, fresh cool water." Poliphilus is then sent to fetch some fresh water: "And I no sooner set my foot upon the step to receive the water but the pissing Boy lifted up his pricke, and cast sodeinlye so colde water upon my face, that I had lyke at that instant to have fallen backward. Whereat they so laughted, and it made such a sounde in the roundness and closeness of the bathe, that I also beganne to laugh that I was almost dead" (quoted in Thacker 1979, 113). *Pneumatica,* a text that dates from the mid-sixteenth century, explains this and many other such water tricks. Renaissance gardens featured paths, stairs, archways, floors, roofs, and even seats that shot water at unwitting passersby (Thacker 1979, 113).

Peeing boy statues and trick fountains are two predecessors of one version of the current "peeing boy" in yard art. Although it is not common, I have seen one contemporary wooden version of a boy to which a garden hose had been attached so a stream of water appeared to issue from the appropriate part of his anatomy. The "joke-sprinklers" that are also part of contemporary American yards may be distant relatives of joke fountains of the Renaissance. Among them are images of cows and cowboys that spray water in more erratic patterns than more ordinary sprinklers. Although primarily designed to water the grass rather than douse people—the spray could catch the uninitiated—joke sprinklers, by emphasizing playfulness, differ from their utilitarian counterparts. Like trick fountains, they are designed to surprise and delight.

The Villa d'Este at Tivoli near Rome is known for its use of water. In his description of its gardens, Christopher Thacker says, "Water, the life of the garden, is openly linked with the idea of fertility . . . originally at the centre of the Organ fountain is the joyously fecund statue of Diana of the Ephesians—many breasted, larger than life, with streams of water gushing from each nipple" (1979, 100). A spraying female nipple was also a theme of joke fountains (Thacker 1979, 114–15). Although many find contemporary yard art to be in poor taste, some of its aspects are tame compared to the ornamental elements in earlier gardens. The wooden cutout of the peeing boy is depicted from the back, and a spraying nipple is not a common motif, although yard art statuary of topless females can be purchased.

After the Renaissance, formal garden design arose and was employed to communicate power and status, especially in France. The garden at Versailles was intended to inspire awe and may have emerged from a case of "garden envy." In 1661 Nicolas Fouquet, France's finance minister, hosted an elegant garden reception at Vaux le Vicomte, his great chateau. Among the guests were Louis XIV and his court. Less than three weeks after the event, Louis arrested Fouquet for corruption and also, perhaps, because of the challenge to Louis's supremacy that Fouquet's party represented. Fouquet had expressed his elevated social standing through the sumptuous development of his gardens, and he used a new, particularly French, sense of aesthetics to do so (Mukerji 1997, 107). His extravagance made the scale of the graft harder to ignore:

Fouquet, the Treasurer when the young king came to power, was only following the lead of previous powerful ministers, namely Richelieu and Mazarin. . . . Fouquet's downfall may have been primarily a political tale about greed, graft, and political disgrace, but the story of Vaux's development and importance to France was different. This grand estate did more than just reveal Fouquet's character; it brought to light the possibility of a French culture that Louis the XIV quickly and enthusiastically embraced. . . . In the seventeenth-century French noble world, where politics was more a matter of performance than words, the glittering qualities of this physical space as a stage for political performance should not be underestimated. . . . At Vaux [Fouquet] built a political stage of staggering proportions and very French novelty. (Mukerji 1997, 106, 110)

Louis XIV took Fouquet's artisans from Vaux and set them to work on Versailles, the apogee of the formal French garden.

Chandra Mukerji argues that Versailles was an "articulation of a territorially based state," and the formal garden helped make the state visible as "a *material* accomplishment" (1997, 304). Mukerji adds that France became a territorial state largely through the construction of fortresses, the presence of which turned French territories into a French landscape. The gardens at Versailles mirrored these military efforts. They were built using military engineering, decorated with military symbols, filled with the evidence of French success, and used for the celebration of French military victories. The gardens were testimony to the power of the state (1997, 306). Moreover, they were a metaphor for the Sun King's power over the physical world and French culture. In addition, the numerous pieces of sculpture at Versailles showed the king to be the era's greatest patron of the arts (Thacker 1979, 158).

Nature, not always cooperative with the demands of king and country, was not subject to quite the level of obeisance that Louis XIV would have wished. Even though much of it was a water garden, water was always in short supply in Versailles. There was never enough to feed more than 1,200 fountain jets. The action of the fountains was regulated to correspond with the movements of the king and court, something accomplished by a "secret" system of whistle-blasts and boys who ran ahead of the king to signal his advent with flags (Plumptre 1989, 18; Thacker 1979, 154).

Formal gardens existed throughout Europe, but during the eighteenth century the rigidity of that approach began to diminish. Its influence in the form of a desire to tightly control nature, however, is still seen in the manner in which Americans maintain their yards. Historically, the movement away from formal gardens began with the advent of rococo, a style that employed lighter, less serious components. The garden at Weikersheim in Baden-Württemberg, Germany, is a good example of rococo playfulness.

It has a formal outline but lacks symmetry. Its unusual statuary initially appears to echo those at Versailles. There are representations of the four winds, the four seasons, and many figures from classical mythology. Several of the sculptures, however, are of servants or personalities of the Court at Weikersheim, all given the features and proportions of dwarves (Thacker 1989, 173).

Playfulness was a theme of earlier gardens, especially those with trick fountains, and it is also an aspect of the yard art that became widespread during the twentieth century (Sheehy 1998, 60). As the whimsical became more dominant and statuary more affordable, yard art ceased to be associated with elite culture and came to be seen as a "lower" form of art.

An even greater challenge to formal gardens than the influence of the rococo emerged in England, where formal gardens were critiqued as too rigid, too arrogant, and too unnatural (Thacker 1979, 182). The English believed that gardens should look more like the countryside, and thus the English landscape garden was created. Despite their emphasis on nature, however, these gardens were still constructed sites subject to human control (Hunt 1999, 85). A fondness for referencing the human past—real or imagined—through artifacts, statuary, or manufactured ruins was also manifest in English gardens, an affinity seen earlier, such as in Renaissance gardens' focus on the classical era. The past continues to be represented in contemporary yard art reproductions of classical statuary and in collections of artifacts, such as the wagon wheels and old equipment, that still adorn American yards.

For many centuries American ground was uninfluenced by European gardening practices, although several cultures in Mexico and South America produced elaborate gardens during the pre-Columbian era. From around 2500 B.C.E. the Incas maintained impressive gardens that included "water channels, pools, and basins, sometimes made of silver and gold" (Huxley 1998, 36). During the twelfth century, the Aztecs had courtyard gardens, extensive and systematic botanical gardens, and royal water gardens (Huxley 1998, 36). Parks were even dedicated to the propagation of rare trees. Tragically, however, the Spaniards destroyed all this (Huxley 1998, 36). When the Pilgrims arrived in North America they found Native Americans to be excellent gardeners who tended "unfenced fields and plots of neatly cultivate crops" in their villages (Huxley 1998, 39). Native Americans also had detailed knowledge of plants; in the East, South, and Southwest they maintained gardens of corn, squash, and beans.

In the non-Indian cultures of early America only a few wealthy landowners debated whether to use the long-accepted formal pattern or try the newer English practices of landscaping (Leighton 1976, 364). Thomas Jefferson was one of the first in the Colonies to create a garden modeled on the English style (Jenkins 1994, 16). George Washington also hired English landscape gardeners at Mount Vernon, which boasted a deer park and a bowling green in front of the house (Jenkins 1994, 16).

Most middle-class Americans had small, fenced front gardens, or their houses were built so close to a road that they had no front yards at all. A garden patch was either in front of the house or behind it. Archaeological digs reveal that household trash was piled alongside front and back doors. Many people had yards of bare dirt, or they left their yards to native vegetation. In the South, many front yards were of swept dirt, clay, or sand (Jenkins 1994, 15), a practice that is probably of West African origin (Westmacott 1992, 103). The first documented American use of the word *lawn* to mean a smooth, grassy ground is from 1733. Many other countries, however, including China and India, eschewed lawns, which were considered as expensive, impractical, aesthetically unappealing, and cover for unwanted snakes and insects (Jenkins 1994, 3).

Even in America the concept of having a lawn did not catch on until after the Civil War (Jenkins 1994, 14). The popularity of lawns was related to the growth of suburbs, which were influenced by public parks. Landscape architect Frederick Law Olmsted, considered the father of the national public park system, was influenced by the landscaping styles of the rural cemetery movement (Jackson 1985, 55). A technological development also greatly assisted in making American lawns an achievable reality: the lawnmower. Grass could be closely cut without the need of scythes or grazing animals.

Frank Jessup Scott's *Victorian Gardens: The Art of Beautifying the Suburban Homegrounds* (1870) helped further popularize the well-mown lawn as a key landscape feature. Stereographs of attractive yards, their grass cut, were found in Victorian parlors across the country (Sheehy 1998, 15). The Centennial Exhibition in Philadelphia in 1876, the World's Columbian Exposition in Chicago in 1893, and the Pan-American Exposition of 1901 in Buffalo introduced thousands of Americans to the concept of a mown lawn and the necessity of having equipment to keep it in that condition (Jenkins 1994, 71).

The American love affair with grass also meant having lawnmowers, which could be dangerous. Virginia Jenkins argues that the mower industry placed performance over safety for many years. By the 1950s the single, knifelike blade of a rotary-power mower could throw stones or debris at a velocity that could (and did) kill and maim. Approximately 140,000 people were injured in mower accidents in 1969. Standards were upgraded in 1972 due to an investigation by the U.S. Consumer Product Safety Commission, which found false safety certification on a quarter of the mowers it surveyed. The National Commission on Product Safety named mowers as the second most dangerous product in the United States, after automobiles (Jenkins 1994, 114).

Many aspects of twentieth-century life involved some hazard—for example, there was a chance of having an accident while driving a car. What is interesting about mowing, however, is that it has the potential to do significant harm but is not an essential activity. Although some procedures necessary to maintain the elaborate formal gardens of earlier centuries must have caused injury, those who were hurt were likely to be injured in the line of duty, executing their jobs. Estate owners were much less at risk than mid-twentieth-century homeowners who cut their own grass. Other aspects of American life court nonessential danger—driving race cars, for example—but those activities are not widespread. Moreover, the wisdom of such pursuits is subject to debate. Some even provide fame and fabulous economic rewards unlike any to be obtained from mowing a lawn. Despite the dangers of doing so, however, little public debate occurred about the wisdom of having a lawn and mowing it. Cut grass became a cultural given. That attitude suggests a high level of technology acceptance and the risks that can accompany technology. After all, as Kenneth Helphand points out, "Most American garden history deals with a period during and after the Industrial Revolution; therefore our gardens are almost all products of a technological age" (1999, 143).

The custom of mowing a lawn also indicates American conformance to a particular aesthetic ideal handed down from European aristocracy. Despite the nation's democratic and antihierarchal rhetoric, many of its customs and behaviors have descended from the class-based systems of early Europe. Contemporary homeowners often explain their yard maintenence practices by acknowledging social pressure or individual aesthetics (Ryden 2001, 12). "It's expected of me," they say. "I don't want to have the worst looking yard in the neighborhood," or, "I just like the way the lawn looks when it's mowed." Although not apparent to most yard owners, one of the reasons why the practice of mowing has become popular involves historical association with elite culture and privilege.

Americans learned about lawn care from magazines and also through advertising. American yards indicate the effectiveness of advertising in creating and perpetuating desires and promoting certain aesthetic ideals, a process that is also part of the reason for the success of Barbie dolls. Gender played a role in strategies for marketing lawn-care products. From the late nineteenth through the twentieth centuries, advertising was directed toward a male audience. When power mowers became more affordable during the late 1930s, they were advertised as masculine machines; indeed, many were sold as recreational vehicles or small automobiles (Jenkins 1994, 109, 127). The word *boy* was part of many brand names: Dandy Boy, Lawn Boy, and Lazy Boy. "Naming these machines 'boy' may have also appealed to the racial stereotypes held by white Americans, as in a Philippino 'house boy' or an African American 'yard boy,'" Jenkins notes. "Such names also may have been meant to suggest class and the presence of servants rather than gender, yet even grass was considered masculine: 'After reading *Lawn Care* you'll discover why Summer's warmed sod, cool nights and gentle fall rains hustle young grass plants into vigorous manhood'" (1994, 128). That twentieth-century description is reminiscent of earlier folk associations of plants and growth with masculinity, for example, "John Barleycorn" is a subject of British folk songs (Santino 1996, 106).

Front yards have been considered male domains as well as reflections of taste, economic standing, Americaness, and even individual character. As Mary Riley Smith says, "The history of American front yards is one of evolution from enclosed, private yards to open, democratic spaces virtually indistinguishable from those on either side" (1991, 15–16). Because Jenkins acknowledges the influence of European aristocracy and American democracy, her description is particularly apt. The English manor house in its parklike setting, she observes, was translated in "American democratic terms to more modest homes on one-acre lots surrounded by trees and lawn" (1994, 25). There are, however, more specific descriptors of the American lawn than the word *democratic*. An even more accurate phrasing would be that having a lawn indicates economic access. Few Europeans of the seventeenth century could finance elaborate formal gardens. More people in America, however, can afford to maintain a yard, so the types of "democratic" ideals a yard communicates may not be that all people are equal but more capitalistic ones instead. Many Americans have greater economic access to material culture.

Even though American yards are similar to each other, varying degrees of status can still be expressed. One can seek standing through having an exceptionally well-maintained lawn, which is thought to demonstrate good taste and imply that its owners command the medium of lawncare more impressively than their neighbors. As Americans shifted from being producers to becoming consumers, their lawns frequently went from workplaces to showplaces:

The economic and social revolutions of the late nineteenth and early twentieth centuries led to the development of national markets for mass-produced goods. These upheavals included industrialization, urbanization, the communications revolution, and the transportation revolution, especially the completion of the railroad network, which made possible the rapid shipment of goods and information from coast to coast and from city to suburb and countryside. A highly protective tariff system and a steady supply of cheap immigrant labor stimulated American's manufacturing capacity. Prices decreased during the last third of the nineteenth century, creating a consumer market previously unparalleled in the Western world. In 1900, more than 75 percent of urban Americans lived in rented apartments. As the average income of urban Americans doubled between 1900 and 1917, thousands of families moved to new homes in the suburbs that were developing around every city. (Jenkins 1994, 64–65)

Drawing on Daniel Boorstin's notion of "consumption communities" that developed in the late nineteenth century, Jenkins argues that advertising along with magazine articles helped create a community of lawn owners who shared a particular landscape aesthetic (1994, 66). The desire to have attractive lawns was created by manufacturers of yard-related products (Jenkins 1994, 115). The yearning for yards also grew out of trends set by cultural arbiters (such as Jefferson and Washington) throughout American history and an ever-present concern with manifesting social standing through material forms (Bronner, ed. 1989), already a well-established tradition in lawns and gardens.

After World War II, lawns were seen as necessary and usual parts of a landscape even as they became more artificial and unnatural. As Michael Pollan observes, "We won't settle for the lawn that will grow here; we want the one that grows *there,* that dense springy supergreen and weed-free carpet, that platonic ideal of a lawn featured in the Chemlawn commercials and magazine spreads. . . . It occurred to me that time as we know it doesn't exist in the lawn, since grass never dies or is allowed to flower and set seed. Lawns are nature purged of sex or death. No wonder Americans like them so much" (1991, 75). Schroeder points out that the advent of air-conditioning has lessened the functional value of a front lawn and increased its decorative quality. "Front yards have become like Victorian parlors and formal dining rooms, expensive, unused, ornamental spaces that need to be kept tidy for the sake of appearances only" (1993, 136).

Along with air-conditioning, the chemicals that are applied to lawns keep people off grass as well. The deployment of chemicals on lawns became widespread after World War II, and it is common to see signs warning people to stay off lawns until the chemical applications on them have dried.

In some cases, moreover, pets such as guinea pigs have died after being allowed on recently treated grass.

The range and potential danger of some of the chemicals that homeowners use in their yards are disturbing in hindsight, but their use reflects American faith—albeit sometimes a dangerously innocent confidence—in science and technology and the chemical compounds they produce. In some cases the degree of danger involved in using a lawn product is unknown to consumers. It took the 1960s, with Rachel Carson's *Silent Spring* (Jenkins 1994, 156) and Vietnam's Agent Orange, to begin Americans' education about the dangers of chemicals. By the middle of the twentieth century the general public had little knowledge of the deleterious effects of chemicals. During the 1940s, for example, isopropyl phenyl carbamate, perfected by the U.S. Army for biological warfare, was recommended as a means of eradicating quack grass. Extremely poisonous (and not terribly effective) crabgrass killers composed of mercury or arsenic were also on the market (Jenkins 1994, 148). Moreover, one could use chloropicrin—teargas—to destroy crabgrass seeds before they sprouted.

Researchers developing chemical warfare agents for use against humans during World War II found that some were efficacious for insects as well. DDT and sabadilla were combined to make a general pesticide (Jenkins 1994, 153). *Lawn Care,* a newsletter produced by a lawn products company, explained that pest control before DDT was much trickier: "[It] generally involved working with poisonous substances, laboriously mixing and applying sprays or choking dusts. Apprehension followed lest a member of the family or a pet be sickened by one of the toxic ingredients. Some treatments had added hazards of explosion and fire" (Jenkins 1994, 153). Chlordane was employed as a pesticide even though in 1950 it was described as "one of the most toxic of insecticides—anyone handling it could be poisoned" (Jenkins 1994, 154).

Concerns about the effects of chemicals continued into the late twentieth century. The commonly used weed-killer 2,4-D caused severe toxic reactions when pets such as dogs walked on grass that had been treated. Diazinon use on golf courses and turf farms was banned by the Environmental Protection Agency because of the large bird-kill associated with it; the agency began phasing it out for lawn use in 2000. In one instance seven hundred brant geese died after feeding on a diazinon-treated golf course (Jenkins 1994, 164). Chemicals like DDT and arsenic were banned for home use (Jenkins 1994, 156). Yet even with the concern about chemical usage, by the late 1980s the average lawn owner was using a higher concentration of chemicals than that used by farmers (Jenkins 1994, 186).

Other environmental problems were created by grass clippings and water use. By the 1990s, many American communities had banned dumping
those clippings in landfills because of the huge amount of space they oc-
cupied. Lawn grass requires about an inch of water a week, and a twenty-
five-by-forty-foot yard requires an estimated ten thousand gallons of water each summer (Jenkins 1994, 186). In arid parts of the United States, such
as the West, watering lawns constitutes an unsound water-use practice. In
Dallas, for example, lawns consume 60 percent of the city's water during
the summer (Jenkins 1994, 172).

Even though it is clear that history (French formal gardens and English
landscape gardens) and science (in the form of herbicides, pesticides, and
fertilizers) have shaped the ideal of an American front lawn, the folk process is also at work. Many people lack formal schooling about how a yard
should look, and many, although they could employ landscape profession-
als, shape their yards by using information gained through folk channels.
They employ what they have learned informally through families, friends,
and neighbors. Homeowners often assume that certain kinds of grasses
should grow in a yard and that weeds should be dealt with in a particular
fashion because of what they saw their parents do. Just as a beginning
quilter might seek advice from a grandmother who taught her to quilt, so,
too, a new homeowner often turns to an informal network of family and
friends with such questions as "what do you do to get rid of dandelions?"
Advertising and the folk aesthetic have taught many Americans that dandelions do not belong in yards.

One often engages in folk customs without much question. Most Americans know nothing of the history of yards, and what they do apprehend
comes from experience. If they are unaware of the historical shifts that
demonstrate that a yard is a created and variable space, they can be less re-
ceptive to change. That conservative aspect of the folk process can perpetuate positive traditions, but it can also preserve less beneficent traditions. If
one learns chemical application from a trusted and loved role model like a
parent, for example, one might be less likely to question whether or not it
is safe to do so ("Dad always used it; it must be okay").

The way many people have learned about yards does not foreground the
variability of landscaping, and alternatives are sometimes met with ridicule
and even hostility. Americans since the 1960s have been increasingly aware
of and concerned about environmental issues as more and more information has become available on judicious chemical use and how to maintain
a chemical-free lawn. Such a change began to be evident in front yards at
the end of the twentieth century. "Alternative" lawns began to spring up,

and the xeriscape approach emerged. This is a particularly fascinating turn of events because it demonstrates the reemergence of the lawn as a political statement, as had been the case with seventeenth-century gardens such as the one at Versailles. The politics this time, however, are quite different. Contemporary yards can become a platform for political debate about environmental safety and responsibility rather than a stage for celebrating the power of king and country. Instead of the politics of state, these lawns express personal environmental politics.

Xeriscape, although often misheard and misunderstood to mean "zero scape," involves creating natural lawns or even "home meadows." The movement is just as constructed—created by humans—as any other landscaping movement I have discussed (Hunt 1999, 86) but distinguished by, among other things, a basis in biology. In a xeriscape, lawn and garden methods are compatible with the environment. Xeriscape conserves water, requires few chemicals, and employs drought-resistant plants. It is a gardening approach to lawns rather than one of traditional maintenance.

Neighbors are not always pleased with front yards that depart from the norms. The latter part of the twentieth century was a time when environmentalism was embraced, but it was also an age when the term *environmentalist* had negative connotations for some people. In some situations, viewer discomfort with more "natural" lawns comes from some level of awareness (and perhaps dislike) of the environmental or "green" politics the yard is supposed to express.

Despite all the historical changes in yard aesthetics, statuary remains a constant. Renaissance and formal gardens made extensive use of statuary, and English landscape gardens had fewer statues but did not eliminate them entirely. In the Victorian era, when yards were fairly common for the well-to-do and the middle class, many Americans turned to European sources for yard statuary. Demonstrating refinement and culture at that time meant drawing on European arts. *Garden Ornament* (1918) by Gertrude Jekyll, the British garden expert, was also popular among American gardeners, who were influenced by the book's many plates of classically inspired statuary. From the 1890s to the 1930s, garden statuary became an important addition to the repertoire of American sculptors, and it helped them expand the market for their work (Bogart 1985, n.p.).

Middle-class gardeners could purchase less expensive copies of classical statuary made of cast iron, lead, stone, ceramic, and plaster. Its use was widespread: "Embellishments of statuary, vases, urns, and outdoor furniture were common to both civic and domestic landscapes. Manufacturers of garden statuary and furniture at the time sold their wares to bereaved families, cemetery operators, park managers, and homeowners alike. The American domestic landscape, therefore, was not necessarily a separate spatial category but shared common design aesthetics and ideology with public spaces" (Sheehy 1998, 24).

During the nineteenth and early twentieth centuries rural cemeteries and public parks provided models for American yards, and as the twentieth century progressed new templates appeared, including lighted displays at world fairs; roadside attractions; miniature golf courses; and amusement parks, especially Disneyland (Sheehy 1998, 34). Many of these sites emphasize celebratory spaces set off from mundane routines (Sheehy 1998, 34). Yard art owners capitalize on that element as well, particularly when they focus on holidays.

A twentieth-century American yard may be visually different from a Renaissance garden or a seventeenth-century formal garden, but there are similarities that may not be apparent at first glance. Distance from nature, for example, is more obvious in a formal garden's design and plantings than a twentieth-century yard's. The desire to control nature was apparent, however, in the twentieth-century's heavy use of chemicals and machinery—and with a significant amount of work and some risk involved. The xeriscape movement at the end of the twentieth century was a nod toward the natural, but that style, and the philosophy that led to it, was not widespread enough to be counted as being responsible for a significant change in American yard habits before the millennium.

The existence of modern yard art thus expresses the influence of classical statuary; worldviews on religion; the gardening methods of Europe; the importance of material culture in manifesting status, politics, and attitudes toward the environment; and public cultural entities such as amusement parks. Lawns also reveal something of the ascendancy of individualism. Historically, distinctive lawns were more available to the wealthy, who used well-executed gardens as evidence of social standing. Because statuary became more affordable, an ever-greater range of individualism was manifest though yard assemblages during the late nineteenth century and throughout the twentieth. Cemetery statuary of the same period also demonstrated the rise of individualism by employing inexpensive materials and technologies.

Unlike some cemetery statues, however, especially those of males, the statues in yards are not generally meant as literal portraits of those who live in a specific house. Many, if not most, yard statues are of stock characters, and neither males nor females are presented as unique individuals. Therefore, yards do not reveal as much about public visibility and the rise of male individualism as cemeteries do. Moreover, unlike cemetery statuary, ary does not usually foster legends. One of the most folkloric aspe art is the process of assemblage, "a category of art, a genre of sculp with found objects, a kind of three-dimensional collage" (Santino 19 see also 1992b and 1994, 36). It involves "juxtaposition of elements t be and often are displayed as discrete units in order to modify, stren or otherwise develop a symbolic public statement" (Santino 2001, 50

Yard Art in a Folkloric Context

Henry Glassie, an eminent chronicler of material culture, argues that assem blage, "the collection of commodities assembled into domestic settings," is one of the key creations in the material culture of industrial civilization (1999, 84). Glassie believes that this collection of commodities represents a victory over the threatened disorder of the industrial era—the flood of goods that threatens to sweep away society—just as stone houses repre- sented a triumph over chaos in the days when people lived close to nature and its uncontrollable aspects (1999, 86).

The task of those who study material culture is to "get up, go out, and find the things that will help us learn how others manage in the world we share" (Glassie 1999, 86). Doing so led me to Bernice and her yard dominated by a central holiday assemblage—which changed seasonally—surrounded by numerous statues and wooden cutouts. The entire yard was framed with bright flowers in beds that also contained statuary. Bernice's comments about her Logan, Utah, yard assemblage and her life taught me, as Glassie says, something of how she manages in the world. Through art, persever- ance, and humor, Bernice managed a life full of labor and difficulty. When I asked if I could interview her about her yard, she pleasantly agreed. It was her wedding cakes, however, that she told me about first when she invited me in and seated me at the kitchen table.

She brought out a fat album that contained pictures chronicling the deli- cate art of a hard-working woman. As she turned the pages, she told me about wedding cakes she had made. She had gotten started after hearing about a family paying $25 for a wedding cake. "I said, 'There's not a cake in this world worth twenty-five dollars.' 'Til after I made my first one. Then I changed my mind!"

Cake-making was hard work: Bernice started on Sunday night in order to have a cake ready for a reception on Friday. She baked it on Sunday and started decorating on Monday. She usually did three cakes a week while raising children and working at a local grocery store. She got home from the grocery store at 7 P.M. and then begin working on her cakes. Looking back on it, she says, cake-making did not pay well. "I never made a nickel. A lot of times I was lucky if I made ten cents an hour." After all those years of standing on her ladder and decorating the top layers, she says, "I can't stand cake! I never make a cake. If someone hands [me] a dish [of cake] with ice cream on it or something, I struggle through it. I don't like cake." Despite the difficulty of the work, Bernice made exquisitely beautiful cakes for years. During that time she also began decorating her yard with statuary, a tradition she maintained for nearly thirty years.

Until her second marriage she did the yard work and assemblage by her-self. Her relationships with other people and her willingness to be a care-taker led to her first yard assemblage. When a disabled woman who lived across the street needed daily personal assistance, the woman's family asked Bernice if she would help. She did so for the final ten years of the woman's life, in addition to making cakes and her grocery store job. As a measure of his gratitude, the woman's husband made Bernice several wooden knick-knacks for her kitchen. During this time Bernice saw a picture of Mr. and Mrs. Santa and their elves, decided she wanted yard art versions of them, bought the plywood and all the material to make them, and enlisted the neighbor to build them for her. That year she won a prize for her Christmas yard decorations. Then, using sheets, she transformed Mr. and Mrs. Santa into a ghost and a witch at Halloween. Because her children have given her some of the statues in the yard, much of the display manifests her social, familial, and care-giving relationships.

Bernice's 120-year-old home with its yard art is well known due to its location across from the tennis courts in a city park. Of living there she laughs, "Oh, I love it. We watch everything that goes on at the park. . . . And I've never seen any really, really good tennis players." The children in the area call her house the "Holiday House" or the "Gingerbread House." A neighbor who works at a nearby school told Bernice that one day, when they were planning a field trip, the students said, "Well, okay, we'll go if you'll take us by [Bernice's] house."

Children are a significant reason for Bernice's yard decorations. "We have people come and take pictures," she says, "and line their kids up [and take their picture]. At Easter, oh, a lot of times, they have little kids in front of all those bunnies and stuff." She reports that the children "as they go by, they say [to me], 'We just love your yard; oh, we just love this place!'"

Bernice and her husband Orange also engage in playful interactions with children. Both costume for Halloween, and Bernice has been known to have some fun with this practice:

There's a little girl—well, she's a senior [in high school] this year, I'm sure. Lives just on the corner, a block north. And when she was about three, her mother brought her over trick or treating. And I always dressed up for Halloween. . . . My husband and I both [do]. And anyway, I was a witch, and I scared her to death. And anyway, the next spring I was out there in the ground bed a working and here come this little girl, and I tried to talk to her, but she wouldn't say a word. Finally, she said, "And, you're the real witch."

And I said, "That's right."

She got on that trike, and she was gone—now! [Both laugh.]

There isn't a day goes by that somebody don't tell us how they like our yard.

Along with reflecting her creativity, sense of humor, and relationships with other people, Bernice's yard art is about creating a space for children in an adult world. It allows adults to engage and share in the delight of the imaginative world that is frequently seen as the realm of children. Front lawns in America often amount to little more than repetitious open swaths of grass with scant variation from the rest of the neighborhood lawns. Yard art like Bernice's transforms those lawns into places that reference an entirely different world—one of fantasy and imagination. The "stage" for yard art—a mown lawn—demonstrates expected neighborhood conformity, but a yard art assemblage can allow spaces that are visually and functionally different from the majority of other neighborhood yards.

Individuals such as Bernice primarily use animals, sometimes the same as found in zoos, and holiday assemblages to create imaginative worlds in their yards. The term *zoo* dates from England in 1847 and is a colloquialism for "zoological gardens" (Sheehy 1998, 81). The precursors to zoos were the collections of rare animals from countries the wealthy considered exotic, creatures displayed in estate gardens throughout Europe. Many estates also kept animals that were not quite so exotic, such as peacocks, cranes, and flamingos. The flamingo is one of the best-known yard art figures (Price 1999, 111–65), and Colleen Sheehy maintains that flamingo displays at zoos brought the bird to the attention of many Americans (1998, 81). In 1957 Don Featherstone, a graphic designer, created a plastic flamingo for a company called Union Products. Featherstone's flamingo was also part of the 1950s' explosion of pink and plastic. *Life* magazine called 1955 the "Peak Year for Pink." Pink toilets and tubs, even stoves, were available, as were pink plastic dishes (Sheehy 1998, 92).

Flamingos are now employed for folk customs such as pranks. Masses of them can materialize on the lawns of unsuspecting homeowners, sometimes complete with cotton balls dyed pink to represent flamingo droppings. Businesses have commodified this folk behavior and sell the number of flamingos necessary for such large-scale pranks or for celebrating a birthday or some other rite of passage. Groups also use flocks to raise money for charitable causes. The flamingos mysteriously appear on lawns, accompanied by a note indicating that they will be removed upon receipt of a donation (Chase 2000, n.p.).

Along with exotic types of animals, more mundane ones such as plastic chickens inhabit yards. Some are also anthropomorphic. One, the concrete or plastic goose, is both mundane and anthropomorphic and frequently gendered either male or female through costume (figure 21). Concrete geese have been popular in the Midwest since the 1980s (Marsden 1995,

Figure 21. Yard goose in bikini designed by Monica.

53); their place of origin has been variously ascribed to Ohio, Kentucky, Indiana, or Illinois.

While driving in the Midwest and Upper South, I saw yard geese dressed in raincoats and hats; Santa and Mrs. Santa costumes; reindeer costumes; and Halloween costumes. There were also husband and wife geese in dresses, top hats, and ties and, standing by a backyard barbeque, a goose in a chef's apron (Modra and Roberts 1998, 82). Handmade signs were posted in some Indiana neighborhoods to advertise the addresses of homes where one could purchase handmade clothing for geese. Amy told me that her mother changed their goose's costumes to reflect the season or family events. When Amy graduated from high school, for example, the family goose was gowned and wore a mortarboard.

Crafters have flocked to the Internet to advertise their "goose wares." It is possible to purchase geese and numerous costumes from individual crafters or from virtual gift stores for geese. There is a grim reaper goose, a ghost goose, a jack o' lantern goose, a cowgirl goose, a cowboy goose, an Easter Bunny goose, an Easter egg goose, a Christmas elf goose, a snowman goose, a leprechaun goose (with a red beard), a turkey goose, a crow goose, a cardinal goose, a Superman goose, a Batman goose, a "bingo lady" goose, and a space alien goose. Catalogs such as the Country Store ("the general store that fits in your mailbox") sell concrete geese as well as Pilgrim outfits, goose earmuffs for winter weather, Miss America costumes, and sunglasses for goslings. Geese clothing references the common components of yard art—holidays, animals, and stock characters such as cowboys. Much yard art is concerned with the humorous or whimsical, and geese have successfully capitalized on that aspect. The incongruity of seeing an average lawn goose dressed as Superman, for example, or a rabbit or the grim reaper can elicit laughter.

Making clothing for geese is akin to sewing doll clothes and dressing dolls, except a goose is usually displayed in a more public fashion and more likely to seem humorous than a doll. It is also easier to make goose clothing than doll clothing because geese have no arms and come in only a few standard sizes (Marsden 1995, 53). Monica, who makes and sells goose clothes in Illinois, says that many customers prefer outfits with arms. Her best-sellers for every holiday and season are dresses that have arms, including items for Mrs. Santa Claus, Mrs. St. Patrick, and Mrs. Valentine. Dresses made from holiday prints are also favored. "I think," she observes, "customers are trying to make the geese look more like people." The "lady witch," a costume that has no arms but does have a witch hat, is the next most popular model among Monica's customers. Lonnie, who sews and sells clothing for geese in Seattle, Washington, reports that her top-selling female outfit is, appropriately, a raincoat: "The yellow rain slicker is a major seller in Washington with all of the rain. I also sell lots of Hawaiian dresses and bikinis. Perhaps the desire we have for warm weather plays out in our geese dressing!"

Monica estimates that 98 percent of her customers are women, and when they buy "male" clothing for their geese the largest-sellers are snowmen and Easter Bunny outfits. Lonnie's only male buyers are purchasing the geese and the geese clothing for their wives. Her customers like sports outfits, especially those of the local sports teams: the Seattle Seahawks (football) and Mariners (baseball). They also purchase fishing and hunting outfits. "Women buying the geese as gifts for men," Lonnie says, "go for the outfit that represents an interest or hobby."

Despite the availability of sports costumes for geese, I saw few of these outfits on geese in midwestern yards. The costuming for the male geese that I saw departed from the stereotypically masculine or macho presentations common in other yard art images. Most outfits were for the male half of goose couples. A male goose's garb often matches the female's; in fact, the males seem to be accessories. Therefore, male geese—most of which are purchased and dressed by women—present a noticeably softer and gentler masculine image than do most other yard art statuary of males.

In some cases a goose marks a female's domestic territory. Chad, for example, told me that his mother had a yard goose dressed as a Holstein cow. Black and white "Holstein" spots were a motif in the decor of her house, especially the kitchen, and she had extended it onto the porch in the form of her goose.

Women often dress geese in a fashion that is whimsical and indicative of caretaking behaviors. Unlike geese in real life, which can be aggressive, yard geese are not meant to be threatening. They often wear evidence of nurturing. Someone has either made their clothes or purchased special outfits for them; dressed them in a manner that is seasonally appropriate (e.g., earmuffs for winter); and changed the clothing to delight others, especially children. Some geese reflect family members or their interests, such as a husband's love of sports. When a mother dresses her goose in a way that shows pride in a child's accomplishments (such as high school graduation) it is a concrete representation of her love.

"In some cases," Monica says, "the geese seem to be a replacement for children that have grown and left the house. In some cases, women who have had all boys use the goose to 'fill the need for a daughter with cute little dresses.' Women just think the goose is so cute. It is a conversation piece."

A goose's ability to meet all these functions, Monica observes, is part of the reason for its popularity. Because geese are frequently used in a way that foregrounds nurturing, whimsy, and caretaking behaviors, male geese are not usually presented in a manner that rigidly follows the stock patterns of other yard art male figures. Even when dressed in more stereotypically masculine clothes such as hunting or sports costumes, the fact that a goose is wearing the outfit lessens its masculine appearance. "Gooseness" works against the toughness implied by "hunterness" or "footballness," and humor is derived from that incongruity. A goose, which is often prey, is dressed as a hunter.

The cross-species dressing subtly pokes fun at human behaviors such as costuming. Other than humans, no other animals engage in masquerade merely for amusement, which is part of the reason it is so humorous to see a goose dressed as another animal. Animal costumes are among Lonnie's favorites. "I enjoy making them look alike but not quite, if that makes sense," she says. "There's something so nonsensical about a goose dressing up as a rabbit or a giraffe. Folks are attracted to the goofiness of it I think, I hope." When she makes her costumes Lonnie tries to get close to depicting the other animal but strives to maintain the goose's identity, because the incongruity of having both present in one form contributes to the humor, or "goofiness" as she says.

Lonnie also notes, however, that she sometimes has to be careful when displaying some species of geese at craft shows. "In the Seattle area, there's a huge problem with Canadian geese pooping all over lakes and lawns, and folks somewhat hate them if it affects them. So much to the point where I had to take the Canadian geese out of the display at one craft show. People are nuts. At the street fair at the University of Washington it was the worst. However, at the same show, there were several folks who actually thought my clothing was for real geese, so figure that into their piece of sanity in the first place."

Both Monica and Lonnie mentioned their interest in the popularity of the geese. Monica maintains that no one single factor accounts for such popularity. Before selling goose clothes, she crafted for more than twenty-five years, making quilts, rugs, and baskets. "I really have been amazed by this phenomenon," she says. "I thought that dressing geese was a craze and would last about three years. That was over eight years ago, and I am still making outfits. In the summer of '98, it went from a hobby to a full-time job. I have four women that sew for me. They might make the entire outfit from my patterns and requirements. They might make the basic dress/body, and I do all the trimming. All I can say is that this 'craze' is still grow-

ing. I do more business each year." Lonnie explains how she entered the
goose business:

A friend attended a conference in Cincinnati several years ago and came back and
told me about the geese. [It] sounded kind of fun to me, so I went on the hunt for a
large concrete goose for my porch. Found patterns in Simplicity but they didn't fit
my goose, so I started to adjust theirs and create my own. Friends enjoyed the goose
on my porch and wanted me to make clothes for them, so they went on the hunt
for geese. Then it was them giving geese as gifts. Soon the concrete ones were too
big of a hassle, so I used the Internet to find pink flamingos and managed to discover that the same company produced plastic geese (Union Products in Maine). I
sell the plastic geese at the shows and really make most of my clothes to fit them.
More and more, folks will show up that already have a concrete goose (usually because they have a relative or visited or lived in the Midwest), and I do have some
outfits available but can always make the same outfit in a size to fit their goose.

Considering costumed geese in the context of the overall patterns found
in yard art—and taking into account Amy's, Chad's, Monica's, and Lonnie's comments—some of the factors that have made yard geese beloved
become apparent. The process of dressing and displaying them allows several inviting aspects of yard art and material culture to emerge in association with one form. Objects that foster caretaking and creative behaviors
are part of the appeal of yard assemblage. Humorous objects are also favored. Animals and holiday images are among the most common types of
yard art. A goose can encompass all of these aspects and embody many of
the things that draw people to yard art in general. A clothed goose allows
any and all components of yard art to be present in one object, to be drawn
upon or not as an owner sees fit. That versatility may account for geese's
ascendant popularity.

Some yard art, such as Bernice's, that uses animal statuary is created with
children and the imaginative world of childhood in mind. Such yards constitute an interesting and significant folk use of space. Free public areas,
playgrounds and parks are dedicated to physical play. Playgrounds occasionally feature whimsical statuary, but most play equipment is meant for
physical activity and often has geometric or abstract shapes. A similar space
composed of concrete forms to embody the imaginative and figurative
world of childhood—and dedicated more to a child's mind—is much
harder to find. In some cases the folk process fills this gap through yard
assemblage that turns fancy and imagination into actual figures on a private but publicly visible lawn. Some adults, through yard art, grant children
a place for the life of the mind.

Because yard art frequently references the world of childhood through cartoon figures, holiday characters, and friendly animals, it is no wonder that figures of children and other little people also populate lawns. Along with statues of animals, statues of little people were among the most common forms of yard art that I saw. Images of children have been part of gardens for hundreds of years. The contemporary wooden cutout of the backside of a boy who is urinating, for example, is descended from centuries-old fountains that show little boys engaged in the same activity. Reproductions of one of the most famous, the Manneken Pis fountain of Brussels from 1619, appear in many gardens:

> The story is that this little child was lost for three days and he was the son of the mayor of the town. The entire town stopped everything to search for the child, and they could not find him. However, at the end of the third day the little boy was found standing on this exact corner with no clothes on doing what he is doing in this illustration [urinating], and the people were so overjoyed that they employed Belgium's best sculptor to model the child exactly as you see it, and they made this now famous fountain. The people love this little statue and its story very much, and at various times of the year the statue is dressed as a military figure, as a political figure; anyone who is in the news might find his clothing in small size on the little boy. (Lynch 1979, 76)

Other art traditions may have laid the groundwork for yard art's boy; one is the nineteenth-century painting tradition of the "naughty child." In these paintings, the child is almost always male and is "shown in the midst of some prank or mischievous or disobedient act. The child's infraction is never terribly serious or delinquent, but rather the consequence of youthful exuberance or lack of self-control" (da Costa Nunes 1987, 225). Public urination is not an act commonly portrayed in nineteenth-century paintings, but wooden cutouts of the peeing boy are rendered in a manner consistent with "youthful exuberance or lack of self-control." An abundance of contemporary folklore celebrates such urinary exuberance in the form of narratives that detail writing names in the snow with urine or dousing campfires with it. Jadviga M. da Costa Nunes notes that changing aesthetics and social ideas at the turn of the twentieth century led to the decline in popularity of naughty boy paintings. The theme lived on, however, in some of Norman Rockwell's illustrations and in popular culture through such figures as Dennis the Menace, who has been the subject of a comic strip, a television series, and a film (da Costa Nunes 1987, 247). Bart Simpson, a character from the cartoon television series *The Simpsons,* is a more recent incarnation of the naughty boy, as is Calvin from the comic strip

Calvin and Hobbes. A sticker of Calvin urinating often appears in the cab windows of contemporary pickup trucks.

No female version of the naughty boy or parallel to the peeing boy exists in lawn art. Girls are limited to stereotypically feminine roles. In some cases a wooden cutout of a little girl does accompany the urinating boy, but her hands are raised to her face in shock and disapproval at the boy's act. In late-twentieth-century yard art, just as in nineteenth-century painting, the naughty child is male. The presentation of boys and girls in yard art is binary. Little boys are shown as active and full of mischief, and little girls are passive in their play and demure in demeanor. Other images of children have also been appropriated by yard art. An 1872 Currier and Ives print by Frances F. Palmer shows a barefoot boy who is fishing (Sheehy 1998, 73), and Jean-Honoré Fragenard painted children as they were swinging. Both childhood pastimes are currently portrayed in yard art.

Ethnic depictions are the most disturbing aspects of yard art, particularly those of black children engaged in fishing, eating watermelon, or dressed as "lawn jockeys" (now considered derogatory in that they recall the antebellum South). Sheehy notes a legend that has sprung up in connection with the statues:

> According to the story, "Jocko," the reputed subject of the statue, was the son of a free black man, Tom Graves, who fought in the Continental Army in the American Revolution. One night after Graves had visited his family on furlough, Jocko tried to follow him back. . . . Finding Army troops but not his father, Jocko helped the men by holding and quieting General Washington's stallion during a winter storm on the very night before Washington crossed the Delaware. Jocko was so dedicated to his task that he froze to death holding the reigns of the General's stallion (ironically, in the very pose adopted by the statue, with one arm out raised). . . . In homage to the boy, Washington promised to commission a statue of Jocko for his home. (1998, 74–75)

There is no evidence, however, that Washington actually had such a statue (Sheehy 1998, 75). Moreover, the story reinforces the disturbing images of docile, faithful, and unquestioning-even-unto-death African American servitude and white insensitivity. It could also, unfortunately, be used to rationalize display of the statue ("it's not racist, it's a tribute").

Many "faithful groomsman" statues were made in America during the nineteenth century; earlier ones of African slaves or "blackamoors" had appeared in Europe during the eighteenth century (Sheehy 1998, 75; Jekyll 1982 [1918], 127, 259). If one of the functions of statues in the eighteenth and nineteenth centuries was to make status material, then having a statue of a servant or a slave could reflect doubly the power and standing of a statue's owner. Today, the coding has changed, and these types of statues are often considered racist.

Significantly, more statues exist of African American males than females, a gender difference perhaps related to the function of status and power. Folklore abounds about the threat of black males to white society, but "owning" an image of an African American male, particularly one happily serving as a lawn jockey or fishing boy, vitiates the perceived threat.

Yard dwarves and gnomes are also more likely to be portrayed as male than female. The popularity of the seven male dwarves in *Snow White* likely contributed to a predominance of statues of male dwarves. Before I consider yard statures of dwarves and gnomes, a review of the folklore might be helpful. By most accounts dwarves primarily come from Scandinavian and German-speaking countries (Briggs 1976, 195). They are traditionally portrayed as humanlike but old and small in stature, with oddly shaped legs and feet. They are said to inhabit underground places, caverns, and dark forests and are sometimes associated with watercourses. They are also believed to have a magical gift for transforming metals into beautiful artifacts or dangerous weapons (Rose 1996, 93).

Dwarves and gnomes are closely linked in folklore. W. Y. Evans-Wentz, an early chronicler of fairy lore, held that gnomes are nature spirits and inhabit one of the four chief elements of nature: earth (1990, 241). As Katharine Briggs explains, "'Gnomes' which is commonly used now is a later term derived rather from obsolete science than from folk tradition. When in the days of Paracelsus the universe was supposed to be composed in different proportions of the 'four elements'—Earth, Air, Fire, and Water—the elementals attached to the earth were the Gnomes" (1978, 84). Moreover, gnomes are thought to live underground and be able to move freely through the earth as though it were air. They are supposed to guard the treasures of the earth, and "in popular tradition, they were called dwarfs or goblins" (Briggs 1976, 193).

Dwarves are perceived as threatening or at least inclined to play mischievous pranks on humans, but those are not the primary associations for some contemporary Americans. Influenced by Disney's seven dwarves, garden gnomes and dwarves are seen as "cute" or "cheery" figures to have on a lawn ("Garden Gnomes Stolen" 1998, 4; Ots and Doherty 1996, 17; Thomas 1997, C5). Many negative folkloric associations are abandoned when it comes to yard art dwarves. Kelly Pentzold-Renteria and her Indiana informant, Jim, view garden gnomes in ways more reminiscent of leprechauns, which are said to be fairy shoemakers. Kelly, a college student, describes Jim as kindhearted, a retired steel industry worker, the father of nine, and a member of the Full Gospel Assembly of God Church ("and you're invited!"). Both Kelly and Jim see the gnome as "a little person thought to live in the forest and . . . thought to be associated with luck." The *Toronto Star* reports that those who own garden gnomes consider them to bring "good luck and wealth" (Paradkar 2000, n.p.), and some garden catalogs also advertise gnome statues believed to carry good luck.

Europeans are particularly fond of garden gnomes, and an estimated thirty million grace the gardens of Western Europe (Dahlburg 2000, A1-A2). A search for news articles about garden gnomes in comparison to articles about pink flamingos makes the flamingos pale by comparison. It also reveals the British press's penchant for comparing politicians (such as Ross Perot) and other public figures to garden gnomes or "crazed garden gnomes," as the case may be.

Historically, statues of gnomes and dwarves existed as early as the fifteenth century in German and Italian gardens (Thomas 1997, C5). The Boboli Gardens in Florence, for example, boast a marble statue of a Medici court dwarf that dates from 1565 (Cleveland-Peck 2000, 7). The earliest known infestation of gnomes in an English garden took place in the mid-nineteenth century. The figurines of dwarves that Sir Charles Isham purchased from Germany were intended as mantel ornaments, but he put them in his garden instead (Ross 2000, I26). Isham, a spiritualist, believed in the actual existence of gnomes, and he regaled friends with accounts of garden sightings (Cochrane 1997, 12).

Advertising helped create a demand for yard art gnomes. During the 1870s a major German wheelbarrow manufacturer used the image of a gnome in its advertising (Thomas 1997, C5). By the 1880s gardeners were asking for outdoor gnomes, and German manufacturers began to produce statues of ones that were bearded and knee-high (Ross 2000, I26). Catalogs from the early twentieth century picture clay gnomes that, true to their folkoric heritage, are depicted as miners, complete with lanterns and pickaxes. Gnomes are now sculpted accompanied by wheelbarrows, watering cans, and flowerpots. In addition, there are fishing gnomes, gnomes who play cards on toadstools, and even gnome orchestras. According to Gunter Griebel, a gnome collector in Germany, "When you look today at the old-fashioned gnomes and compare them to modern gnomes, there is a big difference. . . . In the beginning, they made old men with gray beards. Today, it has been perverted to more or less a child with a beard" (Ross 2000, I26).

In contemporary Europe and America, the increase and variety in gnome statuary were aided by the use of plastic after World War II. In Germany, for example, there are fourteen different garden gnomes based on likenesses of former German Chancellor Helmut Kohl ("Gnome Alone" 1998, 15; see also Dinkelacker 1996). Despite the industry's foray into political figures, fishing gnomes remain the largest-selling version in Europe (Richardson 1997, n.p.), yet another example of the popularity of the fishing motif in yard art.

By the mid-1990s garden gnomes were grabbing world headlines due to the actions of Le Front de Liberation des Nains de Jardin (the Garden Gnome Liberation Front). A popular song of 1994, "Let's Save the Garden Gnomes," by a Strasbourg group named Nains Porte-Quel may have inspired the organization (Geddes 1997, 18).[5] The front's activities are similar to "gnome-nappings" in Australia that David Hult detailed in 1988 and Jan Brunvand described again in 1989. The group's goal is to "protest against bad taste" (Lang 1997, n.p.) and to release garden gnomes into the forest, thus returning them to their natural habitat (Sage 2000, B5). In the late 1990s in Bethune, France, four student members of the group were arrested for stealing 134 gnome statues and two plastic Snow Whites. Publicity surrounding the case allegedly caused gnome sales to rise more than 60 percent in France (Geddes 1997, 18). The group's activities were believed to be the impetus for copycat gnome thefts as well.

The front is rumored to work in groups of seven out of respect for the seven dwarves of Snow White fame ("Gnome Place" 1997, 10). Several gnome-nappings have been attributed to the group. In the summer of 1997, for example, municipal workers from a French village near Limoges discovered a gathering of 115 gnomes in a forest. Officials were able to return nearly seventy safely to their homes. According to a local official, Thierry Chapeau, "All these old people started coming in and claiming their gnomes. . . . And they were so happy to find their little friends. For these people, their gnomes are really their companions. Like children" (Thomas 1997, C5). In 1998 eleven gnomes were discovered hanging beneath a bridge in Briey, France, with a note saying, "By the time you read these few words, we will no longer be part of your selfish world, which it has been our unhappy task to decorate" (Langley 2000, 28). In 1999 the front dumped 143 gnomes on the lawn of Sarrebourg Town Hall in eastern France, and in the spring of 2000 it liberated twenty from a popular exhibit of two thousand gnomes in Bagatelle Park in Paris (Terwillinger 2000, F1). As London's *Sunday Telegraph* described the situation in France:

> Incidents of gnome-napping have increased to the point where a senior police officer declared that "no gnome can now be considered safe." Last week in Lingolsheim, a well-heeled suburb of Strasbourg, 43 gnomes were found dumped

on the grounds of the public library. In Rouen, 68 were recovered from the basement of a house after a week-long police surveillance operation.

    Many gnome-owners have resorted to taking their sculptures indoors at night.
Householders in Gignac, near Montpellier, enraged by the loss of their gnomes,
have formed a vigilante patrol using a truck with an elevated platform and a powerful searchlight to peer over garden walls. (Langley 2000, 28)

There is also a group known as the Garden Gnome Emancipation Movement, believed by European officials to be less menacing than the front
(Langley 2000, 28). Then there is the Association for the Protection of Garden Gnomes, which opposes the activities of the front and believes that
gnomes can live happily in gardens (Geddes 1997, 18). Although the situation in America is not as severe, copycats do exist, according to the *Denver
Post.* One such person describes gnomes as being "kind of like really short
hippies" and espouses their removal to gnome communes where they
could sing "gnome songs, drink herbal tea, prance in circles and drop acid
in peace" (Terwillinger 2000, F1).

    Other gnome-related events during the 1990s included a court ruling
from Recklinghausen, Germany, in 1995 that declared that garden gnomes
neither offend good taste nor lower property values (Swain 1997, 11). A
German group also takes abducted gnomes to landmarks worldwide, photographs them, and sends the photographs to the owners (Paradkar 2000,
n.p.). Gnomes were the subject of one of R. L. Stine's popular "Goose-
bumps" books for children: *Revenge of the Lawn Gnomes* (1995). In 1996 a
garden gnome breached security and mysteriously appeared in the gardens
at Kensington Palace (P.H.S. 1996, n.p.). That same year in Wales, Yvonne
Evans put her parents' two-bedroom bungalow on the market on the condition that the buyer must adopt and care for 191 garden gnomes that came
with the house. Gnome duties included "dressing them each morning—a
two-and-a-half-hour job." Her mother had made the gnomes "special
outfits for St. David's and Christmas Day, sou'westers for wet weather and
sun hats for summer" (Dowle 1996, 36). Of the gnomes Evans said, "They
want to be dressed and fed by ten in the morning. If they're not, there's
ructions. They want to be spoilt with new costumes, and to stay up late.
They wouldn't mind being taken on holiday and would like some brothers and sisters" (Dowle 1996, 36).

    In 1997 garden gnomes hit the big screen in the film *The Full Monty,*
wherein unemployed working-class protagonists steal the garden gnomes
of a comrade who is a member of the managerial class and use them to mock
him during a job interview. In 1999 in Scotland two men were charged with

assaulting another man with a gnome ("Gnome Assault," 4). In 2000 in Sydney, Australia, about 150 garden gnomes were glued to the steps of Australia's Central Bank before its board was to gather for a monthly meeting to set interest rates (Ringle 2000, C1). In 2001 the French film *Le fabuleux destin d'Amélie Poulain* (released as *Amélie* in the United States) featured the classic prank of a pilfered gnome who "sends home" photographs of his travels, the same theme that an advertisement on ESPN sports television used in 2002.

Terry Major-Ball, a one-time gnome manufacturer and the brother of a former prime minister of England, "takes great heart from the success of gnomes," because, he says, "in many ways I equate their struggle with that of the ordinary hard-working man up and down Britain" (Richardson 1997, n.p.). All of these events speak to the ubiquity of the garden gnomes and their ability to symbolize everything from middle-class aesthetics to the struggles of the working class.

Nora, an American in her forties, has described her interest in garden gnomes. She received a pair of them when she was just out of high school: "The gnomes are a gift from my mom, and the idea for the gift came from me showing an interest in gnomes after they became . . . popularized through the book that was released like around '79. . . . I saw the book when I was working in the library [in Illinois]. . . . And, I just thought it was really neat. I like the whole idea, the idea of gnomes existing—these secret, little people that would hide in gardens and out in yards and whatnot."

The book to which Nora referred is *Gnomes* by Wil Huygen and illustrated by Rien Poortvliet, which generated public interest in gnomes in the late 1970s and early 1980s. The volume is an illustration of how popular or mass culture reinvents and generates interest in folk figures. Nora's gnomes, however, not only reveal her interest in those folkloric figures and her appreciation of Poortvliet's illustrations but also refer to family ties and a particular period in her life:

> In addition to the gnomes, she also gave me this little chair. . . . I distinctly remember because it was the last birthday that I had while I was in Illinois, and she had done these gnomes and put them side-by-side by the little chair. And I over-reacted, thinking, "You're thinking I'm a child still! And you don't want me to grow up and leave home." Which I think by that time, she was already figuring out that I was getting ideas about it. And, I'm really just remembering this, but, yeah, that's exactly what happened. She had painted them. . . . she'd buy the casts, and then she would paint them and shellac them. And then . . . give them away as gifts. 'Cause I think a lot of people were saying, "Oh, those are really cute! Those are so cute; oh, I like gnomes!" And so—so the gnome fever stayed around for a couple of years.

Nora complained of being treated like a child, a statement she says hurt her mother. She still sees the gift as emblematic of that moment when she was becoming an independent adult despite her mother's efforts to keep her a child. Nora immediately got rid of the red chair, but even though she does not collect yard art she has hauled around the heavy gnomes for years. Gnomes no longer intrigue her as they did in the early 1980s; she describes herself as being "neutral" on the topic. Although she has discarded several items from her past because of a lack of interest—and admits to feeling "so-so" about the gnomes—she has not disposed of them because they connect her to her mother.

Invariably, all the objects in this chapter are tied into the web of human meaning and experience. Specifically, the gnoming of Europe and the goosing of America, despite their differences, share some of the same characteristics. Both the gnomes and the geese can provide outlets for caretaking. As is apparent from the comments of Thierry Chapeau and Yvonne Evans, Europeans dress their gnomes and use them as child substitutes just as Americans do with concrete geese.

Garden gnomes also share some qualities with the "naughty boy" image; both figures are recognized for cunning pranks and mischievous behavior. Lawn statuary, however, usually does not portray the gnome as being engaged in mischief. There are some statues of bad-boy gnomes sitting on toilets or making obscene gestures, but gnomes are more frequently presented as being at work or engaged in leisure activities such as fishing. Gnome statues have become objects of mischief at the hands of humans who engage in gnome thefts and pranks. In some instances humans—often young males— are mischief-makers, a role that in folklore belongs to gnomes. As statues, garden gnomes represent a tamed version of the naughty boy; pranksters, however, remind us that the naughty boy is alive and well.

Statues of bigger people are also in yards. Ethnic adult statuary follows the same stereotyped patterns as ethnic statues of children. Soldiers and hunters are evident, as are female images, including small replicas of classical statuary, female angels, saloon girls, and granny fannies. Female figures are usually more sexualized than male ones. Occasionally, for example, one sees the male equivalent of a granny fanny. The female version is in a dress, underwear exposed; the male variant wears overalls or jeans. No shorts, no skin, and no underwear are revealed.

One yard artist I interviewed, Yuki, had assembled a large collection of statues of adult figures along with imaginative sculpture of his own. Yuki, eighty-one, is a Japanese American man who has a sense of humor as large as the 5,500-acre pheasant game ranch he ran in western Utah before re-tiring. Originally, he and his wife farmed, but it was "a starvation deal out there," so he started what became a successful game ranch. The "lawn" sur-rounding his house, completely devoid of grass, consists entirely of statues, his own sculpture, and gravel. "I hate yard work!" Yuki says. "I just hate watering the lawn, cutting it, and so forth. I, I just—can't do it!" All of the trees he planted died, and the thin soil is too heavily laden with alkali to be conducive to other plant life.

Instead of conventional plantings, Yuki's own sculpture marks the land-scape. In one piece, the devil holds the decapitated head of a woman. He notes, "Some people like that; some people don't—think it's too gruesome." Yuki had brain surgery a few years ago, and he suffers from a condition that causes the side of his face to hurt all the time. No cure exists, and, he says, "It's bad. It gets worse and worse. And that gets me at nighttime." He can-not sleep at night due to the pain, so he thinks about ideas for sculpture.

Yuki's religious views are presented in his yard. In front of his house are three words that he says describe Buddhism: "love, wisdom, and compas-sion." After these are three more words—"dream, work, maybe"—that en-capsulate Yuki's creative process. Yuki appraises his own work frankly, "See that artwork there? It's just okay . . . it's not bad—even if I say so myself— for an eighty-one-year-old dry farmer, that's pretty good." He showed me a series of humorous sculptures, one of which is his "jackass statue." He worries about the title and apologizes for its "bad language." Another sculp-ture is of a humorous cow in the form of a giant, three-dimensional weather vane, the cow at its bottom rather than its top. The piece moves in the wind, which is plentiful where he lives.

As he describes yet another sculpture, "He's supposed to be a cowboy with a spare-tire middle. That's . . . made out of old machinery parts, water cans, whatever" (figure 22). A Lady Godiva composed of machine parts, one hand hiding her face, rides perpetually across his front yard. Much of his art is kinetic, including people who wave. Yuki laughs and says he would give himself an A in innovation and ideas but a C in workmanship; he does not consider himself a good welder. His "cartoons and comical stuff" hide what he considers a poor handling of form: "You look at that thing, and you wouldn't think of all the poor workmanship in there because it's so funny."

Whimsy and humor are often at the core of Yuki's sculpture and assem-blage. Because he playfully presents the adult form, he sometimes frets about people's reactions to his work, for example, to the one-legged preg-nant woman statue:

Figure 22. Yuki's cowboy with spare-tire middle and a one-legged, blonde pregnant woman, Tremonton, Utah.

Now this is supposed to be my blonde, pregnant, one-legged woman. That's the first one I made. I had it out there on the road. . . . She had . . . that rottweiler on a log chain down here, and the other side was holding up the sign, [the] address. Ooooh, it was good, but too many guys stopped and fiddled around with it. . . . Ohhh, that was comedy. It was something. Ohhh, people didn't just drive by, they stopped and fiddled around with it. Young guys. And I think some of those are kids who are LDS [Mormon] . . . returned missionaries or going, and they had an idea that they don't want anything like that in their town. Yeah, oh yeah, it gets elaborate like that. Kind of fanatical, but they believe that, they're taught that. . . . I thought, "I'm inviting trouble." . . . Took three weeks to build it, and it was out on the road [in front of the house] two days, and I took it out of there.

Some of the sculptures of females, such as the pregnant woman, have funnels for breasts. Because he worries that this kind of detail may offend some of his more conservative neighbors, he took care to build a fence around his yard. The fence makes the statues unapproachable from the road.

Part of Yuki's yard is devoted to three areas of purchased statues, areas he refers to as the western, Oriental, and Occidental sections. The western section includes scenes from the American West, such as coyotes howling. The Oriental section contains images of Buddha, pagodas, and Asian women.

He says that his use of gravel for the yard came from being familiar with Japanese dry gardens. Several statues of Asian women are actually statues of Anglo women that have been modified to look Asian because Yuki had difficulty finding Asian statues (figure 23). In the Occidental section, statues of Jupiter and Venus are painted green. Because the statues are scantily

Figure 23. Anglo statue Yuki converted into Asian woman, Tremonton, Utah.

clad, he surrounded them with images of angels in order, he says, to cut down on offending viewers.

Although Yuki could be classed as an "outsider artist" (Jones 1994, 327), thematically much of his work falls within the patterns of yard art. The purchased male statues in his yard often communicate masculine images of power, such as warriors and gladiators. The statues of women are typically aesthetic or sexualized. Yuki's yard assemblage is art that solves the problems created by a harsh physical environment. It reflects his personality, religion, interest in farm equipment, and ethnicity. It is also an emblem of physical pain being channeled into creativity.

For Yuki, the consumption of consumer goods is bricolage. He buys an item, puts it in a new context, and thus changes its meaning (Hebdige 1989, 102–6). In Yuki's yard a funnel becomes a breast and a piece of farm equipment is a body part. His assemblage reconfigures purchased statues even when he does not modify them in the least. He does not alter the angel statues, but he places them in a new setting. For him, they are guardians not of the ethereal and spiritual but the physical and sensual. He alters many statues, however. He repaints the statues of Anglo women to make them appear Asian, for example, an act that constitutes a critique of the narrow mass-production of race, a critique accomplished through his creative consumption.

In other yards I observed, religious expression was manifest through statues of adult figures such as St. Francis and Mary. The images of St. Francis deviate from stereotypically masculine yard statues. He is presented neither as a soldier nor a hunter but rather a nurturing figure, embracing instead of shooting woodland creatures. Male geese that have been costumed, holiday figures such as Santa and the Easter Bunny, and St. Francis are all types of yard art that do not stereotypically portray masculinity.

Jayne, who has a Ph.D. in biology, works as an aquatic ecologist. She describes the spiritual connotations of the statue of the Virgin Mary in her Logan, Utah, front yard:

> Have you ever read *Les Miserables?* . . . He's really busy all day, and he's always tending to everyone else. But he always had a point, a part of his daily routine was at night, when the housekeepers went to bed, he would go out in his walled garden and walk in his garden. And, just, [to] . . . recompose himself every night that way and look at the stars, and . . . just reflect. And that's what Mary kind of signifies.
>
> I mean it's a very peaceful . . . piece of lawn art really. . . . It's nice to have her like in the summer 'cause she's there, and she's surrounded by the garden. . . . It's more than just having a duck in your yard or a person showing their butt [laughs]. . . . I think it's your Catholic roots, and I'm not that devout, but . . . I think it lowers your

blood pressure looking at them. Maybe it's beyond—I mean, I don't think that happens with my mom's [lawn] goose at home, you know what I mean [laughs]? I think they just do it 'cause they think it's cute, and they can dress them up.

Jayne likes having the statue because Mary is a strong female figure:

These poor women were always just kind of there and suffering with Jesus and were the ones that didn't abandon him after he was crucified. And . . . that's part of the appeal of somebody like Mary. They're very powerful . . . quietly suffering women. [Laughs.] In terms of a gender issue, there's no stronger gender figure than Mary in my opinion . . . for yard art at least. . . . She put up with a lot of crap. [Both laugh.] You know what I mean? Even Elizabeth. Think of Elizabeth. . . . Her kid gets beheaded. We don't hear much about that; these women—you know, you're a mom, I'm a mom—they really suffered a lot. And we just get little glimpses of that in the Bible. But . . . they're always there. They're strong because they never gave up; they didn't go and hide. The apostles all hid after Jesus died because they thought they were going to be persecuted. So it was the women that stuck it out and went into the tomb every day . . . anointed it. . . .

And even the other ones . . . wasn't it Lazarus's sisters that begged Jesus to come and . . . help their brother after he had died? It's always the women that . . . would step up and talk to Jesus and petition him to do what was right. And even— Dostoyevsky has a really great passage in . . . *The Brothers Karamazov.* . . . He talks about the . . . the miracle . . . at the wedding. And they're sitting at that wedding, and they run out of wine . . . and then Mary was the one who said, "Jesus, do something about this." 'Cause she knew who he was.

And he said, "Woman, it's not my time."

Well, Dostoyevsky's point in that whole passage is that that miracle . . . it was almost frivolous in a way because there was no need for that miracle other than joy, to make people happy at a wedding. And I thought, "That's a great way—his first miracle was a miracle of joy." And I thought that's a great way to look at it, and who prompted him for the miracle? It was his mother.

For Jayne, a small, simple statue of the Virgin Mary is evocative of spiritual peace and the strength of women.

The Virgin is also more than just a statue to another woman, Mary, a graphic artist who also has a statue of the Virgin in her Logan yard. She explains that it helped connect her to a place: "It's important to me. . . . I was named after her . . . and I guess it made me less homesick to have that here. And . . . that's what I remember about the Midwest . . . a lot of the Mary statues and the shrines and so on—and to have that here for myself."

Mary collects rocks to build a shrine or grotto around her statue. "Every time I go somewhere," she says, "I like to pick a rock up from . . . where we're hiking or visiting or whatever. . . . If there's something about the rock that

I like, that's why I pick it up, too." Mary also has rock cairns in her yard, and rocks have figured into her artwork. She has an MFA in painting and often paints landscapes and geological formations. Mary explains that rocks and mountains intrigue her because they do not visually change for long periods of time. She sees similar enduring aspects to the figure of the Virgin as well: "She's always there."

Although Mary likes stones because of the issues of time and spirituality that she associates with them, she has also contemplated surrounding her statue of the Virgin with an up-ended bathtub because she appreciates these kinds of shrines, too. "Well, on the one hand, in a way," she says, "it seems sort of tacky, but yet it's a sincere expression of someone's faith and sort of reusing and recycling something, and it was a creative—whoever started it, it was a really creative thing to do." In Mary's case the statue evokes at least three significant aspects of her life and art: place, time, and spirituality. She also admires "bathtub shrines" because of the ingenuous practicality that the recycling represents.

Randee's mailbox in Garland, Utah, a solution to a problem and an expression of identity, is a welded sculpture of a cowboy on a horse (figure 24). The front of the mailbox is the horse's hindquarters, so mail is inserted literally into the horse's backside. Randee, a skilled welder who has taught welding for many years, creates a lot of ornamental objects that have western themes. "One time the mailbox got run over—got knocked over," he recalls. "And I thought, 'Well, I'll build one they can't run over.' . . . I needed a mailbox, and we decided to just build a horse. I was just going to build a horse. But then we put a cowboy on it by the time we got done."

Like Yuki, Randee uses art to solve a problem. In his case, climate is not a difficulty but vandalism is. The mailbox also manifests Randee's sense of humor, interests, and occupation. Randee owns a horse arena, his entire family rodeos, and he is a rodeo clown. "I always wanted to be a cowboy when I grow up," he says. "It [the mailbox] kind of ties in; I like cowboys and horses and to ride and rope and do stuff like that. And I like metal, and I like to build stuff with my hands. So it's kind of . . . a breed in-between to do both." Like many other yard art forms such as costumed geese, Randee's mailbox expresses aspects of his personal and his family identity. In this sense the domestic (what is inside the house) is often extended to the yard.

The mailbox elicits a lot of positive reactions, but "I get cussed a lot," Randee admits. "It'll scare the hell out of you at night, driving along down there. It scared me twice. You think it's a damn horse out in the road." His mail carrier has never commented on it, but several people have told Randee that he has created the perfect receptacle for junk mail.

Figure 24. Randee's mailbox, Garland, Utah.

Like other forms of yard art, Randee's mailbox is used in seasonal displays: "Oh, we have a lot of fun with it because we'll dress it up—do different things. Dress up . . . a Santa Claus and that at Christmas time and make a scarecrow out of it at Halloween . . . so it's fun. We change the color of it every year or two . . . just so it changes." Although the cowboy is a stock figure that appears in many forms in yard art, in Randee's case the figure is specific to his life. It reflects his skills, interests, and identity and is also variable. It can be turned into a seasonal figure such as Santa Claus.

In Colorado ranch country I photographed a ranch entrance gate decorated with western subject matter. On its top rail are metal silhouettes of two team ropers roping a cow, and the gate itself consists of wooden boards that indicate the ranch's brand, the Two Bar X (figure 25). Martha, who made the gate, says she intended to create one that fit into the regional ranch gate tradition, but she also wanted it to be unique. "You know how gates always have the cross bars? Well, I didn't want to do that, so that's why I came up with the brand in there, and it seemed to work pretty good. . . .

Figure 25. Martha's ranch gate, Elbert, Colorado.

That gate was so long, and I didn't want to do—you know how gates are . . . purposely half-and-half. You open them up. Well, I didn't do that with that gate . . . but I did a little gate along with the big gate. . . . So I made it a lot different than any gate around. . . . It is a little traditional, but it's . . . not like most of them up there."

Martha created the silhouette of the ropers "just for fun." She is a sculptor and was also just starting out in competitive rodeo team roping at the time. "My husband [at that time] was a team roper, so instead of just sitting on the sidelines . . . I'm not very good at that—I just want to dive right in and do the same thing. That's what I did." Because her husband was a header (he roped the cow's head), she became a heeler (she roped the cow's hind feet), which is harder to do. Martha's gate is a pragmatic form that is creative and reveals her interests.

The gate has a western theme that some of her sculpture shares as well, but she does not consider it in the same category as her artwork. When she sculpts, she says, it is necessary to weigh the market value of a piece, along with cost and other factors as well. The gate, she observes, "was more of a fun, whimsical thing compared to the actual business of art."

Like the ranch gate, Martha's sculpture often reflects her interest in animals:

> I lived with horses, I did the team roping, [and] watched a lot of the horseshoeing. Just everything around me was very western, that's why . . . I did that kind of sculpture, just watching horses out in the field and what they do—what their pecking order was and what they did on their own. [Laughs.] I kind of tried to capture that: how people and horses interact. [I] try to, try to say a little story with the piece. And I kind of got into the old cowgirls. . . . I just started reading about them. And then I started getting more information and doing more research. They just intrigued me, so that's why I did that [sculpture] series of them in the rodeo.
>
> Yeah, I wondered about the girls that were roping . . . and of course it all went back to the women back in the early 1900s, the Wild West show, the rodeo. . . . It just intrigued me. Then of course I lean toward the feminine side; women doing the rough and tough western things.

Cowboys are common figures in the western yard and on its perimeters, but Martha's team ropers also reference a masculine sport in which their creator, a woman, participates.

The western practice of putting a cowboy boot on a barbwire fence is at the heart of yet another type of perimeter yard art I saw and photographed in Colorado. It is customary to mark a fence post with an old boot as a means of locating a place that might be otherwise hard to distinguish. Related versions of that folk practice exist. People have been known to throw shoes over electrical wires to celebrate a sports victory, sexual encounter, or mark territory. Trees also become the home to pairs of shoes, items of clothing, or other objects (Preston 1996).

Along a stretch of barbwire fence in central Colorado I saw the boot-on-the-fence custom gone wild. Hundreds of shoes were massed along the fence, but even had they not been the place would still have attracted attention. It boasted an older home and outbuildings, and, near the main house, a smaller house heavily decorated with signs, old CDs, guitars, and whatever else could be nailed to a wall. This turned out to be Paco's house.

When I visited the house the first time I was greeted by Yeager, a black lab, and Norma, who had a broad smile and ready sense of humor. Norma and Paco were among several tenants who lived on-site at the time. One of the first things Norma said was, "Do you want to meet Merrill?"

"Sure," I said.

I stepped in the front yard and met Merrill, Norma's young, uncastrated pet bull, who licked our knees with great gusto and abandon as we talked. Because Merrill could not be ignored, he was a major topic of conversation. Norma told me that she had debated whether to get a great dane or a bull. She ultimately decided upon a Holstein bull and named him Merrill Lynch after the investment firm whose symbol is a bull. Merrill slept each night curled up by the steps leading to the front door of the house. One night the barn caught fire. A police officer who was passing saw the glow of the fire and stopped at the house. He opened the gate and walked toward the front door, waking the bull. Merrill rose from his dark corner and frighted the officer, who rang the doorbell and sputtered, "Jesus Christ! That's the biggest dog I've ever seen!"

As I looked down the fence that had hundreds of shoes hanging on it, Nora said, "We're not crazy or anything, you know." The housemates had thought it would be funny to hang a lot of shoes on the fence. They were going to use only boots but decided that would take too long because "you just can't find many cowboy boots these days." Norma estimated that the epic shoe fence had begun a couple of years before we spoke. To create it the housemates collected shoes from the garage sales in a nearby subdivision. On that hot day at the end of July I walked the length of the fence and counted 276 shoes. I wondered if the well-heeled residents of the comfortable subdivision ever drove by and were startled to see a pair of their shoes dangling from the fence. Paco, the instigator of the shoe fence, explained its origins:

A lot of folks will put shoes on their fence; that's an old tradition. . . . I had this one pair of boots that I just really liked; I had them for years, rebuilt a few times, and they finally were just . . . gone. So I hung them on the two poles by our gate as kind of a little marker. And then . . . I met a girl that worked at the Stampede; that's a big local saloon in Denver. And, it's two levels, and she worked in the upstairs part; they used to dress up like characters of the Old West. And I was downstairs talking to some people. [Laughs.] Well, she looked over the railing, and I guess she didn't think I should be talking to this particular girl, so she took a boot off and threw it at me. And here we are, we're right by the dance floor— it's hard—the boot hit; [laughs] all my friends . . . the people that are around me are looking at me to see what was going to happen [laughs]. And so, being a typical male, I just—I tucked it up under my arm, and I yelled up at her, "I'm gonna hang this on my fence post, and when you think you're woman enough to come and get it, you know where it is!" [Both of us laugh.] And so I kept it. . . .

[Laughs.] [She came to get it,] but when she came, she . . . hung the other boot on the other side . . . on the fence. So then . . . I have Pac-ettes, and it's like "Paco and the Pac-ettes," it's girls that go way back with me, that are real close [to me]. They're . . . my favorite one, my musical Pac-ette, my heart, "Tall Pam," "Little Pam," we have all these different girls that are Pac-ettes. And so, two of the Pac-ettes just happened to stop by, and they said, "What's with the boots?" [Laughs.] . . .

I told them what had happened with Michelle and . . . they said, "Well, she can't get away with that." [Laughs.] And so, when they came back they put some shoes and boots on the fence. And then it just kind of got out of control. Like a buddy wanted to meet one of my Pac-ettes, and he put a pair on there. And then it just got a life of its own.

I talked with Paco and Norma separately, but both wanted to know if I had seen the "sections" of the fence, including a sports section, a ski section, a section of women's pumps, and a section of children's shoes. I had, and they were impressive. Also attached were golf shoes, flippers, and even fishing poles, skis, ski poles, and ski boots (figure 26). Toy trucks were parked near the portions devoted to clusters of children's shoes, and Miss Piggy of Muppets fame presided over a section of high heels that teetered atop a row of posts (figure 27). Boots flanked a headless Barbie doll. A wire sculpture of a man's face towered over a single, scarlet, high-heeled pump and a cowboy boot, and a plastic flower whirligig turned in the breeze close by. Bedroom slippers, animal skulls, and roller skates also adorned the barbwire. Paco says that many strangers have contributed to the fence:

I still, to this day meet people that talk about it and tell me about a shoe they put on, or a story about their families. It's pretty neat. . . . Some people would put them on the fence, and then other people would come and put them on my porch, and leave a little note asking you if it could go on the fence.

And one little girl—it was so cool—it was Fiona, and, oh, I can't remember the

Figure 26. Ski section of the Fence of Shoes, Parker, Colorado.

Figure 27. High-heel section of the Fence of Shoes, Parker, Colorado.

other little girl's name. But . . . one was about three, I think, and the other one was just four or five, and they had come out and knocked on the door with their mother and asked if they could . . . hang these shoes on the fence. They're like little patent leather dress-up shoes; there was a couple of them, two pair. And I said, "Sure." And then they asked if they could take a picture with me down there, and they were just so cute. And I went down there with them; we hung the shoes. [Laughs.] And the littlest one had these little, sparkly shoes on, all glittery. And they were like brand new, and I kept teasing her, going, "Boy, those would look so pretty on the fence." [Laughs.] Like I was trying to talk her out of these little . . . she wasn't about to give those up!

But it was just so cute; I mean I must've asked her three or four times. And her mom, we were all laughing about it. She was real shy and cute, and then . . . I don't know if it was a year later. I can't remember the time frame, but I came home and out on my porch were those little sparkly shoes that were all scuffed and worn. She had obviously outgrown them, and left them, and they left a photograph. A little picture of them. That was so cool. . . .

These [high school] girls . . . each wanted to put a shoe on this little sign that said "Fence of Shoes." And they wrote all this cool stuff on their shoes, and it was pretty neat. One of them was talking about art. She was going to college, and art was going to be her major. And then she went through this little philosophical thing around the sole of the shoe about art: "What is art?" . . . It was pretty neat. . . . It's funny how this has really become a little—I just—I don't know, it sounds corny but, it's really meant a lot to me personally in life. I mean . . . you get a little blue sometimes at everything that happened to us on it, but . . . it was really neat meeting all those people. And the sense of community that something like that can create with people that don't even know each other. . . .

And those are the kind of things that were neat . . . people would just knock on the door, or you'd run into them in the store or somewhere, and they'd tell you, "Hey, did you see our shoe?" [Laughs.] . . .

I think for . . . the little resistance that we had from basically that one lady, I got more support from the community. I couldn't believe how—it almost became like a little symbol of the old Parker. The Chamber [of Commerce] even put it in their magazine for the year. You know how they have their annual magazine? It's one of the landmarks in Parker. I thought that was way cool. . . .

The people from whom Paco leased the property sold it to a developer, and Paco had to move. The land would be subdivided as "Old Town Parker." "Which is funny," he laughed, "'cause there's never been a town out here. There's never even been like a station for the old trains or the stages to stop or anything. This has just been—it was a dairy farm. But that's the way they—I guess they call that 'progress.'"

When, according to Paco's estimate, the fence had more than seven hundred shoes on it, the housemates were asked to remove the shoes on the long fence south of their house because of complaints. Paco recalls what happened:

> It was exactly the . . . first week of June [that we took it down]. Because . . . we have a carnival for Parker Days . . . and I had these . . . pages from the county. I had like twelve pages of violations, and all this stuff. So they were gonna fine me a hundred dollars a day for each one [violation] and ten days in jail . . . if I didn't do all this stuff. And, I had about twenty-six little business in the back . . . they're local people where they couldn't have things in front of their house and stuff. They're like landscapers and fence people and stone masons and things like that. So they said I had to throw everyone out; take down my shoe fence and . . . I couldn't park my tractors in my front yard anymore, or I couldn't have any of my equipment here. It got real ugly. . . .
>
> We're on forty acres, and it's part of a hundred-twenty-acre parcel. So we're not in anyone's homeowner association or anything, but it just takes one call from someone to the county to . . . get things going. . . . So I—the reason I remember the date is that the Chamber of Commerce called me because Parker is growing so much. Where they used to put the carnival up was under construction for like a little three-story high-rise in Parker, in Parker Station they call it. So they called and asked if we had about five or seven acres that the carnival could live on and set up . . . come out, before they set up for Parker Days, and they were going to stay about a week to nine days longer. Josie . . . she's passed away since then—she was one of the founders of Parker Days. [Laughs.] And she calls me, and I'm like, "Josie, I'm in all this trouble with the county, remember?"
>
> And she goes, "Oh, yeah, don't worry about it then."
>
> And I said, "Nope, everybody wants a carnival, but nobody wants to see a carnie." I said, "You call those boys and give them my mobile number. They're more than welcome here." And they moved in overnight . . . but they started coming in, and it was already dark when they started moving in, and it was like a train or something. It was awesome—all the vehicles; they had the little Volkswagens and stuff that people actually live in: the semis, the buses, campers, and then all the rides and everything, and the booths.
>
> So the next morning, you know, when Parker woke up [both laugh], we had a whole community out here. It looked like we'd built a subdivision. So the county came out and videotaped us. So we were in trouble for that too. But we got support from the town and from the Chamber and everything. So they just made it as part of my deadline [to remove everything]; they just kind of added that on. [Both laugh.] . . .
>
> It was funny when Channel 7 [television news] . . . came when they were making me take them [the shoes] down. And they wanted to film us with the county here, and the county wouldn't come over here. . . . They had to be in their offices

with their representatives and stuff [laughs]. So they came here in the morning and interviewed me, and then they went to the county, and then they came back in the afternoon, and they did their editing process. And then they did the video, and then they did a live remote when the news came on. So I got to see all the unedited stuff from the county. [Laughs.] It was kind of cool. I felt kind of stealth [laughs]. . . . They were pretty decent really. I mean it's the kind of thing that once someone complains, and it gets going, they just have to do their process. She [the woman who complained] just thought it—hurt property values and it was tacky.

And so . . . one of the quotes that was so funny—I was watching in the news van [laughs], and one of the representatives from the county—the interviewer asked him why I had to take them off the fence. And he says, "Well, there's no discarded materials on a fence line."

And he [the interviewer] says, "Well, a lot of people think of this as folk art." It's not discarded materials.

And the [laughs] [county] guy goes, "Well, I know nothing about art." [Both laugh.] It was—and they didn't leave that . . . on the TV.

But it was hilarious! I thanked them for not; I said, "Oh, man, if you would have left that in there, I would have been in so much trouble." That guy would've caught grief everywhere he went. His buddies, they'd go to lunch, and they'd say, "Oh, look at that picture or that sculpture." And then they'd say, "Oh, yeah, that's right, you don't know anything about art!" [Both laugh.]

And so it's just funny because it kind of summed up the whole case of the "real world" or the . . . special people that decide what is art and what isn't. He was totally by the rule book. It's like, "Oh, I don't know anything about art." . . .

Yeah, well, I'll tell you if I owned the property—I just lease forty acres—and if I owned it, I would have gone to the Supreme Court. I mean I would've called CBS *Sunday Morning* or somebody to come and help me. But when you don't own it, what can you do? . . .

It was kind of sad to take it down. And, so, impromptu when the shoes came off the fence, at that same time we made a float and we entered it in the Parker Days parade. It was called "The Fence of Shoes" float. And we won a blue ribbon; we got "best parade theme." . . .

It was pretty cool; we took . . . t-posts and we welded on the bottom of the t-posts, so they'd fit into the pockets on the trailer, and we . . . extended them every four or five pockets away. And then we took Bronco [referring to the Denver football team] orange wire . . . like sprinkler wire . . . fourteen-gauge. . . . This is the big thick one, and we did Bronco orange on the top, Bronco blue in the middle, and then Bronco orange on the bottom. And then we put the shoes on them like they were hanging on a fence. And . . . we had straw bales . . . I don't know if you remember my porch where I got all the weird stuff on my porch? I had that pink beauty parlor chair up on the top [of the float]; I was like a captain with a pitchfork. [Laughs.] And my good friend for twenty-eight years, Kermit . . . he's a quadriplegic—he was at the other end of the trailer with his wheelchair on there. And we had every age from little infants to old grandparents. It was cool. It was . . . a fun thing.

The Fence of Shoes was a vital form of community art that resembled the work of the fine artist Christo, known for his large-scale environmental wrapping of objects such as the Pont-Neuf in Paris. Christo's art is described as challenging "our habitual perception" of familiar landscapes and as causing "buildings we pass every day without seeing suddenly become the focus of awareness" (Schellmann and Benecke 1988, 11). The Fence of Shoes functioned in much the same fashion. It also cleared a space where, as Paco said, strangers created a sense of community through art and humor. It was a private act in a public place that "opened . . . a dialogue on what the cultural landscape was to look like" (Preston 1996, 14). Moreover, it gave children and adults equal access to a mode of creation and expression as well as a visual product. Christo's work is characterized as "an ongoing dialectic with powers that are indifferent or antagonistic to art" (Schellmann and Benecke 1988, 13). The Fence of Shoes prompted a similar conversation. It also provoked class and aesthetic clashes, as the complaints and the county's actions attest. The fence raised questions of what constitutes art and who gets to create it. Anyone could participate in the art of the Fence of Shoes, and that lack of discrimination may have made it harder for some officials to regard it as art.

The fence was also a reference to gender and became a means of cross-gender, romantic communication. Its origins were in an exchange between a man and woman in a bar. In one case leaving a pair of shoes on the fence became a hopeful way for a man to meet a woman. In addition, the fence provided an example of the manner in which gender is a frequently used organizational category and means of differentiation in American culture. Specifically, a sexy row of women's high heels pranced across a portion of the fence, and more men's shoes appeared than women's in the sports section. Those who assembled the display were having fun and not commenting on gender. The incongruity of high heels being on a fence, or skis lashed to barbwire, could be interpreted as poking fun at a number of societal conventions. The fact, however, that many shoes on the idiosyncratic fence were grouped according to the gender of who had worn them suggests that it exerted strong influence as a basic cultural and perceptual category. It also indicates that gender stereotypes (such as men being associated with sports) are still pervasive in American culture despite some claims to the contrary. People are so used to seeing (or literally stumbling over) such images in public and private spaces that they often do not think about gender implications, and stereotypes are often perpetuated subtly and unknowingly.

Although the shoe fence was unique and had fewer human figures on it than most other kinds of yard art I examined, it still exemplified some of the larger patterns. The world of childhood was emphasized, and animals were even given some space. Adults were pictured directly. A sculpture of a man created by a friend of one of the housemates hung near a Barbie doll.

Paco's comments, and yard art in general, raise still more questions: What are the definitive features of art, and how much does money, rarity, and elitism have to do with defining it? Statues of classical figures, for example, appeared in Greek, Roman, and Renaissance gardens (where they would likely be considered fine art) and are part of contemporary yard art displays (where they are likely considered kitsch). That designation is aided by the fact that these forms became mass-produced during a period, the late 1800s through the twentieth century, in which "high culture" was isolated and differentiated from mass or popular culture (DiMaggio 1991, 374). Lawrence Levine explains the distinction as being aided by the fact that the late-nine-teenth-century quest for political order was paralleled by a desire for cultural authority: "The new meanings that became attached to such words as 'art,' 'aesthetics,' and 'culture' in the second half of the nineteenth century symbolized the consciousness that conceived of the fine, the worthy, and the beautiful as existing apart from ordinary society. . . . The taste that now prevailed was that of one segment of the social and economic spectrum which convinced itself and the nation at large that its way of seeing, understanding and appreciating music, theater, and art was the only legitimate one" (1988, 228, 225, 231).

Art, as it is now seen in Western culture, is a separate category of cultural production frequently defined—in part by a group of elites, what Paco calls the "special people who decide what is art and what isn't"—on the basis of perceived uniqueness, rarity, aesthetic value, mastery of form, intellectual value, and separation from everyday life (Pocius 1995, 413, 417). Fine art is usually expensive art; its price testifies to its worth due to originality and exceptional qualities. Therefore, a reproduction of a Greek statue does not hold the value of the original because it is no longer as rare. Reproductions may lack the impact and power of the original for other reasons as well. They are usually rendered on a smaller scale and may not be displayed in a manner that shows a command of basic design and aesthetic principles. In addition, many yard artists and homeowners would never think to call their assemblage or even their own sculptures "art," and they recognize their lack of schooling in the elements of design. Yuki, for example, gives himself a C in execution of form and handling of materials.

Behind this discussion of the aesthetic rises the specter of class. Taste often functions as a marker of class, both as socioeconomic level and quality: "classy" (Storey 1998, 210). Refined aesthetic taste frequently involves appreciating art that emphasizes form over function; "popular" and "folk" art are viewed as doing the reverse (Bourdieu 1984, 5). The display of an object in an art museum deemphasizes its prior functions, and it becomes pure form (Bourdieu 1984, 30). Pierre Bourdieu believes such aesthetic views legitimate social and class differences (1984, 7). Paco is aware of such distinctions based on taste and class, as he indicated in comments about the "special people" and the carnival workers. He allowed the workers on the property because he recognized some of the class biases they face ("Everybody wants a carnival, but nobody wants to see a carnie").

Much of contemporary yard art's concern with humor also excludes it from the category of fine art. Aesthetic "distinction is not just established by the object of admiration but how the object is said to be admired. Popular audiences are said to display their pleasure to emotional excess, whereas the audiences for official or dominant culture are always able to maintain respectable aesthetic distance and control" (Storey 1998, 215; see also Levine 1988, 229–30). Laughter, especially in connection with the visual arts, usually is not perceived as expressive of appropriate distance and control. Fine art has a long tradition of serious treatment of subject matter, and art museums are not known for having noisy galleries filled with mirth and laughter. Moreover, given the traditional emphasis on mastery of the schooled elements of design, it is obvious why yard art has not been the subject of serious study within elite fields of art. It generally does not fit the parameters for that genre and tends toward the carnivalesque.

I do not think yard art should be studied within this elite tradition out of some democratic concern or inclusive impulse. It is, however, worthy of attention on its own merits. Yard art can be analyzed in terms of principles of design and aesthetic execution, but I am more interested in seeing it in another way—as a behavior. Such an approach allows consideration of the profundities and necessities of art as a verb, a way of solving problems and addressing issues in everyday lives rather than in just the lives of people like Christo or Pablo Picasso. Moreover, both elite and non-elite art can be studied as behavior.

I call for an aesthetic and analytical gaze that looks not just at form but privileges behavior when seeing an object. This is an attempt to reconfigure the aesthetic gaze so it does not have to set up class distinctions. Looking at art as a behavior can be done with any kind of cultural product, whether its emphasis is on pure form or on function. Specifically, art is a problem-solving behavior, whether those problems lie on canvas or in a landscape too alkaline to support vegetation, such as Yuki's yard. Therefore, I define "art" as a problem-solving or issue-addressing behavior that emphasizes the aesthetic in its execution.

Considering yard art as part of historical and folkloric contexts has allowed me to sort out some of the possible functions it serves. Informants, for example, continually point to its whimsical and humorous nature.[6] In many cases that folk process combines the visual with the humorous on lawns like Yuki's in the form of what I term a "site gag." The expression is a pun evocative of a visual image (sight), a particular place/yard (site), and humor (the gag) merged into one form.

Yard art assemblage like Bernice's creates new, semipublic spaces for the imaginations of children and others. Warmth and unpretentiousness are also communicated. Jayne, who describes herself as a minimalist when it comes to yard decorations (her statue of the Virgin is the only piece of yard art she owns), comments:

Why not? If it makes people feel good, let them do—it's their yard. . . . In Florida where we lived there was yard art that I did love, and it was a whole group of pigs . . . a mother pig with . . . these baby pigs behind it, and it was so cute. I loved going by there, and seeing those black and white pigs. . . . Because I think it's very unpretentious, so it's kind of like, 'Oh, these people must be fairly normal, they put this yard art out' [laughs]. . . .

I think, too, it is . . . a welcome mat. If you have something like that in your yard, like pigs, or somebody's butt . . . you're not saying, "Stay away!" It's kind of—we're so isolated now as a culture, we hardly even know our neighbors. And that's like putting in your front yard, "Hey, I'm a friendly person that has a sense of humor!". . .

I don't know. If you were lost in the middle of the night and saw someone with a butt in their yard and a house that didn't have one, I'd probably go to the one with the butt in it [laughs]. . . .

I think cute to me . . . is tied to being unpretentious, I really do. And it's like, they put this stuff out and on some levels, intellectually, we say, "That's gaudy" or "that's really ugly." And it's so ugly and gaudy that it becomes cute. . . . An eight-year-old . . . could stand side by side with a grandmother . . . and they'd have the same opinion. And I think that's kind of cute. You know what I mean? . . .

When we go home, like my nephews and my—even my daughter go out . . . and check that goose out, and it gives them something to talk about. And we don't have a lot of statues in our personal lives. Think about it, it really—they are statues. They are art; it's a form of art. So yeah, you're sharing art, so why wouldn't it be? It wouldn't be any different than looking at a painting with your grandmother or anybody else. . . . At the most basic level, it's just a piece of art. And so why wouldn't you—and especially if you get to change its clothes. . . . "Wooowho! Let's go change the goose's clothes!" [Laughs.] . . . That's fun. "Geez, this must be cool; Grandma has this on her porch. This is great! Let's go change those clothes." [Laughs.]

When I was growing up—actually, this reminds me, at Christmas, my dad would decorate our house . . . use . . . the same amount of electricity they use in San Francisco now. . . . And he made these deer, reindeer and a sleigh, like a full-sized sleigh. And he'd hoist them up on our roof, and there's something about that—ritual, and getting those things out and putting them on the roof, I mean it was something you did together.

Wow. Okay . . . you think about it: as a kid, isn't it kind of cool? Like, "My dad is taking time to make little tiny reindeer and the little sleigh, and he's gonna paint it, and it takes him two weeks to paint it, and then he's gonna get up on the cold roof and hoist that sucker up!" [Laughs.]. . . There's definitely a connection there. So I imagine it's the same with other types of yard art.

Jayne's comments also indicate that lawn art can sometimes create a space for children, and she suggests that yard art can facilitate connection between children and adults. Paco describes this type of intergenerational communion when he talks about some of the things that happened at the Fence of Shoes.

Nora says that yard flamingos, frogs, and deer evoke "warm, fuzzy" feelings and fond childhood memories. Although Nora owns almost no yard art other than her gnomes, she confesses that she likes to go to places that sell yard statuary: "I love to go to places that sell. . . . 'Cause one, it amazes me that people would even think about it. But it's almost like a flood. It's like going to a toy store again. Or getting the Sears catalog at Christmas. It just, it's like it all comes kind of flooding back at you, and you think, 'Oh, yeah, that's neat, that's neat!'" Such visits take Nora back to her childhood world of imagination, possibility, and magic. She had wanted yard art statues of animals so she could pet them and have them talk to her, especially because she was not around animals much while growing up in the suburbs of Chicago.

Nora and Jayne's comments indicate that yard art can be seen as a kindness to the imagination. It can nurture. That nurturing may take the form of supporting the imaginative life of a child, or, like some of the geese that Monica's costumers dress, it expresses caring behaviors after a child has left home. In these instances form has a comforting effect. In recognition of this function, and without condescension, this kind of yard art could be seen as functioning as "comfort art." Fine art that has the same intent could be described in the same way.

Because of my concern about the class implications of aesthetic evaluations, I have thought long about employing the phrase *comfort art*. I use it for two reasons. First, it is an honest description of an important, if sometimes overlooked, function of art. And, second, it is a type of a behavior that can be found in all levels of art, elite included, so it is a place of potentially rich intersection among varying kinds of aesthetic practices. Expressions that provide humans with solace, valuable aesthetic and cultural creations when found at any level of culture, are reminders of why art is so important—it works.

Yet yard statuary can be a way to make a consumerist, status-oriented statement of worth. Consumerist consumption can also critique, however, as is the case with Yuki.[7] The yard art forms discussed in this chapter indicate that gendered images in yards remain fairly stock and stereotypical. Attention to folklore complicates the picture. Folklore helped me realize that I often see an inventive mix of both the ingenious and the mundane in gendered forms that grace lawns. Michael Owen Jones describes the urge to create "as a condition fundamental to being human" (1987, 55). This chapter's discussion of yard art is also testament to the useful necessity of art and whimsy in solving problems and aesthetically addressing the issues that arise in everyday life.

3
Barbie and Her Consorts: Baked Barbie, Forgotten Ken, and Flushed G.I. Joe

Issued in editions of billions, she is the ultimate piece of mass art. . . .
Mattel copyrighted Barbie's face as a piece of sculpture. . . . It was one
of those watershed moments, like Elvis's return from the army or the
arrival of the Beatles in 1964.

—M. G. Lord

When adults recall being children, they often remember the sensory
pleasures associated with play, such as the sweet, poignant taste of
autumn's darkness during a late-season game of kick-the-can, or the
destructive precision of a well-placed firecracker, or the satisfaction
of a prank played on an unsuspecting sibling, or the stolen time in
the otherworlds of "let's pretend," or the numinous beauty of
fireflies, captives of canning jars and the summers of childhood.

When I talk about children's folklore and folk behaviors with college students, they usually revert gracefully to the worlds of their various childhoods. Their stories come with the delight and intensity that looking back on the games of youth democratically affords most people, including those who have had painful childhoods. Even students who belong to the latter category can usually smile at these narratives, whether their own or someone else's.

My students relate account after account of the simple yet profoundly sentient delight afforded by a well-wrought game of capture the flag, king of the mountain, kickball, jump rope, or pickup football—or of the epic spitball that not only made it to the roof of the high school gymnasium but was also still to be found there at the twentieth class reunion—and indeed was the highlight of that reunion. Popular culture figures into the stories of play. Students recall favorite toys such as *Star Wars* figures and the television shows they took into their imaginations and acted out in backyards and living rooms.

Always in this mix are stories about play with Barbie and, occasionally, G.I. Joe; Barbie's official boyfriend, Ken, is rarely mentioned. The narratives intrigue me because of their humor and the range of important themes they raise. One young woman confessed to domesticity gone awry, for example. As a child she liked to take the heads off her Barbies and bake those heads in the oven. Another student's brother would torment her by taking the heads off her Barbies and flushing them down the toilet. One woman who disliked Barbies and did not want her sister playing with them gradually took all the sister's Barbies and hid them. She filled the tanks of three toilets before being caught. Barbie also perennially received crew cuts at the hands of the little girls who would later became my college students.

Adult themes, ranging from sexuality (Lamb 2002) to metaphysics, also surfaced in stories I heard about Barbie. One student, for example, recalled that her male cousin, in an attempt to annoy her, placed Barbie in compromising—and confusing to her child's mind—sexual positions with G.I. Joe. Upon hearing of these stories and my interest in them, a colleague told me that she, at age seven, had her first major existential and metaphysical moment while playing with Barbie dolls. She had wondered, as she was creating scenarios for them and scripting their behavior, if a higher power or a being of some sort did something similar with humans.

The two most prominent forms of Barbie folklore that I encountered, both of them recognized relatively recently as types of folklore, are personal-experience narratives detailing play experiences with Barbie and electronic folklore about Barbie that circulates, mainly via e-mail. The personal-experience narrative is regarded as folklore not because of content, which can contain traditional elements or be highly idiosyncratic, but because of the process of narrating individual experiences. The act of telling these personal-experience narratives is a traditional and customary behavior (Stahl 1977, 14, 17, 19). The accounts I examine also detail folk behaviors: children's play customs that are informally learned and thus part of folk culture. By the end of the twentieth century the Internet had joined the fax machine as a means of passing along folklore to informal networks of family, friends, and co-workers. The Internet is a major vehicle for transmission of urban legends, rumors, jokes, and humorous lists.[1]

Until I heard this folklore I admit that my interest in Barbie was minimal. I certainly did not collect all things pink and Barbie. In fact, Barbie did not overly intrigue me when I was a child. I had one doll I thought was Barbie, but I have discovered—during the process of my research—that it was actually Barbie's friend, P.J.—Twist 'n Turn P.J. to be quite exact.[2] With the exception of my "Barbie," I generally eschewed dolls, especially baby dolls, in favor of playing with stuffed animals.

I must admit, however, that Barbie afforded me many pleasurable hours of play—construction play to be specific. My sister, the neighbor girls, and I dug an entire village, complete with houses containing individual rooms and swimming pools, out of the ground beside our garage. My father dubbed the site "Mole Village" and ultimately filled it in with dirt because he feared someone, namely him, would fall in and break an appendage. Using dirt, conifer needles, grass, and leaves, we also constructed a fairly extensive highway system for our Barbies and their cars. I realize now that Barbie provided an outlet for my burning—but unspoken—desire for Tonka trucks and a big hill of dirt upon which to play with them. My play reflected my world and interests, which is a common pattern in the accounts I have collected and one I will discuss later in this chapter after I have considered Barbie's form.

Pattern, Gender, and Barbie

Barbie came from the decade that saw an explosion of plastics, an emphasis on the color pink, and the creation of pink plastic flamingos. Ruth Handler, one of the founding members of the Mattel Toy Company, created Barbie in 1959.[3] Handler had noted that her young daughter and the girl's friends liked playing with paper dolls of adults, but no three-dimensional adult dolls were available on the market. Through their play, the girls were imagining what their lives as grown-ups would be. Handler thought that having an adult doll available to girls might help them deal with the changes their bodies underwent at puberty, such as breast development (Stern 1998).

Observing children's play behaviors gave rise to the idea of Barbie, but it was a German sex doll that helped give her form. Handler was traveling in Europe when she found the inspiration for Barbie in a shapely doll named Lilli that cartoonist Reinhard Beuthien created in 1955. Lilli's cartoon antics with men appeared in the *Bild Zeitung,* and she was also issued as a doll (Lord 1994, 25). The doll was a kind of three-dimensional version of a pinup poster. It was Lilli that Handler saw while shopping in Europe, and by means of Lilli's plastic body she found the nascent Barbie.

Previously, Handler had mentioned her idea for marketing an adult doll who had well-made clothing to Mattel designers, who were male. They told her that it was impossible to create a doll like she envisioned and sell it at a reasonable price. "Frankly," Handler said, "I thought they were all horrified by the thought of wanting to make a doll with breasts" (Lord 1994, 30). Handler gave her Lilli doll to Mattel engineer Jack Ryan, who had been at one time Zsa Zsa Gabor's husband. He had also created the bodies of the Hawk and Sparrow missiles during the cold war (Ockman 1999, 78). Ryan had a prototype doll made in Japan, but it had nipples, which he "daintily" filed off (Lord 1994, 33). Thus Barbie, named after Handler's daughter, was born with an adult figure and nippleless breasts that have remained controversial ever since.

Body parts were also at issue with the inception of Barbie's boyfriend Ken in 1961. Lord describes Ken as "a gnat, a fly, a slave, an accessory of Barbie," which is an accurate assessment of Ken's second-class status compared to Barbie's. Even the narratives on Barbie's box seem more developed than those on Ken's package. When the Ken doll was being created, Handler wanted a "bulge" in his groin, but male executives at Mattel did not. They ultimately compromised with a very modest bump, what Lord refers to as Ken's "genital abridgment" (1994, 11, 49, 78). As Steven Dubin, a sociologist, observes, "Barbie's prominent breasts are still the lightning rod for controversy; the quandary over Ken was what Mattel gingerly referred to as the 'bulge' or the 'bump.' The corporate decision? Hapless Ken became a eunuch, distinctively embodying Gertrude Stein's dictum, 'there isn't any there there'" (1999, 21).

Those who have written about Barbie have had fun with Mattel's squeamishness when it came to dealing with genitalia. Barbie and Ken, however, are not the sole creations of Mattel and the latter half of the twentieth century. The patterns they follow in presentation of form and gender are similar to those of other types of material culture, especially nineteenth-century cemetery statues. Ken and Barbie, along with G.I. Joe, continue established patterns.

There are several parallels with nineteenth-century cemetery statuary. Just as Barbie is more prominent and ubiquitous than Ken, for example, so, too, are nineteenth-century cemetery statues of women more visible than those of men. That is in large part due to their sexualized bodies. Barbie and the statues are alike in that their breasts, which are commonly eroticized, are among the most noticeable parts of their anatomies. Barbie's breasts generally attract more print than her other body parts. The breasts on cemetery statuary usually command attention because of being the sexualized part of bodies most likely to be nude or emphasized by revealing drapery. Like Ken's elliptical genitals, the genitals of cemetery statues of males could also be described as not having any "there there." Finally, statues of soldiers in cemeteries have a brother in toyland, G.I. Joe, which demonstrates the enduring and common male cultural role of soldier (figure 28).

Figure 28. G.I. Joes.

Even though the temptation is to link Barbie, Ken, and G.I. Joe to the prudery and cold war militaristic tendencies of the 1950s and 1960s, they are also more recent manifestations of the same types of fine-art traditions and conventions discussed earlier. These traditions include making the female form symbolic of idealized beauty and either downsizing male genitalia or referencing them symbolically, as with Ken's and G.I. Joe's bumps.

During the classical era, which influenced many later artistic conventions, large penises signaled a negative and animalistic nature, and "dainty" penises were the rule for male gods, heroes, and athletes. Mattel's Ken, Hasbro's G.I. Joe, and fine-art nudes have something more in common than just their sex. They all emerged from art and social conventions that are hundreds of years old and frequently downplay, in public traditions, the appearance of male genitalia.

Woe to those forms that violated this genital convention. They could come under attack or even be castrated, as were the nude male statue on Oscar Wilde's grave and Mattel's anatomically correct doll of 1975, Baby Brother Tenderlove.[4] Just as the penis on Wilde's statue was covered by a plaque, so, too, some store owners placed a sticker over the penis shown in the photograph of Baby Tenderlove on the box. Some consumers, however, were not appeased by such precautions. Just as the genitals on Wilde's statue were hacked away, so, too, a group of women took to a toy store in Louisville, Kentucky, and actually castrated the dolls (Lord 1994, 101).

In-store castration was not the only protest action prompted by a Mattel doll. Barbie has been at the center of many such events, including the activities of the Barbie Liberation Organization (BLO). During the early 1990s that group claimed responsibility for swapping Barbie's and G.I. Joe's talking mechanisms in some stores.[5] Barbies were made to growl things like "Vengeance is mine!" and the Joes would twitter "Let's go shopping!" and worry "Will we ever have enough clothes?" (Lord 1994, 252). That BLO switched the dolls' voices obliquely points to the fact that Barbie is indeed a gendered stock character. We generally know what she is supposed to say, and "Eat lead, Cobra!" is not it.

Steven Dubin notes, "Barbie (along with Mickey Mouse) is as close as we have to a global litmus test for being human: If you fail to recognize her, you're hardly of this world. That's why a trendy coffee bar in New York City's Chelsea district tags its bathroom doors with her and pal Ken, replacing the prosaic international symbols for female and male" (1999, 19). As Dubin's comments indicate, the dolls' adult bodies provide them with some degree of implied universality. Just as cemetery statuary has stock characteristics, so do dolls. It is the stock nature of the dolls, especially Barbie, that leads them into trouble. A doll's generic human body—which is generally the same from doll to doll—seems to imply that she is Everywoman, but of course she is not. No woman has Barbie's body in real life with the possible exception of Cindy Jackson, who has spent more than $100,000 on some twenty plastic surgeries in her quest to look like Barbie (Dubin 1999, 26).

Much has been written, performed, and exhibited about the body image problems to which Barbie allegedly contributes.[6] As Wendy Singer Jones notes, "The majority of Barbies . . . have activities and accoutrements that emphasize the body" (1999, 94). Research concludes time and time again that Barbie's body is unrealistic. Mass media accounts purport that her measurements would equate $38 \times 18 \times 34$" in a human (Uhlenhuth 1997, A1). The possibility of having a body shaped like Barbie's is less than one in a hundred thousand; the chance of having a body shaped like Ken's is one in fifty (Norton et al. 1996, 287). Translated into human form, Barbie's measurements are considerably smaller, especially in the waist and at the hips, than the composite of a fit woman soldier known as "Army Norma," whose figure is based on those of more than two thousand African American and white female recruits. When Barbie's height is scaled down from the fashion model height of 5' 10" to Army Norma's height, 5' 4", Barbie measures $32 \times 17 \times 28$" and is "clinically anorexic to say the least" (Urla and Swedlund 1995, 297).

G.I. Joe's body has also received scrutiny. Harrison Pope argues that "our society's worship of muscularity may cause increasing numbers of men to develop pathological shame about their bodies, to become obsessively preoccupied with working out, and to take dangerous drugs, such as anabolic steroids" ("Boys' Toys" 1999, A7). Pope measured action figures and scaled those measurements to the height of an actual man. The original G.I. Joe would have biceps of about twelve inches, similar to an ordinary man. A G.I. Joe Extreme would have biceps of about twenty-six inches, larger than any bodybuilder in history (Pope, Olivardia, and Gruber 1999, 68). These bodies are the result of recent fitness trends and influenced by fine-art traditions: "Following ancient models, painters schematized the male figure in terms of muscle structure, in order to convey a powerful body which appeared armoured and under control" (Smith 1996, 173).

For years Mattel has responded to body-image concerns by explaining that although Barbie is nowhere near the size of a person, she wears fabrics that are scaled for people. Thus, her waist had to be disproportionately narrow to appear proportional when she is dressed (Lord 1994, 12). In 1998 Mattel finally reconfigured some Barbies, thickening their waists and hips and decreasing their breast sizes.

Barbie's measurements are not the only aspect of her body that has provoked condemnation, however. Even though Mattel subsidized Shindana Toys, which "produced ethnically correct playthings long before they were fashionable" (Lord 1994, 15), the company's track record concerning race and Barbie often comes under fire.[7] Scholars such as Ann duCille point to Mattel's stereotypical construction of ethnicity (1999, 127, see also 1994). The arguments against Barbie and her problematic measurements are clear, but her exact impact on children is not so certain. "But if I am critical of Barbie as a vessel of ideology," Jones observes, "I refuse to condemn her as necessarily harmful for little girls." She then cites the creative uses to which Barbie is put by everyone from lesbians to gay men to little girls (1999, 104; see also Rand 1995; Shapiro 1999, 121–23; and Stern 1998).

Ironically, Barbie's most notable flaw is her perfect body, a problem apparent to many consumers who refuse to purchase her for that reason. Barbie's biggest public relations challenge lies in the fact that her greatest strength—the idiosyncratic uses to which she is put—is not nearly as universally obvious as are her faults. Her idiosyncratic nature is most clearly observed through informal folk channels, as when, for example, children play with her or engage in narratives about such play. The meaning of her form is not located in, or visible solely from, her body itself.

Like cemetery statues and several yard art figures of females, Barbie is yet another sexualized, stock female figure but more individualized than the others. Individualization is also fostered to some extent in the way Mattel constructs and markets her. The company has created hundreds of versions of Barbie, including Asian American, Latina, African American, and international Barbies. Barbie's careers have included fashion model (her first career), ballerina, stewardess, teacher, doctor, airplane pilot, Olympic athlete, aerobics instructor, cowgirl, corporate executive, veterinarian, and paleontologist. There is also an *X-Files* Barbie, a *Star Trek* Barbie, a Marilyn Monroe Barbie, and a Harley-Davidson Barbie.

Like the cemetery statues, Barbie embodies youth, ideal beauty, and Caucasian characteristics. Barbie doll gender patterns depart in some notable ways, however, from those found in cemetery statuary. For instance, Barbie is more individualized than Ken and G.I. Joe. Cemetery statues of males, by contrast, are more individualized than those of females. There is a progression from cemetery statuary to yard art to Barbie in terms of expanding individualism and widening the range of gendered roles, especially those associated with women. Barbie is at the most liberal end of that continuum. That she is the "best" of these female forms suggests that American culture still has a long way to go before the female image is envisioned and embodied in everyday, visible venues in a less stereotyped and more realistic fashion.

Depictions of both genders frequently remain stock, whether in cemetery statuary, yard art figures, or among the dolls. In terms of age and ethnicity, women portrayed in yard art are cast in more diverse roles than those in cemetery statuary. Still, the roles remain fairly stereotypical, for example, a "good girl" or an older female who is literally the butt of a joke, as is the case with yard art granny fannies. Barbie dolls demonstrate more individuated personas and a greater range of gender roles than yard art or cemetery statues. That pattern is ironic, because cemetery statuary might be considered as more directly linked to real people. As yet, however, it does not commonly make real-life individualism and a range of women's occupations visible. Barbie, despite her plastic superficiality and perfect body, portrays various kinds of women and female occupations; she also evinces more ethnic diversity and less age variation. Barbies are invariably young, whereas images of older women can at least make an appearance in cemeteries or yards.

Cemetery statues elicit a genre of folklore that is more communally shared than Barbies and yard art do. The statues trigger legends and third-person narratives, whereas yard art prompts pranks (and sometimes even organized groups of pranksters like the Gnome Liberation Front), the custom of assemblage, and personal-experience narratives. Similarly, Barbie dolls inspire play behaviors, personal-experience narratives, communally shared electronic lore, and even, in a few cases, ludic pranks—such as those instigated by the Barbie Liberation Organization—informed by gender politics and a sense of playfulness.

If Barbie is the most progressive and least stereotypic of the three types of widespread, gendered material culture, why does she engender the most controversy? It is because, first, she is the most ubiquitous of the three types of material culture; second, she appears in the most intimate of human spaces—the home; third, she shows up in the hands of what are supposed to be the most impressionable inhabitants of that home—children; fourth, she still needs further refinement in terms of representing the lives and bodies of actual adult women; and, fifth, she bears some of the weight of the negative historical associations made with female sexuality and fashion.

Barbie's pervasiveness and the intimacy of her ubiquity make her noticeable. Yard art and cemetery statues lack the same amount of print and television advertising exposure. It is Barbie's high degree of visibility that lends itself to a fuller response to her—and a critique of her. When Barbie is placed in historical context, however, it is apparent that some of the things about her (and how she is played with) that caused so much controversy in twentieth-century culture are not novel at all.

Barbie in Historical Context

A watershed period for the production and purchase of toys in America was the nineteenth century. It was the same century that saw an increase in cemetery statuary as well as the period when lawn statuary began to be affordable for the middle class. It is helpful, however, to understand at least a brief history of toys, particularly dolls, before the advent of mass production during the nineteenth century.

In ancient cultures such as the Greek and Roman, dolls were given moveable limbs that were jointed and held together by cords. In Japan, festivals involving dolls—the Girl's Festival, for example—have been a significant part of the calendar for centuries (Fraser 1966, 39). In medieval Europe, children played with rag dolls and simple clay dolls, some modeled after knights and their horses or even ladies with falcons on their wrists. German dollmakers were at work at least as early as 1413, and dolls were even familiar enough to be referenced in literature. Martin Luther used the term *doll* as a metaphor when rebuking women for their vanity (Fraser 1966, 66).

From the sixteenth until the beginning of the nineteenth centuries, dolls were used as models to display fashionable clothing. That practice was finally replaced by drawings of clothing, made possible largely due to lithography (Ariès 1962, 70). Children in some Native American cultures played with dolls and other miniature accouterments, such as bows and arrows and, later, images of horses. In 1585, when English colonists came ashore on Roanoke Island, they brought dolls as gifts for the native population (O'Brien 1990, 11).

Some current criticisms of Barbie can be put within a larger historical context. For instance, one contemporary charge is that play with Barbies—which now begins around age three for American girls (Lord 1994, 71)—may rush little girls too quickly into the adult world (Cross 1997, 231). Karin Calvert's examination of the material culture of childhood in America between 1600 and 1900 shows the culturally constructed and historically variable nature of such a view. Before 1750, adults wanted American children to grow up quickly because they felt that childhood, especially infancy, held too many dangers. They pushed children beyond infancy as quickly as they could. Now the concern is the reverse—that children will grow up too rapidly. The nineteenth century fostered the idea that the imagined "joy and innocence of childhood" should be prolonged and protected as much as possible (1992, 8).

Some aspects of toys that are commonly assumed to be contemporary often existed in earlier eras. Much is now made of the fact that Barbie is an adult doll and a fashion doll. Dolls, however, have been associated with fashion for several hundred years. From Colonial days onward they were meant to introduce little girls to the world of fashion, dressmaking, and entertaining (Calvert 1992, 117). Mattel—without complicating the issue by considering some facets of girls' entertainment with Barbie, such as the play that mutilates her—has promoted her as having a didactic function. Little girls can practice good grooming and hygiene with Barbie, which is also not a novel use for a doll (Formanek-Brunell 1993, 179).

In today's world Barbie may be seen as one of the most controversial dolls of all time. Many feminists have criticized her, and discord has plagued her from her plastic beginnings. As bumper stickers proclaimed during the late-twentieth and early-twenty-first centuries, "I want to be Barbie; the bitch has everything." The bitch-goddess identity has been with Barbie since her inception, although in a less humorous fashion. During the 1960s she was characterized as a "perfect bitch" (Stern and Schoenhaus 1990, 63) and criticized for having a "predatory" nature. Men worried that she would turn little girls who played with her into a generation of "independent" and "viperous" women (Mitchell and Reid-Walsh 1995, 152, 154).

Earlier dolls were sometimes linked to witches. Philippe Ariès notes, "The ambiguity of the doll and the replica continued during the Middle Ages" (1962, 69). In some instances dolls were used as evidence against women accused as witches (Fraser 1966, 86). Barbie as a bitch and Barbie as a cultural threat come on the heels of hundreds of years of negative press for dolls in general.

Female dolls were also employed to display women's fashions. Since the Middle Ages fashion has been linked to the moral corruption of women, even though men in certain historical periods were just as involved in fashion as women (Hughes 1992, 138). As Diane Owen Hughes observes, "Fashionably dressed women—'painted coffins with rotten bones,' an English critic described them—thus become the ultimate symbol of a too transitory material world corrupted initially by Eve's sin" (1992, 144). Hughes quotes from a seventeenth-century text, but her description of the fashionable woman as "the ultimate symbol of a too transitory material world" could just as well apply to Barbie, who began as a fashion model, as to the women of the seventeenth century. Anne Hollander, an art historian, says that the anti-fashion literature is "enormous, thunderous, scathing, and centuries old" (1994, 24). Moreover, the constant "element of fiction in it [fashion] makes it smack of inauthenticity, pretense, and pretention," and its "important imaginative function . . . is often blindly ignored" (1994, 21, 20). Fashion's history of negative associations may form part of the context for the unfavorable way in which Barbie, a female fashion doll herself, has been seen.

Perhaps the amount of hair Barbie sports these days does not help the situation (figure 29). Mattel, having discovered the salability of "hair-play" factors, has created bigger and bigger hair for Barbie, and that adds to some parental concerns (Thomas 2000a, 80–83). Although little girls like to play with her voluminous locks, parents worry about the cultural messages it communicates. They have expressed dismay, for example, over Totally Hair Barbie, who, one parent said, looks like a "professional fourth wife" (Lord 1994, 185).

Hair has a history of erotic associations—consider, for example, Lady Godiva. In addition, both eroticism and hair have historic links to witchcraft:

> Witches traditionally muss up their hair when they are preparing to engage in witchcraft. As late as the seventeenth century. . . . Europeans, historian Barbara Walker tells us, actually believed witches "raised storms, summoned demons and produced all sorts of destruction by unbinding their hair." In Scottish coastal communities, women were forbidden to brush their hair at night, lest they cause a storm that would kill their male relatives at sea. St. Paul, one of history's all-time woman-haters, was scared of women's hair; he thought unkempt locks could upset the angels. (Lord 1994, 77–78)

Next to her perfect plastic physique it is her mane of hair that defines Barbie's very being. The negative associations with witches and fashion, in addition to the linkage of hair and sexuality, may provide the historical backdrop to some concerns about Barbie beguiling children and about whether play with her causes them to deal with adult issues before they are ready. When the age-old discomfort that sometimes appears in relation to dolls is coupled with contemporary concerns about body image and parental control, it is a wonder that Barbie's press has not been even more negative.

Despite historical links to negative figures like witches, Barbie tames when compared to other figures in the toy world. She is not violent like G.I. Joe, nor is she the type of plaything that Antonia Fraser identifies as the "grotesque toy," which appears throughout history. "In Czechoslovakia," Fraser observes, "the devil is simulated with a forked tail and a pitchfork, and sometimes is shown carrying off naughty children to be roasted. . . . The guillotine toys of the French Revolution were so popular that Goethe actually asked his mother to send one for his son" (1966, 54). Such toys continue to appear on the market. In 1964 a toy company sold a guillotine, complete with beheaded bodies, but it was removed from toy stores after seven months. During the 1980s Cabbage Patch dolls were satirized in the

Figure 29. A mermaid Barbie with long tresses.

form of the grotesque Garbage Pail Kids, who included Arline Latrine, Heaving Heather, and Destroyed Lloyd, all emphasizing body fluids and violence (Cross 1997, 228).

The nineteenth century brought toys and mass production together in America (Fraser 1966, 142). The century was pivotal in both the history of toys in general and dolls specifically. Parents tended to give boys more toys than girls during this period, and those girls did receive "required quiet, careful handling and often encouraged solitary play indoors" (Calvert 1992, III, 112). Historically in America, boys' toys have been intended for more active games than girls' (Calvert 1992, 81), a pattern still maintained in twentieth-century toys like G.I. Joe. Significantly, the expression "boys will be boys" dates from the nineteenth century (Calvert 1992, 113).

Despite the emphasis on quiet activities and play with dolls, fewer than a quarter of a thousand girls surveyed in 1898 said that dolls were their favorite toys (Calvert 1992, 115). The toy preferred by both boys and girls was the hoop, which fostered active play. Children in the late twentieth century also cherished toys that enabled action (Csikszentmihalyi and Rochberg-Halton 1981, 96). In diary entries of 1841 and 1842, twelve-year-old Eliza Ridgely of Baltimore recorded her passion for hoop play. She also "threw snowballs, rode sleds, played catch and King George's troops, and after one morning of paper dolls 'walked out with the boys and Aunt Ellen with our bows and arrows.' She also had a penchant for wrestling matches. . . . 'After dinner I had six fights or wrestlings, three with Isabel Laroque and three with Lizzy Berny, in all of which I laid them flat and conquered them both'" (Calvert 1992, 115–16).

Some boys' play of the nineteenth century might be surprising now. Many little boys played with dolls, as is indicated by photographs and memoirs from the era (Calvert 1992, 117). In a survey published in 1896, G. Stanley Hall found that 76 percent of the boys he surveyed played with dolls (Formanek-Brunell 1993, 28). Few soft, cuddly toys were available in the era, and some types of dolls satisfied that need for both boys and girls:

> In a world where nearly everyone was bigger and stronger than the small child. . .
> doll play gave children a pleasant sense of superiority and control in a world that
> rarely permitted them such feelings. A young boy who craved the comfort of close
> contact and companionship had little choice but a girl's doll, and many moth-
> ers seem to have recognized the need and indulged the child. By the end of the
> century, when a renewed interest in children's make-believe produced a market
> for soft stuffed rabbits, bears, Brownies . . . most little boys found satisfactory al-
> ternatives to dolls, and their ownership among this group declined markedly.
> (Calvert 1992, 117)

According to Miriam Formanek-Brunell, however, male dollmakers, among them Thomas Edison, did not generally understand or consider such needs of children when manufacturing dolls. The machine was their model, and they worked on issues such as indestructibility and mechanization (1993, 40–41). In addition to male dollmakers, there were also women who manufactured dolls. Formanek-Brunell, for example, describes Martha Chase, who produced dolls in accordance with her social reform beliefs and her direct observation and interaction with children (1993, 62–63). Chase is also well known for the teaching mannequins she developed to assist in nurses' training (Fraser 1966, 244).

Women like Chase were interested in creating soft, portable, durable, realistic, and safe dolls. The concern for safety led several women inventors to patent and produce cloth dolls (Formanek-Brunell 1993, 68, 70). They also "reversed the appearance of generations of European dolls" and made dolls that resembled children instead of adults. Sometimes they used their own children as models (Formanek-Brunell 1993, 71). When Ruth Handler had the idea for the Barbie doll while watching children play, she was following in the footsteps of female doll manufacturers of the preceding century.

"The doll," Ester Singleton observed in 1927, "is a greater stimulant to the little girl's imagination than to her maternal instinct" (v–vi). Formanek-Brunell argues that there is much evidence that girls resisted codified doll games, and she has challenged the "widespread assumption that attributes minimal agency to girls whom we *still* assume slavishly played in socially prescribed ways" (1993, 7, 6). By the end of the nineteenth century, however, doll-play was, at least in some part, imbued with consumer values. The increase in popularity of dolls after the Civil War reflected many cultural changes, including "increased affluence, new consumer outlets, smaller family size, and greater emphasis on imitation of adult social rituals and the formalized play it encouraged" (Formanek-Brunell 1993, 15).

Funerals were one adult ritual that children recreated with dolls. Doll funerals were common in the latter half of the nineteenth century, and middle-class parents of the era generally did not find the practice morbid. Death and dying were imbued with romanticism during that era—it was the same period, after all, that produced romanticized surrogate mourner cemetery statuary. Although society considered grieving and mourning to be a proper part of the female realm, mimicking feminine aspects of grieving was not the only, or even the primary, attraction of holding funerals for dolls. "In the numerous doll funerals . . . it was not the passive grieving that provided doll players with pleasure. Doll funerals probably appealed to girls in part because . . . the staging of doll funerals was an expression of aggressive feelings and hostile fantasies. . . . Girls . . . changed the emphasis from the ritualized funerals to cathartic executions" (Formanek-Burnell 1993, 31–32).

Such funerals may have also functioned, like legends about the cemetery statues can, as a means of exploring the mysteries of death. Statistics on child mortality were not uniformly kept during the nineteenth century, but 10 percent died in infancy at the turn of the twentieth century. Moreover, children commonly had to cope with the deaths of friends and family (Shapiro, Schlesinger, and Nesbitt 1968, 3). That reality informed their play. Although mortality rates have dropped and doll funerals are no longer such a widely recognized convention in play, they do still occur. Death also enters into how some children play with their Barbies. One woman, for example, told me about a granddaughter who keeps a bag of "dead Barbie" parts. The adults around her are not attuned to which Barbies are dead and which are alive, but the child knows, and she carefully keeps, stores, and sometimes buries the parts of the dead Barbies.

Just as nineteenth-century doll funerals could be an active, exploratory, and aggressive form of play, Formanek-Brunell observes that some girls who played with dolls developed a sense of self that was anything but submissive and passive. There was, for example, Sarah Bixby from southern California, who skinned, dressed, and boiled rabbit meat for her doll, Isabel. Another little girl attacked a friend named Harry who had bitten a hole in her doll. She "grabbed him by the shoulders . . . ready to fight to the death [for] her rights, [when] he burst into cries for help" (1993, 33). Both events occurred long before the days of Barbie's We Girls Can Do Anything! slogan.

Many turn-of-the-twentieth-century doll manufacturers worked to reify the notion of a good girl who quietly played with her doll. Along with the introduction of teddy bears, which were popular, more and more toys were being produced and consumed. The dollmakers became nervous about threats, even toyboyism, to their market. Unlike earlier dollmakers, Mattel tried to encompass tomboyism and even encourage girls to venture into previously male-dominated arenas. As early as 1965, and long before the first woman in space, Mattel created an astronaut version of Barbie (Tosa 1998, 125). In what some see as relatively superficial ways the company also tried to connect the doll with feminism through such things as Barbie collector cards about feminist history (Mitchell and Reid-Walsh 1995, 148).

Linking a doll with feminism is not a new concept and was much more radically accomplished early in the twentieth century by Rose O'Neill, who created the Kewpie doll. By World War I, Kewpies were the best-known popular culture figures in America (Formanek-Brunell 1993, 117). Just as Mattel's marketing of Barbie uses elements of folklore such as fairy tales, customs such as holidays, and legendary creatures such as fairies, mermaids, and angels (Thomas 2000a), O'Neill also drew upon folklore as an inspiration for the Kewpie doll. Kewpies were based on O'Neill's baby brother and on her childhood belief in an Irish "elf." Like Barbie's predecessor, Lilli, Kewpies began life as cartoon figures, albeit less risqué than Lilli: "An educated woman with a social conscience, O'Neill designed politically conscious and benevolent Kewpies who, like their creator, carried suffrage placards, debated the opposition, and vigilantly watched over working-class neighborhoods" (Formanek-Brunell 1993, 188). O'Neill used the Kewpies to illustrate many pro-suffrage cartoons and postcards (Formanek-Brunell 1993, 129).

Kewpies were drawn naked and had wings like cupids' but no genitals. They were male, but they were androgynous-looking little males and often assumed caretaking roles and wore clothing such as aprons that is usually and stereotypically assigned to the feminine realm. Formanek-Brunell acknowledges that because of these traits, and given the nineteenth-century fine-art tradition that dictated that most nudes be female, many people assumed that Kewpies were girls (1993, 126). When male dollmakers turned the Kewpies into dolls, they made them into feminine figures, reversing what was one of the more radical and interesting gender presentations in doll history. Formanek-Brunell says of O'Neill's creations, "As feminists or as their supporters, the Kewpies were an unusual amalgam of the New Woman and emancipated New Man" (1993, 130). Unfortunately, the doll versions of the Kewpies did not continue in that way. O'Neill's Kewpies did provide, however, a much earlier and a more directly political take on gender and social issues than Barbie.

Sales of baby dolls increased after the turn of the century as the birthrate declined. Realistic dolls like the Bye-Lo-Baby, supposedly modeled after a three-day-old infant, appeared on the market in 1923 (Cross 1997, 77). The 1930s produced the Shirley Temple doll. It was during this era that the first major alliance between toys and the film industry developed, foreshadowing what was to come during the latter half of the century. In connection with the release of *Snow White,* Walt Disney developed a strategy of licensing images that "now dominates children's culture" (Cross 1997, 107). Radio also became a conduit for the growth of the character toys.

The first part of the twentieth century saw the decline of utilitarian toys as ones that were fantasy-oriented became more popular. Superhero figures powered children's play even further into the realm of fantasy. The generation of children born after World War II was the largest in American history to that date. For the first time, children took control of toy selection, something traditionally the purview of parents.

During the 1950s—the decade when Toys "Я" Us stores opened their doors—television gave children power to influence the purchase of toys, and in 1955 the *Mickey Mouse Club* changed the way toys were sold. Before then, many were advertised in magazines geared toward adult audiences. The Mouseketeers, however, marked the initiation of advertising directed at children—an approach employed ever since (Cross 1997, 164). Significantly, Mattel took the lead:

> Ruth and Eliot Handler risked their family business to purchase three commercials every weekday for a year on the *Mickey Mouse Club*. This flew in the face of conventional wisdom. Everyone knew that profit from toys did not warrant such expensive advertising and that commercials were effective only at Christmas and then only if directed at their purchasers—adults. Mattel's opening advertisement in the autumn of 1955 was for the burp gun. . . . Within six weeks of commercials, a deluge of orders for the guns reached Mattel, causing a shortage at Christmas. (Cross 1997, 165)

When Barbie arrived on the scene in 1959, she, too, was advertised on the show. Test-marketing indicated that mothers were not nearly so positive about Barbie as were their daughters, and it was those girls who made the doll a success (Cross 1997, 170–71). Soon doll companies that had not bought advertising time on television disappeared. Two hundred companies manufactured dolls in 1959, the year of Barbie's debut; by 1969 there were only sixty. Baby dolls dropped from 80 percent of the dolls made in 1959 to 38 percent in 1975 (Cross 1997, 174). The postmodern princess of plastic had arrived, and she had decisively deconstructed dolldom.

Barbie's influence even extended to G.I. Joe, who appeared in 1964. "Someone at Hasbro is supposed to have said, 'How about a doll for boys that concentrates on accessories like Barbie?'" (McClary 1997, 194). Even though Joe was marketed as "America's Moveable Fighting Man," he shared with Barbie the critical feature of being a dress-up doll with a lot of accessories. Stan Weston, who pitched the concept of G.I. Joe to Hasbro, had been taught the "razor and the razor blade idea" by Eliot Handler of Mattel. That company based Barbie marketing on the following premise: The doll is analogous to the "razor," and the accessories are the "razor blades" that continue to sell long after the doll (Michlig 1998, 17).

Hasbro was cautious about the G.I. Joe concept; the worry was that parents would not buy dolls for boys (Michlig 1998, 27). That concern was addressed at a semantic level. The doll was never referred to as a doll but as a "movable fighting man" or "an action figure" (Michlig 1998, 28, 38). For the first prototype of G.I. Joe, Hasbro employees "beefed up" a Ken doll

(Michlig 1998, 32). Christened G.I. Joe ("Government Issue Joe"), a name popularized by Ernie Pyle during World War II, the doll invaded American toy stores in 1964 (Santelmo 1997, 23).

War toys and toy soldiers were hundreds of years old by the time Joe made his debut. Earlier in the century, many boys' toys were technologically oriented miniatures. They helped train boys to imitate the adult world of work and technology. Cap, pop, spring, and air guns had been available since the nineteenth century, but "toy guns were still relatively rare before World War I, and no advertisers encouraged mock combat between children. . . . Shortly before and during World War I, toy guns became more prominent as the nation prepared itself for war" (Cross 1997, 110–11). Later in the century, the "combination of aggressive marketing of toy guns and general anxiety about crime in the gangster-ridden 1930s produced a negative public reaction" (Cross 1997, 112). During the mid-1930s in Chicago, for example, a bonfire was held to protest violent toys, and toy guns from more than sixty Chicago-area schools were collected and used as fuel.

In the late 1960s G.I. Joe was critiqued as promoting violence, and he faced a firestorm—Vietnam:

> By 1967 as the Vietnam war heated up and adults such as Benjamin Spock attacked war toys, sales decreased. Beginning in 1970 Hasbro responded by transforming the "fighting" Joes into an "Adventure Team." Joes searched for sunken treasure and captured wild animals. . . . In 1976, with the Vietnam War in the past, G.I. Joe became "Super Joe" and shrunk to eight inches (because of the higher costs for plastic). . . . From 1978 to 1981 the "Great American Hero" disappeared from the store shelves to be pushed aside by an even more fantasyful line of toys based on George Lucas's *Star Wars*. (Cross 1997, 177)

Joe had his ups and downs during the final decades of the twentieth century, but Barbie, unruffled by Vietnam, continued to sell. By the end of the twentieth century, Mattel maintains, two Barbie dolls were being sold somewhere in the world every second ("Twin Fates" 1999, 121).

If the media invades homes and shapes consumers, the consumers fight back and rework mass-marketed goods—including Barbie—whether or not Mattel likes them doing so. Mattel, however, is frequently aggressive in trying to silence artistic depictions of Barbie it does not like. The company, for example, sued Tom Forsythe, whose photographs show Barbies being cooked, sliced, or diced in kitchen appliances. According to Forsythe's attorney Annette Hurst, Mattel has taken legal action against more than sixty-five artists (Rosenzweig 2001, n.p.).

Mattel tolerates some artistic refashioning of Barbie, however, and Craig

Yoe's anthology (1994) of Barbie artwork, which Mattel authorized, exemplifies how she has been reconstructed in the fine arts. Some of the pieces rely on humor. Rick Tharp's photograph *Put Another Shrimp on the Barbie, Mate,* for example, shows a supine and nude Barbie, raw shrimp draped over her upper torso in roughly the form of a dress. Other artists depict Barbie as an icon—and a primal one at that. In Brian Sheridan's photographs, a series of Barbies parodies the stone statues on Easter Island.

Some artists in the anthology explore Barbie's connection to other famous idealized female forms in art history. Emily Cohen's *Birth of Barbie* portrays Barbie on the half-shell—an image made famous hundreds of years earlier by Sandro Botticelli's *The Birth of Venus.* Marian Jones provides a photographic play on Marcel Duchamp's *Nude Descending a Staircase,* with a naked Barbie, complete with multitudinous hair, flouncing downstairs. Finally, Joel Peter Johnson has painted her as that most holy of women, *La Barbie Vierge.*

Such artwork expresses Barbie's connection to all levels of culture, whether folk, popular, or elite. The pieces place her as an idealized female figure within a long artistic tradition of perfect female forms; they indicate that, like yard art, she invites playfulness and whimsy on the part of adults as well as children; and they demonstrate that people, whether children or adult artists, continuously and insistently apply individualized meanings to her.

Mattel is aware of the way people personalize Barbie, and it tries to sell that concept in various ways. Children, for example, can go to a Web-site and design a Barbie to their own specifications. Barbie represents a kind of commodified and rampant individualization. We often seek to make personal and human uniqueness more visible through the use and display of mass-marketed goods, a process visible in yard art assemblage as well. Such goods also provide a channel for individual creativity. In a fashion parallel to the different ways individual children play with Barbie and the variety of roles they create for her, Mattel thus produces more and more different kinds of Barbies.

Mattel's Barbie actualizes what folklorist Jack Santino identifies as serialization in consumer goods. In *New Old-Fashioned Ways,* he argues that serialization is central to consumerism: "It is increasingly clear that a primary distinctive feature of mass consumer culture, with its ongoing need for the appearance of novelty is the underlying principle of the serialization of virtually everything. . . . We see the periodization or serialization of mass cultural products that are not themselves periodical or temporally sequential in nature. . . . This periodicization of mass-produced consumer goods may be a distinctive feature of industrial, commercial culture" (1996, 69). He then convincingly documents how pervasive products of consumer culture, for example, music, comic books, and even food packaging, use traditional events such as holidays because of the serialization and, therefore, relative novelty they lend to the products. Santino demonstrates the manner in which traditional forms such as holidays "are of the utmost importance to contemporary, postindustrial, existential, postmodern life" (1996, 151).

Mattel's marketing of Barbie supports Santino's thesis. She is serialized to sell. Making her new and different is the crux of a marketing plan that employs traditional elements (such legendary creatures as angels or mermaids) and events (holidays) (Thomas 2000a). With Barbie, the ongoing and larger cultural interest in distinctiveness and individualization is merged with consumer culture's need for novelty. Encompassed in a form such as Barbie, the nineteenth-century's emphasis on individualization meets twentieth-century serialization.

In a discussion of Frederic Jameson's view of the postmodern condition and the manner in which holidays have become commodified, Santino continues:

> Jameson talks of how in the postmodern situation the terms "cultural" and "economic" "collapse back into one another and say the same thing, in an eclipse of the (Marxist) distinction between base and superstructure that has often struck people as significantly characteristic of postmodernism in the first place" (1991, xxi). In this sense, then, the phenomena we have surveyed indicate the postmodern condition. . . .
>
> This is true as far as it goes, but it must be remembered that while these mass-produced artifacts can be viewed as mere simulacra of directly engaged, participatory ritual and celebration, *these objects are used. While these artifacts may function as a substitute for sociability, they are just as often the medium, or the excuse for it.* (1996, 148–49, emphasis added)

Clearly, Barbie is also used as a medium for children's and adults' sociability and creativity.

All three types of material culture (cemetery statuary, yard art, and Barbie dolls) that I discuss in this book have nineteenth-century ties. They are part of the emergence of a culture of conspicuous consumption. Even as mass-produced goods of consumer society threaten to overwhelm them, however, Americans continue to use the same material forms to express individualism. As Santino says, we need to examine the ways store-bought items "acquire meaning, and how their use is more important than their origins or mode of production" (1996, 156). Narratives that concern play-ing with Barbie are an excellent means for doing just that.

Barbie is "an education in consumption" (Cross 1997, 173) and yet some-thing more. She is a plaything that can reflect the specific and idiosyncratic lives of those who play with her. A Barbie doll and play with her often be-come part of the unique narratives of childhood.

Barbie and G.I. Joe in a Folkloric Context

When I first contemplated writing about Barbie, I planned to present a more negative picture of her than I have done in this book. After all, she was easy. The Bimbo-Goddess of Blondeness, Plastic, and Perfect Physiques seemed ripe for intellectual trashing—or so I thought until I started paying atten-tion to the folklore about her. Although still deserving of criticism—and the folklore I examine herein often does critique her—I realized as I thought about the lore that Barbie evokes more cultural complexity than I had been aware of initially. In this section, I will examine some of the folklore about Barbie and discuss the intricacies it reveals.

Stories about play with Barbie answer a question: What do real children and adults (the folk) do with Barbie? Some accounts of playing with Barbies reinforce the effectiveness of Mattel's marketing strategies. Several field interviews, for example, emphasize hair-play as an attractive aspect of Barbie. But folk Barbie is not as predictable as I first thought, nor does she follow the storylines Mattel has created for her.

In the diverse stories of play that follow, Barbie appears as a wife and mother, she cross-dresses in Ken's clothes, or she lies around naked on the bedroom floor all day. She is an equestrienne; she is also Godzilla and a mother to G.I. Joe. She packs a toothbrush gun in games of cowboys and Indians and plays hide-and-seek. She is a fashion model, a soap opera star, a hostage, and a member of the Cleaver family. She consoles a child about the dysfunction in his family. She shops, goes to college, makes sushi, has sex with aliens, gets pregnant, and works at jobs ranging from babysitter to dentist to stewardess to architect. She participates in race-car driving, camping, dating, swimming, mountain climbing, and movie watching.[8]

The doll as a reflection of her owner's interests, family life, and worldviews is apparent in an account one of my folklore students collected from a twenty-year-old biracial (African American and white) male acquaintance:

> Anthony played with both Barbie and Ken dolls as well as G.I. Joe dolls. He had a total of ten dolls (one Barbie, one Ken, and eight G.I. Joes). He said that he began playing with dolls around the age of five and continued to play with them until

he discovered girls at the ripe (old) age of nine. . . . He said that he played with his dolls from the moment that he walked into the door from school until he went to bed of a night. He played a variety of games with his dolls.

He played the usual war games with the G.I. Joes in which the Barbie and Ken dolls were "Godzilla-like creatures" that wanted to destroy the city by dancing atop the houses in the village and crushing them. He also played house many times in which Barbie and Ken were mother and father to his G.I. Joes. He also played instances of cowboys and Indians with his dolls. His Barbie and Ken dolls would ride other stuffed toys of his as horses and use toothbrushes as guns. He would also play Navy Seals with his dolls in the bathtub and toilet. He laughs in remembering how much trouble he got into when he flushed his favorite G.I. Joe down the toilet and his mother had to call a plumber to retrieve it (or at least try). He remembers that his mother "beat the piss" out of him for attempting this stunt. He told his mother that he was only trying to see if G.I. Joe could swim as well as he could. He would also have his dolls conduct scavenger hunts through-out the house and outside. He would have his brother leave little hints everywhere about the whereabouts of his "captive." He would then search for hours to find the "hostage." He said sometimes his brother would put them in impossible places, and it would take him forever to find them. In these instances, he said he would give up, and his brother would make him cry by not telling him where they were until two or three days later. He would also conduct fashion shows with his Barbie and Ken, and his G.I. Joes would be the critics of the outfits.

He often mimicked adult roles and TV shows. His favorite memory was mim-icking sex scenes from soap operas. He said that his Barbie and Ken dolls would be the stars for the show, and his G.I. Joes were the camera crew. He said he would be entertained for hours playing this type of game. He said that he learned the most about sex by watching soaps and mimicking what they were doing on TV. His dolls also mimicked the Cleaver family. . . . He said that his family was very dysfunctional and . . . playing this . . . took away the hurt of knowing that his family was so bad off and had so many problems.

Anthony's recollection of childhood play with dolls is at once poignant, complex, and creative. It provides an example of doll-play wherein the child's family life is projected in the play. But Anthony did not specifically mimic his family, which he described as dysfunctional. By using tele-vision's Cleaver family as a model, he created and manipulated a positive family through his dolls. In this fashion his play extended his concerns about family and became a way of addressing family issues and comfort-ing himself about them. He also played war games with his dolls, follow-ing the stock script associated with the G.I. Joe doll. His doll-play was not stereotypical, however; for example, defying her ultra-feminized origins, Barbie would become a powerful aggressor, Godzilla. She was also a cowboy. Anthony had her return to her origins as a fashion model, but Ken and G.I. Joe participated as well. The G.I. Joes assumed a role Hasbro probably never dreamed of for them: fashion critics.

Anthony remembered his brother doing things to the dolls that caused conflict, a theme that arose in other narratives as well. It seems to be related to a common type of family narrative among my students, accounts of the activities siblings used to harass each other. In addition, his narrative raises the theme of children's play based on popular culture, a thread in the doll-play of some but totally ignored by others. Anthony acted out scenes from television soap operas, which involved all his dolls, and used the dolls and the soap operas to explore sexuality and the human body, another major theme in playing with Barbies.

An interview I conducted with a six-year-old white girl, although very different in content and detail from Anthony's account, demonstrates a similar structure: the projection of her interests and activities onto the doll. According to the narratives I collected, play with Barbie is used to reflect and expand the interests, worldviews, and experiences of her owners. I call this play process mirroring and extension.

The little girl's two-and-a-half-year-old brother, who likes both Barbies and Tonka trucks, was also present during the following interview. I had observed both children's play behaviors on numerous occasions and knew the kinds of things they did when they played with Barbie dolls. In some cases I repeated the girl's answers because I was concerned that she would be hard to understand on tape. She spoke softly, and her brother, seeking attention, jabbered a great deal in the background:

> Jeannie: Do you know what the name of this Barbie is that you're holding? No? This Barbie is naked. Don't throw her at me.
> Girl: That['s] on tape [the reference to nakedness]!
> Jeannie: That's okay. . . . How come she's naked?
> Girl: [Loudly.] I COULDN'T FIND HER CLOTHES.
> Jeannie: How come you took her clothes off?
> Girl: I wanted to.
> Jeannie: Was it fun to take her clothes off?
> Girl: I can't answer that one.
> Jeannie: Why not?
> Girl: I don't want to.
> Jeannie: Well, you [can] tell me—.
> Girl: I DON'T HAVE AN ANSWER FOR IT!
> Jeannie: Okay, do you like dressing her?
> Girl: Yeah. . . .

Jeannie: What do you like about this Barbie?

Girl: That it spins.

Jeannie: That it bends?

Girl: SPINS.

Jeannie: Oh, that it spins.

Girl: [Sighs loudly.]

Jeannie: What do you like about your Ballerina Barbie?

Girl: I like to play with it. . . .

Jeannie: What kinds of things do you like to play with your dolls? What kinds of things do you have them do?

Girl: Have fun.

Jeannie: Have fun? What's having fun?

Girl: I can't explain that one.

Jeannie: Do you play with them in your [doll]house?

Girl: Yeah.

Jeannie: What do they do?

Girl: I forgot.

Jeannie: Well, think about it; if you were going to play with them in your house, what might they do? Would they have dinner? Would they—

Girl: Dinner?

Jeannie: Yeah, do they pretend like they're big people? Do they play with your animals?

Girl: Play with animals.

Jeannie: What do they play with the animals?

Girl: [Sighs.]

Jeannie: What do they play with your animals?

Girl: They play games with them.

Jeannie: They play games with your animals?

Girl: Uh huh [yes].

Jeannie: Like what kind of games?

Girl: Hide-and-seek and stuff.

Jeannie: They play hide-and-seek with your animals? That's pretty neat! Do they do that very often, or do the animals mostly play by themselves?

Girl: Fairly often.

Jeannie: You do it fairly often?

Girl: Uh huh. . . . What's the next question?

Jeannie: Do you ever pretend that your Barbie is an adult?

Girl: Uh huh [yes].

Jeannie: What does she do when she's an adult?

Girl: Have dinner and stuff.

Jeannie: Have dinner and stuff. What else? What other stuff do adults do that your Barbie does?

Girl: Read stories.

Jeannie: She reads stories? Wow, that's pretty neat!

Boy: She's [Barbie] looking at you!

Jeannie: She's looking at me, is that what you're saying?

Boy: And me!

Jeannie: And you, huh?

Boy: [My sister.]

Jeannie: And [your sister]. Okay. Does she do anything else that adults do besides read? What are her favorite kinds of books?

Boy: [Delighted.] She's spinning!

Girl: I don't know.

Jeannie: Does she ever pretend she's in a TV show or anything like that?

Girl: No.

Jeannie: Do you have a favorite doll between your twirly one [a fairy Barbie that spins when you pull a string on her back] and your ballerina one?

Girl: Ballerina.

Jeannie: Why do you like ballerina?

Girl: Because it has a pretty dress.

Jeannie: Have you ever heard of Ken?

[The girl shakes her head no.]

Jeannie: No?

Girl: Uht uh [no].

Boy: See? I, I squashed—I bumped into my leg!

Jeannie: Do you ever build any sort of house for your doll? [Girl shakes head no.] Do they live in your log cabin?

Girl: Uh huh [yes].

Boy: [Loudly.] WHERE'S MY CAR SHIRT?!

Jeannie: Do you ever make any clothes for them?

Boy: WHERE'S MY CAR SHIRT?!

Girl: How am I supposed to do that?

Boy: WHERE'S MY CAR SHIRT?!

Jeannie: Be creative. . . .

Boy: [Softer.] Where's my car shirt?

Jeannie: What's your favorite toy to play with?

Girl: You mean out of Barbies?

Jeannie: No, out of anything in your room. What toys do you like to play with the best?

Girl: My dog toys and my unicorn ones.

Jeannie: Your dog toys and your unicorn ones?

Girl: Uh huh [yes]. Like that unicorn [points to a stuffed unicorn].

Jeannie: Oh, yeah. What do you like to do with your dog toys and your unicorn?

Girl: They play together, and sometimes they play hide 'n seek.

Jeannie: Sometimes they play hide 'n seek, too. And they play together?

Girl: Uh huh [yes].

Boy: We [he and his sister] play hide 'n seek. We play hide 'n seek!

Jeannie: That sounds like lots of fun. What else do you like to do? What else do you like to play when you're in your room?

Girl: Are we going to all be on TV?

Jeannie: No, this isn't going to be . . . on TV. But [I] might use it in a book, if that's okay.

Girl: Okay.

Jeannie: What else do you like to play in your room?

Girl: After this, can I just say stuff into it [the microphone]?

Jeannie: [Nods yes.] But don't you like to paint and draw? What are your favorite things to do?

Girl: Paint and draw.

Jeannie: Didn't you have a Barbie birthday cake once? Didn't you ask for a Barbie birthday cake?

Girl: Yeah, I did.

Jeannie: How come you wanted a Barbie birthday cake?

Girl: I DON'T KNOW! I just saw it; it was the only one I liked. . . . So I wanted it for my birthday.

Boy: I just got a Teletubby cake! At my house.

Jeannie: Yeah, [he] got a Teletubby cake for his birthday—he wants—that's what he wants, I guess. Do you know other little girls who play with Barbies?

Girl: Unt uh [no].

Jeannie: You don't. Okay. Ever thought about taking the dolls apart?

Girl: NOOOO!

Jeannie: How come your Barbie, your Ballerina Barbie, is so beat up? Isn't she missing an arm or something?

Girl: And a leg.

Jeannie: And a leg?

Girl: YEAH! I DON'T—THEY JUST CAME LOOSE, OKAY!

Boy: See? See? See?

Jeannie: [To boy.] What do you think about that? Oh . . . don't do that to [your sister's] doll. So what do you think about the Barbies in [my] bag?

Girl: I like them.

Jeannie: How come you like them?

Girl: Because they're pretty.

Boy: I like them, too!

Jeannie: Do you think they're smart?

Girl: Yeah.

Jeannie: What makes you think they're smart?

Girl: They look smart.

Jeannie: How do you know when somebody's smart?

Boy: They're cute!

Girl: I don't know.

Jeannie: [He] thinks they're cute. [The girl laughs.] Do you ever style their hair and do stuff with their hair?

Girl: Yeah, sometimes I do. . . . How many more questions do we have?

Jeannie: We're pretty well done.

Girl: Are we done?

Jeannie: So do you think Barbie looks like the grown-ups that you know?

Girl: I don't know any that look like Barbie.

Jeannie: You don't know any grown-ups that look like Barbie?

Girl: Unt uh [no].

Jeannie: How are the grown-ups different than Barbie?

Girl: They're real.

Like Anthony, the six-year-old projects the activities of her life onto Barbie. For example, she says her Barbies play hide-and-seek, a game she frequently plays with her brother. She also describes reading as being among her dolls' "adult" behaviors. The adults in her family read often, both individually and to the two children. The girl tired of my questions (and wanted to play with the tape recorder) and made it clear that her play with Barbie focuses on fun. She also demonstrates awareness of the fantasy elements involved in such play when she comments that the doll does not look like any adults she knows; they are real and the doll is not. Finally, like Anthony's, the girl's account of her play shows awareness of the body and some of the taboos associated with it. Even though nudity is not a major taboo in her home, she has picked up on enough cultural taboos and public/private distinctions and practices concerning the body to be embarrassed by my questions about the doll's nudity, especially because I was taping our conversation. More disturbing was the fact that part of Barbie's appeal was based on the fact that the girl saw her as pretty. Her two-year-old brother has not yet learned to make many of the cultural distinctions that his sister makes. When he plays with Barbie, he appears primarily to be enjoying her form; he picks her up by the hair and throws her a lot. During the interview he was delighted when the doll's body began to twirl.

In an interview I did with Sally, a twenty-three-year-old white woman, some of the same themes and issues came up, although the details of Sally's accounts were quite different from Anthony's and the six-year-old's. Like them, Sally mirrors and extends her world through doll-play. She grew up in Hawai'i, where she and her friends localized their Barbies: "There's no Polynesian people in the media. And so I think that people in Hawai'i take something that's meant to be something else and make it their own. Because even with Barbie, like everyone in Hawai'i wears like t-shirts and board shorts, and you cannot buy t-shirts and board shorts for Barbie. But you can at the swap meet because there's somebody who is handy with the sewing machine."

Sally's play with Barbie evinced regional foodways as well; her Barbies made sushi. Not only did Sally's Barbie mirror the place where Sally lived in terms of clothing and foodways, but the doll also reflected and extended her interests at the time in her life when she played with Barbie. That was common among other informants. Kim, a twenty-one-year-old African American woman, comments, "When I went to sleep, they [the Barbies] went to sleep. When I woke up, they woke up." When Kim was spanked so were her dolls, and when her parents argued so did her Ken and Barbie. As Shelley, a twenty-two-year-old white female, sums it up: "What didn't we have them [our Barbies] do? Really Barbie did everything we did, and everything we dreamed of doing."

Jessica, a twenty-year-old white woman who collects Barbies, recalls hating "Barbie pink" and loving Tonka trucks as a child. She played "prom" a lot with her Barbies: "There was a lot of prom going on then because they got to wear the huge dresses. . . . Sometimes they'd forget Ken. As a girl and as a teenager, I was one of those kids: 'Who cares if the boy comes? If the boy comes, the boy comes, but it's not that big of a deal.' Girls are like—they get crushes, and that was never really me. But Ken, I had him; he was there. He served a purpose, but we'd go to the prom without him."

Jessica's parents were teachers, so she also played "school" frequently with her dolls. Not only did Jessica's play reflect her interests and her parents' occupations, but the family also incorporated her fondness for Barbie into her upbringing and training. When Jessica, for example, wanted a Barbie Cadillac, her mother offered her a nickel if she would walk her brother to school and a quarter if she would not sleep in her parents' bed at night. Jessica learned to save money, and stay out of her parents' bed, in order to get a car for her Barbie. As an adult, Jessica uses some Barbies in her collection in a playful fashion reminiscent of some yard artists. For example, she creates indoor Halloween assemblages with her *Addams Family* Barbie dolls for visitors to enjoy (figure 30). Jessica was uninterested in boys, which her play revealed.

Sally used Barbies as an extension of her passion for horses:

My favorite toys were . . . horses. Like that was what I REALLY played with—was My Little Ponies and Breyer Horses. . . . [Barbie] was always like having to sit Ken down to tell him that either she had purchased another horse, or she was expecting a baby. . . . She was always saying like, "Well, I've purchased a new Arabian, Ken."

And Ken's like, "Again? We can't keep feeding them!"

"I know, but he's so handsome!"

And they'd go out to the pasture and lean against the fence, and the horses

Figure 30. *Addams Family* Barbie and Ken.

would gallop around, and then it was horse time. So they just owned the estate where all my horses lived. . . .

It all goes back to the horses, really, because I had a whole bunch of little fences and stuff for the horses. . . . I also had a My Little Pony Pretty Parlor thing that opened up into like a place you could stand the horses while you groomed them. And so I would attach that to the whole bunch of little fences, and then we could make Lego things, and then incorporate the dollhouse. My mom, I'm sure, just saw a huge, multimedia mess on the floor, but we saw this world. . . .

I had a friend who also had a lot of My Little Ponies, and she was much wealthier than I was . . . so I was kind of jealous of how many she had. And she didn't comb them. . . . I would ache at her neglect—it was probably my first, my first feelings of animal rights and wanting to do humane work for pets and animals—because I felt like she was so mean to leave her My Little Ponies' tails in snarls. . . . I always felt sorry for my toys; like I wanted to make sure that—not to hurt any of their feelings. And if I got a new one, I wanted all the old ones to know that I still liked them. So I didn't want Barbie to be naked because it would be cold and undignified, and I didn't want her to be embarrassed with Ken and the horses around.

Sally's play with toy horses was a venue for expressing concern for animals, a trait that stayed with her into maturity. Doll-play also allowed her to exercise such social skills as empathy and thoughtfulness when she worried about the "feelings" of her toys.

Another informant demonstrated a similar interest in horse-play. As a child, Deb used dolls to mirror the activities focused around her younger siblings, and she employed Barbie as an accessory for her "tomboy" personality:

When I was little (five or six), I would play with baby dolls. I would carry them, feed them, and change them. I believe this was in direct response to the activities that were occurring in my family at this time. My mother had two more children after me. To me my dolls were real. I would take them for walks. Rock them when they cried. Read to them and feed them. It was especially fun when my mom would let me use the real baby clothes for my dolls. I felt extremely grown up.

Later on Barbie had her impact. I had become somewhat of a tomboy, and so off came Barbie's and on went Ken's clothes. I'm sure Freud would have a lot to say about that! When I was little I was obsessed with horses. There's no other way to put it. I collected Breyer horse statues and Barbie became the equestrienne. I think I need to mention that I am a brunette, so I always liked Francie [a Barbie-family-and-friends doll] better because her hair was dark like mine. My cousin and I would construct barns for the horses out of old apple crates. You can imagine our disappointment when we discovered that Barbie's anatomy did not allow her to "ride" the horses. I do believe we ditched her soon after that.

Deb recalls getting rid of Barbie because her body proved unsuitable for the kind of play that interested Deb. Her account of spurning the doll because Barbie's body was not functional for play was not as common as narratives of parental rejections of Barbie. Amy, for example, a white woman in her twenties, said she had not played with Barbie as a child. Her mother felt Barbie's body was unrealistic and therefore the doll was inappropriate, a conviction she demonstrated by purposefully running over some Barbies with her car.

Using Barbie to explore sex and anatomy, particularly adult physiology, is another common theme in the Barbie stories. As Jessica observes, "There was always the . . . anatomy lessons from your Barbie; you know, 'What are THESE?'" As Janet, a thirty-five-year-old Hispanic woman, says, "Of course, you wouldn't want Mom and Dad to see the things you really wanted to do with Ken and Barbie either. As you got older, Ken and Barbie would go off and be sneaky, too, you know. It's so funny; you'd go outside and play, and when Mom and Dad went around the house, then you'd let Ken and Barbie kiss."

Barbie's body is also a topic in Sally's narratives and, for her, raises issues of gender, ethnicity, and sexuality. She began one section of her interview by talking about a childhood play group:

> When I visited my grandma in Idaho, there was a neighbor girl that came over and played Barbies with me, and she—I didn't know what a date was—like, I was probably eight, and I didn't know what "date" meant. But her Barbies were always going on a date, and my whole . . . reference for date wasn't—it was like a little wrinkled fruit. I didn't think that it was like an outing. So I never knew what she was talking about until way later. . . .
>
> I had a[nother] friend who lives in my grandmother's town. . . . And he was three years older than I was, so it was a strange play group anyway, but he was the one who introduced a real sexuality to Barbie and Ken that I previously had not thought about.
>
> I had the twin-size dream bed . . . and he was always like putting Barbie and Ken together. And I would say, "There's only room for one. There—it's a small bed; it's not like a party bed." And he would always try to fit all of them in there. So I think he just knew more than I did. . . .
>
> He was probably nine, and I was probably six, so I didn't know. I just wanted Barbie the horse girl. And I remember, oh gosh, I think that he came from a troubled home now that I think about it 'cause I think that I remember Barbie and Ken fighting because Barbie slept with someone else. Like, I—gosh, I feel like this is so Freudian or something. . . . There was a lot of sexual stuff that he did. . . . That was new to me though . . . I think he probably had sex stuff going on with my

horses, too. Leaving them mounted or something. And that was another thing, like I was too little to really think it was dirty or anything like that: "That's how he plays; meanwhile, Barbie's purchased another horse." . . .

And he actually had an older sister who was a teenager who got pregnant out of wedlock. And so he had sort of a fascination with pregnancy from a young— so I would always have Barbie announce that she was expecting, and it would be like, Ken would be like "Yaaaay! We're gonna be a family!" And when he had Barbie announce that she was pregnant, Ken would stomp out of the room and be really angry. And he would actually make her pregnant; he would like put cotton balls underneath her outfits and stuff. . . .

I was like, "Let's go back to the horse thing. Why are you—? Okay, she's pregnant, but she, she can still ride" . . . he was so knowledgeable on pregnancy. . . . "She's not far along enough yet; she can still ride horses." . . . I didn't understand most of it until way later.

Again, Sally's play reflected her lack of sexual knowledge at the time, whereas her friend's play mirrored what he knew about sex. They were modeling what they had seen in their home environments, and the dolls became a means for exploring gender difference, sexuality, pregnancy, and social issues.

The dolls provide vehicles for some children to contemplate another body-related issue: What it is like to be in a visibly recognizable ethnic body. Although Sally is white, she grew up in a predominantly Asian population in Hawai'i:

Sally: For me, Barbie was the other blonde girl; she was the only—for a lot of my friends, I was their only blonde friend. And she was the only other person I'd met, like there were some blonde people on TV, but those aren't—those aren't real. Even Barbie seemed more real than, than people on TV. So it was kind of like me and Barbie. And I thought of her as a friend, and yet, at the same time, what everyone thought was beautiful—even what I thought and still think is beautiful is not the blonde Barbie. It's the more, the more Asian Barbie is by far the more attractive one to me. And that was the standard that was around me. She was the one I wanted, even though I related to the . . . blonde one. . . . And I kept waiting for my hair to go dark. And even into high school I kept thinking my—any day now my, my hair will grow dark [laughs], I just have to grow into it. It never happened. . . .

My high school graduating class was 227. And there were several people who were half Caucasian, and their other half was Hawaiian or Philippino or Japanese, but DOUBLE haoles . . . I can think of four of us. . . .

Jeannie: Did you ever feel like your beauty wasn't the ideal beauty?

Sally: Oh, completely. Completely. When prom time came around I was too tall and too busy. There was nothing demure about me. . . . When prom time came around, all the short Asian boys wanted to ask all the pretty Asian girls, and I wasn't Mulan. . . . And there wasn't anyone for me . . . twice I was asked to a dance . . . but all the other times—like probably six other times total—I asked my own date. . . .

And my boyfriend . . . was half Chinese, half Japanese, which is weird enough as it is in Hawai'i. . . . His parents didn't like me, and REALLY discouraged it, and were very polite but not—.

Jeannie: Because of ethnicity?

Sally: Yeah. They were embarrassed that their son would be dating a haole girl. And I kept, that was around the time I kept waiting for my hair to go dark. [Both laugh.] I kept thinking I was going to wake up with brown eyes one day, and it just didn't happen. . . .

[Barbie] helped me have a hope that in some other state or planet or country or something—that somewhere far, far away, tall and blonde was beautiful. But not here and now. . . .

I thought that when I was like thirteen, and then way later when I was in high school and dateless and feeling UGLY and really bad. . . . And as I got more comfortable with who I was, I didn't want to leave because I was used to being a minority, and I was used to people petting my hair, and saying, "Oh, it's . . . so silky." And making weird comments like that. . . . And I, I wanted to like escape that when . . . I was upset in my younger high school years, and I wanted to be like everyone else. But then later, I think I started to enjoy it. And so I'd just be like, "I can be, I can be me and be different." . . .

Jeannie: And so you said that you're still today attracted to the darker Barbie?

Sally: Totally. . . . Oh, I'm probably just racist, and I try not to be. [Slight laugh.] Everything that I grew up with—which was what was pretty—was Asian and sometimes Polynesian, but usually, usually Asian. And everything about straight, shiny black hair and angled eyes and coffee-colored skin is so attractive. And everything about the culture that I grew up with—about ritual and foods being meticulously placed, and everything is deliberate: all of that is attractive and comfortable to me. All of that is familiar. I like Kira [an Asian Barbie doll]; I like the Asian face molds best because—like one of your students from the folklore class said, "It looks like a half-hearted attempt to be Asian." But that's what everyone in Hawai'i looks like because everyone is like Asian and haole. And so she looks familiar; she looks like my friends, like when my high school friends—there's me and a bunch of Kira faces around me. And so she's the pretty one, by far.

I like the . . . newer African American ones that have curly, curly hair because it looks Polynesian to me. Like the Generation Girl Nichelle looks really Polynesian to me. I KNOW that she's supposed to be black, but I'm pretending in my mind [slight laugh in voice] that she's someone I know [laughs]: that they're my familiar friends, that they look like what's beautiful where I'm from. . . .

And Ken, my Ken was haole, so we said he was with the military. And he was just like temporarily living in Hawai'i when he had met his love that was a local girl. [Laughs.] That's all I really remember—but I also remember, my friend who's Hawaiian, she's Hawai'i-Philippino, and she's got very dark skin, and she had an African American Barbie. It was probably Christie, and she knew that that wasn't her. She knew that Christie wasn't meant to be Hawai'ian that she was meant to be African American, which was like a rarer minority than haole in Hawai'i, and . . . you just don't see African Americans very often either unless they're with the military . . . I remember her saying really clearly that "I wouldn't mind being black. It doesn't"—and I remember looking at her 'cause I hadn't even thought about it. I was—I was too busy dealing with being blonde to even think about that. She was like, "Aaaaah, I wouldn't mind being black, especially if I can be pretty like this person—like this doll." But I don't remember much conversation after that; I just remember being like, "Yeah. Sure." And I was so busy trying to be local that I couldn't even think about another minority besides myself. But my friend did.

Sally's Barbie dolls helped her feel better about her physical features and enabled her to think positively about ethnic diversity. Barbie's message, however, seems to be that ethnicity is all right as long as it fits some sort of cultural beauty ideal. When Sally says that blonde, Barbie-style beauty is valued elsewhere (the mainland), she reveals awareness of the dominant vision of beauty that Barbie represents. Both Barbie's positive and negative aspects are evident in Sally's account.

Kim, the twenty-one-year-old African American, recalled having ten Barbies and one Ken. Her comments suggest the importance of children having dolls that reflect a variety of ethnic backgrounds, including the child's. All Kim's dolls were white, something the dolls themselves would "complain" about. Although her grandmother tried to help the situation by explaining that the dolls were "light-skinned" African Americans, Kim's favorite doll was the one with the darkest skin and hair.

Both ethnicity and body image issues continue to affect Sally's accounts of Barbie, and she is critical of the manner in which Mattel handles these issues. Even though she likes some aspects of Barbie, she does not buy all that Mattel markets along with Barbie. She discussed her attitude toward her body during puberty and Barbie's role in the way she thought about her body:

Jeannie: So you were saying developing breasts was awful because—.

Sally: It was! I was so embarrassed; I just wanted to slump all the time. . . . And I was in ballet, right when I started high school, so like seventh—eighth grade into there I was taking ballet and jazz . . . tons and tons of dance. And it was horrible and embarrassing . . . because I had to strap myself in [laughs] . . . to avoid off-rhythm bouncing or anything. . . . 'Cause I knew I was taller than everyone else but having breasts made me feel bigger and fatter all over than everyone else. I heard boys talking about boobs, but the girls they wanted to date, like the pretty, sexy girls they wanted to date, were like my stick-ballerina friends that didn't have any curves at all; they were just like little mini ironing boards . . . with long, long hair. . . .

Jeannie: What do you think about the reverse kind of issues? . . . You know Barbie's been accused of making little girls more likely to have this unrealistic body image.

Sally: Probably.

Jeannie: Encouraging anorexia. What do you think about that?

Sally: Probably. Because my flat-chested Asian friends talked about how they wished they had breasts! Although . . . I couldn't understand that because they were exactly what everyone thought pretty should look like. But they—but I guess because of the media, and that probably includes Barbie as a standard of beauty—said that attractive women should be busty. So I'm sure that it does that; I'm sure that it makes people insecure.

But I think that you have to play with them at a certain age. I don't think that at age six, you are absorbing those messages quite as much. I don't think. I like to think not . . . I think if girls played with Barbie when they were eleven that it would be much worse. . . . Because that's right when you really are consciously deciding how you should look and how you should be, and how cute should your hair be and what color lip gloss will your mom let you wear, and when you're six, you're not thinking about being cute quite as much. . . . Playing with a skinny doll might start to make young girls think about body image because she is a fashion doll, but I don't think it has quite the impact yet when the kids are young. . . . That's what I think and hope. . . .

[However,] some [Barbies] I think are so dumb! . . . I wish she wasn't always dumb. I can still hum the "We Girls Can Do Anything!" [advertising] campaign . . . but it sounded like they were asking for confirmation from an idiot. "We Girls Can Do Anything, RIGHT, BARBIE? Please help me out here." [Laughs.] It was catchy and everything, but I would like to see Barbie really do everything. And I feel like it's always very superficial. . . .

There's new dolls called Smarties. . . . There's actually an attorney, and Destiny the Doctor and Valerie the Veterinarian and Emily the Entrepreneur, and they're really brainy dolls and they come with a storybook describing how to become the career that the girl has. And the doctor comes with scrubs, and the attorney comes with a little law book, and they all come with their little framed degrees that you can post on, I don't know, your Lego building as you play with them. But I don't know if that's just adults pushing politically correct stuff onto children; I don't know if kids would really get into it. 'Cause the attorney does have really short hair. . . . So there's no hair-play value . . . which is . . . a . . . real play value. And so I don't know if I'm just too media-aware; I'm thinking too hard to like those dolls better, or if those really would give positive messages absorbed by a six-year-old. I don't know. . . . Is it totally produced so the parent can like them, or is it toys really produced for—that kids can really get into. . . .

[Smarties] have their own Web-site. The Web-site . . . has a glossary . . . of Smartie words that all girls should know. And it's "degree" and "grad school" and all these different words. . . . I thought, "Those are words that I want my daughter to know." But again, I don't know if it's . . . really for the kids or is that for the parents?

The [Barbies] that I like the most are the ones where they . . . created a whole persona for her—like Becky in the wheelchair; she's the high school photographer and stuff. Those are the ones I like the most, where there's kind of a character that's not stupid . . . not a dumb-girl character. Not just "Pretty in Plaid," but "Thinking in Plaid." . . .

And I really like Nichelle, the Generation Girl, and she's the one that wants to be a model. All the Generation Girls have kind of dippy aspirations, but she wants to be a model, and I guess that doesn't bother me because I think the world needs more beautiful black women, so—with REAL African American hair . . . it's real curly hair. So I think it's okay for her to have a dippy model-wannabe profession because we need to think that's beautiful more. So that's okay, that one's okay to me. I hate all the Hawaiian ones.

Jeannie: You said something nice [earlier off the tape], "This is a sacred dance not a hairstyle."

Sally: Exactly. You grow up in Hawai'i dancing the hula, and it is so intense and it's so personal. And I had a teacher, a *kumu,* he would always say, "Hula is life; there's nothing that we live that we cannot dance. There's nothing that we go through that cannot be expressed with this dance." And . . . I was in hula from preschool . . . until even after . . . my first three years of college . . . my whole life. And those drums and everything—it stirs up something in me—it is so emotional, and it is so special, and it is so personal.

And it's not meant to be done sloppily; like my *kumu* would say, "If you can't do it right, you need to sit out. If you're too tired to dance it properly then you should sit down." . . . There's inaccuracies, like Hawaiians don't wear grass skirts, Tahitians do. And so, like with the Hula Hair Barbie that has a tassel-y looking skirt . . . that's not even right.

But there are so many things I learned, like you should treat your skirt with respect—the skirt that you practice hula in—because even if it was just your ugly practice skirt, never let it touch the ground; you should not kick it around because you're putting your self in the skirt. You're putting your *mana,* your power in the skirt. And you, you've worked and you've sweat, and you would never disrespect your work. And I just don't see that same kind of awe and reverence portrayed in Hula Hair Barbie. [Both laugh.]

And she just hurts my feelings, and the back of the box talking about . . . the sweet pineapple-scented air and these dolls with these really crooked, deformed arms trying to do some artificial hula gestures. It hurts my feelings because I think of what my *kumu* said, "If you can't do it right, sit out. If you're not going to put all of yourself into it, then don't do it."

And that's [laughs] kind of what I want to say to Mattel is "leave that alone . . . that's really emotional for a lot of people." And I'm just a little white girl that grew up there; it's not even pumping through my veins . . . but it is for a lot of people. And I think it's hurtful. And at least now the Barbie that's labeled Hawai'i Barbie is not Hawaiian Barbie, but she's just more like mainland-girl-gone-to-visit-Hawai'i-as-a-tourist Barbie. That's . . . better because she can be ugly—tourists are often loud, so I can forgive that. If she wants to wear an unfashionable swimsuit and be at Waikiki, that's her place. But not when they start trifling with the truly sacred, I guess. It bothers me.

Although Sally found Barbie helpful in some ways, she argues, like several scholars, that certain dolls demonstrate a lack of cultural sensitivity. She also thinks that Mattel could improve stereotypes of Barbie's supposed lack of intelligence. Finally, she says, Hula Hair Barbie, who has "artificial" gestures and "crooked" arms, represents an inversion of the sacred nature of the hula. For those like Sally who know about the hula, the doll is hurtful and troubling. In addition, she thinks Hula Hair Barbie sends the wrong message to those who are not aware of the sacred nature of the hula.

Janet noted that she liked the fact that Mattel marketed multi-ethnic Barbies. It was important, she said, that she had black Barbies when she was a child. She also thought Mattel could sell Barbies of varying body shapes rather than rely on the "typical model" body. She did not worry much about that body image's impact on her own daughter, however, because she engaged in imaginative play with Barbie (figure 31). "You know," Janet remarked, "I've seen them put girl clothes on the boy Barbies. California–San Francisco man . . . I don't think it's a worry for me."

Although some accounts of playing with Barbies were fairly conventional and followed consumerist and stereotypical gender roles, several examples did not stay within typical gender boundaries. A thirty-two-year-old white male who maintained that he would not let his sons play with dolls, for example, had himself played with them as a child:

I never had any Barbies! They belonged to my older sister, and she made me play with her! We played all of the time. I used to take the legs and arms off just to make my sister mad. Sometimes I would take off their heads and tell her the dog did it. Sometimes it was fun though. I would load them up in the back of some of my

Figure 31. Barbie dolls dressed by Janet's eight-year-old daughter.

trucks and take them to the backyard and pretend like I was selling them. Bad guys would buy them, and then I would be a good guy and rescue them.

When . . . my sister would be gone, I used to go into her room and play with her Barbies. I would change their clothes and talk to them. We would go for drives and do fun stuff. But I never let her know about it. She would have told all of the guys that I liked dolls.

Even though he says his sister "made" him play Barbies, he also played of his own volition, which suggests that Barbie can be an attractive toy for some boys. Jessica, too, said that her brother was sometimes an unwilling participant although he did participate:

My brother is four-and-a-half years older than me, so he would play until they [the Barbies] died. That was always the rule: we'll play until they die. . . . There's the stairs to the basement, so we'd pack up the Barbies, and they were going to the Grand Canyon. So we'd drive over, and he's "Oh, Thelma and Louise"! And he'd kick them, and they'd fly! And they'd be dead. And sometimes he'd play nice you know [laughs.] . . . Sometimes he'd be really nice, and he'd get a chair out, and we'd put a blanket over it, and it would be a mountain, and they'd go camping. And he'd be really good, but if he didn't want to play . . . then he'd kick it [the Barbie car], you know. That was really funny.[9]

Rusty, nineteen, was much more relaxed about playing with Barbie than the previous male informant:

Our dolls were talented; they got to go swimming in our aquarium, rock climbing, and get caught in a cave; they got to fly around in space in little space ships, and they even got abducted by sex aliens.

Our dolls were like normal dolls; they had sex all the time and saved the Pretty Ponies from the Troll People. They played a lot of TV shows like *Melrose Place* because they were always having sex and lots of babies.

Barbie always lived in boats, palaces, and mansions. She always wore sleazy clothes or Ken's tuxedos. Our Barbies were tough, except when I threw Barbie against the wall and her neck broke. One time I put clear nail polish on her face to give her a shiny complexion, but when I took it off with nail polish remover, her whole face came off, too.

Barbie always played with My Little Ponies, He-Man. . . . And Barbie's kids were always the Muppet Baby toys from McDonald's Happy Meals.

Such narratives indicate that Barbie invites imaginative play—sometimes normative, sometimes inversive—for both girls and boys.

In addition to Janet, I also interviewed her eight-year-old daughter (figure 32). Everyone in their family, including both parents and her younger brother, plays Barbies with the eight-year-old. Janet said her husband is

BORDERS

BORDERS BOOKS MUSIC &
050 North Main Stree
Logan, UT 84321

(435) 787-0678

STORE: 0563   REG: 01/78 TRAN#: 7202
SALE   02/07/2004 EMP: 00039

NAKED BARBIES WARRIOR
                    SOFT   21.95
Order#.6837

            Subtotal   21.95
            UTAH 6.35%   1.39
    Item   Total   23.04
            VISA   23.34

ACCT # /S XXXXXXXXXXXX0319
                AUTH: 00/670
NAME: KIMBERLEE J. CHRISTENSON

CUSTOMER COPY

02/07/2004 04:45PM

Check our store inventory online
    at www.bordersstores.com

Shop online at www.borders.com

Figure 32. Janet, her daughter, and Barbies.

particularly creative in how he plays with the Barbies. He gets into character, for example, and also makes up accents for the dolls. As the girl describes
playing with her father, "We pretend some of his Barbies are sick, and some
of my Barbies are helping them try to get better." Not only does the eight-
year-old have fun with her parents, but her play also allows a reverse of the
family's power and care-giving roles. She and her dolls dispense aid and
advice to her father, who, in turn, helped her with a Barbie computer program until she learned to do it on her own.

It amuses the eight-year-old and her mother to remove the heads from dolls and put them on still other dolls. The girl also says that sometimes she puts pillows under her Barbies' clothes and pretends the Barbies are pregnant. Once, she admits, she loaded the Barbies into the microwave but did not turn it on. She has a Dorothy of the *Wizard of Oz* Barbie whose bare feet have little red lights in them to illuminate ruby slippers. Dorothy Barbie talks and says things such as, "Toto, we're not in Kansas anymore." When I asked the girl how she played with this doll, she said, "I . . . make her look like a witch with scraggly hair . . . I pretend she's the witch, and I get a boy Barbie and dress him up in an outfit to make him look like the scarecrow or a tin man." Although she uses characters from the film, she is creative in inverting roles. The heroine is turned into the villain, a powerful and dramatic role for her to explore.

She also likes to make school buses out of chairs and benches for her Barbies, and she sometimes pretends having slumber parties in Barbie's house. She had difficulty with a friend while playing Barbies:

> Jeannie: Your mom was just saying that you have the problem of trading toys and getting your toys mixed up, when you play with your friends. Do you . . . ever get in any fights?
>
> Girl: Uh huh [yes]. Stacey, she bosses me around with them. She says, "How about your Barbie picks on mine?" and stuff like that.
>
> Jeannie: Really, so what do you say when Stacy says stuff like that?
>
> Girl: "I always have to be someone like a robber and stuff, so I'm getting tired of it. I don't want you to boss me around."
>
> Jeannie: That's a good thing to say. Then does she stop?
>
> Girl: Yeah.

With her mother, the girl negotiated the conflict that the play had brought about. Such play also permitted exploration of the female body and issues such as pregnancy. Although her Barbies assumed some traditional roles (as waitress, teacher, and stewardess), her play with them was creative, which allowed her to interact with and receive positive attention from the entire family.

One college undergraduate and mother, Sue Ellen, watched and documented how her nine-year-old daughter plays with Barbies, an activity that demonstrates a mixture of traditional and nontraditional play:

> [She] talks to her Barbies, and she talks for them. Barbie is very well-adjusted—she is very versatile. Barbie has done everything from mountain climbing to being a babysitter. She drives race cars, rides horses, teaches school, goes to college, is an architect [and] an airline stewardess, and [she] even practices dentistry.

Barbie's looks change as dramatically as her occupations do. Sometimes Barbie has long, flowing hair. Other times she has a teased, punk-looking ponytail. Of course there are times when Barbie has suffered at the hands of a brutal beautician [my daughter] and has no hair.

[My daughter] is just as attentive to her Ken dolls as she is to her Barbies. Ken drives the pink Corvette, babysits, shops, and does dishes. Ken and Barbie date—by going for drives, going to the movies, and by working out together. There are times when they are married. Their marriage is very '90s. They both work; sometimes they work together by sharing an office, and sometimes they have not so stereotypical jobs: "I have to fly to Eygpt today. I should be back Sunday," says Barbie.

"That's fine dear. I have to be at nursery school all week," Ken answers.

The girl, who is white, often creates a fairly feminist world for her dolls. Hers is one of the few accounts in which Ken also has a starring role.[10]

Jennifer, twenty and white, played with Barbie in traditional and non-traditional ways. Sometimes the play involved her brother's wrestling figures, which would either serve as boyfriends or as maids to her Barbies. Traci, twenty-six and white, describes herself as a tomboy and had two Barbie dolls and "lots" of G.I. Joes. I encountered several men who played with Barbies, but Traci was one of only a few women who detailed prominent play with G.I. Joe. She hated her Barbie dolls and would not play with them but liked to play with the Joes. She lived on a farm and often pretended that her Joes were farmers.

When Linda, thirty-seven and white, played with her Barbie as a child, her favorite type of play involved Barbie accidents. Linda's Barbie was blown up, run over, drowned, and taken apart. Several other narratives described doll destruction. Elizabeth, white and in her twenties, told me that she had liked to burn her Barbies at the stake. Siblings perpetrated a lot of doll abuse. For example, Ty, a nineteen-year-old male, said he used his Joes to "beat up" his sister's Barbies; Craig, a forty-eight-year-old white male, reported that he used his army men to "blow the heads off" of his sister's Barbies.

Discussions of dolls also generated stories of play with G.I. Joe, although such narratives were not as frequent or as developed as stories I heard about Barbie. Dwight, a nineteen-year-old white male, had approximately 150 G.I. Joes when he was a child and played with them daily. Play revolved around good guys versus bad guys. He had the dolls assume the roles of generals, commanders, medics, sergeants, lieutenants, and corporals. Dwight created a swamp in the yard so he could use Joe's "water vehicles" and boats. He also deployed the dolls in the bathtub. In addition, he would turn areas of the house such as the couch or under the kitchen table into battlegrounds.

War play and violent play dominated when G.I. Joe was involved. Common themes in the narratives concerned war and destruction, and often Joe himself was annihilated. Nathan and Matt, twenty-one-year-old white males, provide typical descriptions of things that small boys would have their dolls do. Nathan's Joes would "bash each other, shoot and kill each other, and kick each other in the groin." Matt would have his dolls shoot each other in addition to kicking and trampling each other.

I encountered such comments over and over in relation to Joe. Terry, a white, twenty-nine-year-old, would have his dolls fight and blow each other up—the hand grenades and bombs were made of Play Dough. Firecrackers were also a favored method of Joe destruction. Russell, a forty-two-year-old African American, had three G.I. Joes when he was between ten and twelve:

> My friend Rob and I used to play war all the time. We would use our trucks to make roads in Rob's sandbox for our army guys to drive on. We dug trenches, we made tents from cardboard. We would create specific missions that our soldiers would have to go on. One day they would have to rescue other guys from the enemy. The next day we would rig booby traps to catch spies.
>
> I had the G.I. Joe Jeep and a tank. I used my other trucks and a bulldozer when they needed other types of transportation. I had a tree house in the backyard, and I would set up camp for Joe and his buddies underneath it. Rob and I had our own guns, helmets, grenades, and other army gear. We were all involved in the fighting.
>
> We used to yell, "Gotcha!" "You're dead!" It was not uncommon for Joe to lose his head one time and an arm the next. We thought this was pretty cool. We got into fights fairly often because no one wanted to die.
>
> I would say, "You missed me, you jerk!"
>
> To which Rob would yell, "Did not!"
>
> Typical boy stuff. I don't remember physically fighting about it, but someone usually got mad, picked up his "men" and headed for home.

Russell, who grew up during the Vietnam War, would watch television news reports of the war each night and then use his dolls to act out what he had seen. His narrative reveals imagination and creativity in doll-play, which he and many other informants recalled with obvious pleasure. It also, however, dramatically raises the issue of how war-play affects young children.

Hasbro, the company that created G.I. Joe, has experienced a small amount of internal conflict about war-related matters. In 1966, for example, one of Hasbro's Action Soldiers of the World series caused some concern within the company. At issue was the inclusion of a Nazi Storm Trooper in the series. Some argued that "no company—especially one with the Jewish heritage of Hasbro—should commemorate this purveyor of brutality" (Michlig 1998, 74). The company, however, made a disturbing decision: The doll was already in production, so it was allowed to stay in the line. The "Nazi doll" has gone relatively unnoticed in toy history. For a sense of toyland's double standards of gender, consider the outcry had Mattel produced Nazi Barbie.

G.I. Joe was pushed aside in 1977 by action figures from the film *Star Wars* (Michlig 198, 190). Joe disappeared from the market in 1978. His production was reliant on petroleum-based products, and the costs of producing him had become prohibitive (Michlig 1998, 185). Kenner's *Star Wars* action figures were wildly successful and cheaper to produce than Joes (Michlig 1998, 190). G.I. Joe was reincarnated in 1981 as a 3¾-inch plastic figure that resembled *Star Wars*-type figures (Michlig 1998, 195).[11]

Narratives about play—even play with G.I. Joe—also detail the deployment of *Star Wars* figures. For example, Dustin, white and twenty, played with Joes and *Star Wars* figures. Both were engaged in battle, but G.I. Joes "died" more often than the *Star Wars* figures because Dustin liked to bury them in his sandbox. Usually, "good guy" dolls defeated the "bad guy" dolls, but Dustin also occasionally let the bad guys win.

"Good guy versus bad guy play" was another dominant theme of recreation with G.I. Joe. Variation existed, but not as much as in play with a Barbie. David, a twenty-two-year-old African American, played with Joes in conventional ways when with his brothers. They would have fights and line up the dolls and play *Sunday Night Football.* When he played with the Joes by himself, however, the play was atypical. David would have them act out favorite television game shows such as *The Price Is Right, Name That Tune,* or *Win, Lose, or Draw.* On Sundays he would dress them up and sneak them into church.

Some male informants said they had not played with G.I. Joe, nor did they like him. A twenty-four-year-old white male said his father would not allow him to play with toys like G.I. Joe because they were dolls and therefore not "masculine enough." The father did not want him to become a "sissy," so he played "boy-type" things like Matchbox cars or "pretend" guns. His experience is exemplary of how toys are considered to have genders:

> The toys children play with are designed to be sold as girls' toys or boys' toys. Girls are given dolls and doll houses; boys get trucks and building blocks, and are told that they are "sissies" if they want to play with girls' toys. These labels come origi-

nally from adults, for it has been noted that, at age two-and-a-half, many boys prefer dolls and doll houses; they are urged away from them because parents consider them to be girls' toys. Parental responses are quickly absorbed by the children, who shortly thereafter display quite different toy and game preferences. Advertisements, salespeople and other agents of socialization all reinforce these cues from parents. (Kimmel 2000a, 124)

My students succinctly refer to the gendering of toy store aisles as "the pink and the not-pink." Consumers can tell which toys are intended for which gender by the colors of the packaging.

Other men reported a very different kind of antipathy to Joe, unrelated to the fact that he is a doll. After collecting a G.I. Joe narrative from an acquaintance, for example, Michael, who is white and in his twenties, responded to the narrative by saying, "I think [the informant who played with G.I. Joes] was a bully when he was younger. I remember most of the G.I. Joe guys would always try to mimic the army and either punch you or kick you. I'm pretty sure that's why I hated G.I. Joe figures. Not only I thought this. Ron, who was listening [to the informant] also saw the G.I. Joe–players acting as bullies."

Michael's comments indicate that some boys are disturbed by the violence they see and experience in play involving G.I. Joe. After hearing so many descriptions of creative play with Barbies, I thought I would see more variation in play with Joe than I did. Although creativity and pleasure are present in the accounts of such play, the gendered play role Joe encourages appears more restrictive, in general, than that of play with Barbies. Barbie play deviates more from Mattel's storylines than Joe departs from his Hasbro soldier-action figure script.

Joe is also controversial because some see him, like Barbie, as promoting an unrealistic body image for children. G.I. Joe, however, does not appear in electronic folklore as much as Barbie does even though he is critiqued for being a war toy. Neither is Joe the subject of as much "e-lore" as Barbie. He is not seen as Everyman but rather as one specific type of man, a soldier. Neither as successful as Barbie nor as pervasive, Joe's particular role tends to remain with him in play, making him less a tabula rasa than Barbie.

Although I have discussed the play behaviors connected with G.I. Joe and Barbie, folklore about Barbie also reveals that many adults do not leave dolls entirely behind as they mature but continue to manipulate them, especially Barbie, at a folk level. Dolls continue to be a source of interest in playful adult venues, such as the parodies, humorous lists, and jokes that circulate via e-mail.

One e-lore list that found its way consistently into my electronic mailbox concerned Barbie's fortieth birthday. The list intrigued me as a folklorist because I received different versions of it. Although the oral tradition fosters variation, e-lore's mode of transmission encourages senders to press a key and forward an item, exactly as it is, to friends. The fact that variation occurs, however, even in cyberspace, suggests that it is a significant process. Some have acknowledged that they occasionally alter material before forwarding it. They tell me that they make changes—ranging from correcting spelling and punctuation to altering or adding to the text—to reflect what they think. The e-lore excerpt that follows has appeared in slightly varying forms under various titles, including "Possibilities Abound as Barbie Turns Forty," "Over Forty Barbies," and "The New Over Forty Barbies."[12] "Over Forty Barbies" is shorter than the "Possibilities Abound" version:

> ** Bifocals Barbie. Comes with her own set of blended-lens fashion frames in six wild colors (half-frames too!), neck chain and large-print editions of *Vogue* and *Martha Stewart Living*.
> ** Hot Flash Barbie. Press Barbie's bellybutton and watch her face turn beet red while tiny drops of perspiration appear on her forehead! With hand-held fan and tiny tissues.
> ** Facial Hair Barbie. As Barbie's hormone levels shift, see her whiskers grow! Available with teensy tweezers and magnifying mirror.
> ** Cook's Arms Barbie. Hide Barbie's droopy triceps with these new, roomier-sleeved gowns. Good news on the tummy front, too: muu-muus are back! Cellulite cream and loofah sponge optional. . . .

This list has an interesting history. Marion Abbott maintains that she wrote a humorous piece about Barbie turning forty for the *Washington Post* (Abbott 2000, n.p.). Soon after the article appeared, she began to receive e-mail from friends who forwarded the story back to her without knowing that she had written it: "A later version added Divorced Barbie while my own Single Mother Barbie had gone the way of the delete key. The mutation after that featured Post-Menopausal Barbie." A video clip was added to yet another chain-letter version. Punctuation errors crept into the electronic version, and Abbott found that her chances to sell the article had been reduced to nothing. Her work, she maintains, has been robbed of its integrity, and she has been denied due credit by "people with a dramatically over-exaggerated sense of entitlement when it comes to altering others' work." Were she to revise what is now "an author-less, amorphous bit of . . . folklore rocketing around cyberspace," Abbott observes, she might add

Internet Barbie to the list, "complete with copyright handbook and intellectual property lawyer" (Abbott 2000, n.p.).

In this case, a written, mass-media document has entered the folk process. The reverse is more frequent. The mass media takes a story or legend from the oral tradition and uses it in a film, for example. The Internet creates a conduit that makes it easy to "folklorize" something from popular or mass culture. Thus the Barbie list becomes anonymous; even though it once had an author, it now exists in multiple "cyber-lore" versions. I have also heard of teenagers who, before the widespread availability and use of e-mail, composed similar, oral parody lists about Barbie and sometimes wrote them down.

Other e-lore in list form also circulates about Barbie, such as "Barbies We'd Like to See":

> Admin Barbie: Works twenty-hour days for little pay (80 percent of Admin Ken's salary) and is the lowest on the totem pole despite being the one that actually runs the group. Comes with mini-laptop. Pull the string on her back and she'll schedule a meeting with your other dolls, replace the toner cartridge in the laser printer, coordinate a re-org and a move, and order airline tickets for Director Ken. . . .
>
> Bag Lady Barbie: Complete with shopping cart; wearing everything she owns.
>
> Barbie Bobbit: With knife, Ken had better watch out.
>
> Barbie Brown Simpson: Slashed neck and bloody body, carton of Ben & Jerry's Cookie Dough included.
>
> Battered Wife Barbie: Comes with a restraining order to serve to Ken.
>
> Birkenstock Barbie: Finally, a Barbie doll with horizontal feet and comfortable sandals. Made from recycled materials.
>
> Bisexual Barbie: Comes in a package with Skipper and Ken. . . .
>
> Black Barbie: Once your Ken doll goes black, he'll never go back.
>
> Blue-Collar Barbie: Comes with overalls, protective goggles, lunch pail, UAW membership, pamphlet on union-organizing and pay scales for women as compared to men. Waitressing outfits and cashier's aprons may be purchased separately for Barbies who are holding down second jobs in order to make ends meet.
>
> Boulevard Barbie: With cheap makeup, short skirt, and high heels.
>
> Bow-wow Barbie: The ugliest Barbie you've ever seen.
>
> Breast Implant Barbie: Now Barbie's a D-cup.
>
> Brunette Barbie: The only Barbie with a brain.
>
> Bulimorexia Barbie: Also no different in appearance from regular Barbie.
>
> Cancer Patient Barbie: Remove the wig and Barbie's bald.
>
> Crack Addict Barbie: Pipe included, sugar may be used to simulate crack cocaine.

Dinner-Roll Barbie: A Barbie with multiple love handles, double chin, a real curvy belly, and voluminous thighs to show girls that voluptuousness is also beautiful. Comes with a miniature basket of dinner rolls, Bucket o' Fried Chicken, tiny Entenmann's walnut ring, a brick of Sealtest ice cream, three packs of potato chips, a t-shirt reading "Only the Weak Don't Eat," and, of course, an appetite. . . .

Feminist Barbie: Has unshaved legs and armpits.

Homegirl Barbie: Truly fly Barbie in midriff-bearing [sic] shirt and baggy jeans. Comes with gold jewelry, hip-hop accessories, and plenty of attitude. Pull cord and she says things like "I don't think so," "Dang, get outta my face," and "You go, girl." Teaches girls not to take shit from men and condescending White people.

Lesbian Barbie: Barbie with a butch.

Lipstick Lesbian Barbie: Actually no different in appearance from regular Barbie.

Melrose Place Barbie: Comes complete with her Barbie Dream Apartment, where Skipper and the rest of the gang live rent-free. Other accessories include a bottle of vodka, silk sheets and an arrest warrant.

Mobile Home Park Barbie: Comes complete with hair in rollers and pregnant. Accessories include two toddlers. When you pull the string on her back she asks where her gov't support check is. Some Mobile Home Barbies come with surprise Ken or G.I. Joe since they often give her surprise visits when they come into town. . . .

The humor of this list is often biting. Many items (such as Bulimorexia Barbie), like those on "Over Forty Barbies," can be understood as a critique of Barbie's unrealistic figure and the "life" that Mattel creates for her. By incorporating women like Nicole Brown Simpson or Lorena Bobbit who have been involved in well-known crimes and adding references to social problems (crack addiction, alcoholism), the list also emphasizes that real women do not live in Barbie's dream house. Blue-Collar Barbie, Bag Lady Barbie, Mobile Home Park Barbie, and even Crack Addict Barbie introduce a class critique of Mattel's doll and the conspicuous consumption that marketing it encourages. The list satirizes Barbie's "body beautiful" by not only including Bow-wow Barbie and Breast Implant Barbie but also women who are ill (Cancer Patient Barbie), overweight (Dinner-Roll Barbie) or those who have rejected traditional feminine fashions (Birkenstock Barbie and Punk Barbie). The list implies that even some television characters are more true to life than Barbie:

Murder, Barbie Wrote: Whenever this elder stateswoman of the Barbie-set (she's twenty-seven!) arrives in the playhouse, all the other dolls mysteriously disappear.

My So-Called Barbie: She faces the same troubling issues as regular teens who don't have huge wardrobes, perfect bods, pools, and ponies.

Navy Pilot Barbie: Comes with a body bag, wrecked fighter jet sold separately.

Oprah Barbie: Push a button on her back and this Barbie actually speaks! Hold your very own talk show with topics like how tough math class is, Ballerina Barbie's struggle with bulimia, Kens who wear Barbie's clothes.

Our Barbies Ourselves: Anatomically correct Barbie, both inside and out, comes with spreadable legs, her own speculum, magnifying glass, and detailed diagrams of female anatomy so that little girls can learn about their bodies in a friendly, non-threatening way. Also included: tiny Kotex, booklets on sexual responsibility. Accessories such as contraceptives, sex toys, expanding uterus with fetus at various stages of development, and breastpump are all optional, underscoring that each young woman has the right to choose what she does with her own Barbie.

Punk Barbie: Has rings in all sorts of strange places.

Quantum Physicist Barbie: Yeah, right.

Rabbi Barbie: So, why not? Women rabbis are on the cutting edge in Judaism. Rabbi Barbie comes with tiny satin yarmulke, prayer shawl, teffilin, silver kaddish cup, Torah scrolls. Optional: tiny mezuzah for doorway of Barbie Townhouse. . . .

Robotic Barbie: Hey, kids, experiment with an autonomous two-legged walking machine! After falling over she says "Control theory is hard. Damn these spike heels anyway!"

Roseanne Barbie: The dark side of the American dream is explored with this doll, which shows what happened after Barbie graduated from high school, married too young and ate too much.

Sister Mary Barbie: This spiritual Barbie comes with jointed knees and neck for genuflecting and praying, mini-rosary beads, a mini-bible, and a black sequined nun's habit (after all, she's still Barbie). Pull the string on her back and she says nothing because she's taken a vow of silence.

Teenage Single Parent Barbie: "Welfare check" from Mattel mailed each month. . . .

Transgender Barbie: Formerly known as G.I. Joe. . . .

This portion of the list incorporates real-life situations and occupations, ranging from being a single mother to a nun. Barbie is infamous for having an adult body, but the dolls on the cyberlist, such as Our Barbies Ourselves, are reminders that she could be more physically accurate. By including Transgender Barbie, Butch Barbie, and Lipstick Lesbian Barbie the e-lore may also be critiquing the heterosexual construction of Barbie and Ken. I have also received, via e-mail, a series of photographs in which Barbie has been reworked along thematic lines similar to those in "Barbies We'd Like to See." There were, for example, images of Goth Barbie and Lactating Barbie.

E-lore such as "Over Forty Barbies" parodies Mattel's penchant for creating numerous Barbies and Barbie lifestyles. Santino's theories about the importance and ubiquity of serialization in postmodern culture are applicable (1996, 148–49). Serialization is a significant part of the marketing of Barbie and structures the folklore about her as well. It gives form to Mattel's Barbie and to the folkloric parodies of her, which may again be another indication of how seminal and endemic serialization is to late-capitalist cultures (Santino 1996, 69).

The lore parallels Mattel's use of television and film stars in marketing (e.g., *Baywatch* Barbie, Rosie O'Donnell Barbie, and *The Addams Family* Barbie and Ken). The shows parodied, however, are *My So-Called Life,* a television series of the 1990s concerning a less-than-perfect teenaged girl, and *Murder, She Wrote,* another late-twentieth-century series in which a female senior citizen was the protagonist. By selecting these shows to highlight, the list emphasizes the fact that images of an older woman and a less-than-perfect teenager are ones Mattel chose not to market in Barbie form.

At the time that the "Over Forty Barbies" list pointed to Barbie's perpetual youth, the doll itself turned forty in "real life." The list was a reminder that real women who turn forty do not share Barbie's plastic, perpetually preserved body but are subject to physical and lifestyle changes.

Although both lists are humorous critiques of Barbie's limitations, they present stock figures, just as many of Mattel's constructions of Barbie do. The stereotypical figures differ, however, from Mattel's infinite incarnations in that they are grittier and often darker. They are still, however, stock images. Moreover, the genius behind the concept of Barbie as an adult female figure who lends herself to play is apparent. Both adults and children are attracted to Barbie—in part because she is a portrayal of an adult woman—and use her in play, whether it is little girls creating lives for Barbie in their bedrooms or adults creating more realistic lives for her in sardonic cyberspace parodies.

In fact, children's play with Barbie and adult folkloric wordplay have a lot in common. The parodies—which are created by adults and circulate among adults—show the same kind of behavior that children often demonstrate when playing with Barbies. Both groups often place Barbie in what they deem to be real-life situations. Children's play usually does not critique Barbie—but it sometimes deconstructs a stereotypical vision of her—although many parodies do. Yet the play process is similar for both young people and adults. The e-lists emphasize that Mattel's Barbie ignores issues such as aging and sexuality yet also demonstrate the energy that has gone into compiling playful, imaginative details. The lists are thus evidence of satirization as well as a sense of play. The practices of adults and children reveal that a three-dimensional gendered form, a doll, is a significant and useful vehicle for "playing with" and thinking about the lives of females in American culture.

Other e-lore addresses the idea of a better or more realistic Barbie. Instead of listing different Barbies, however, it creates and develops one type in some detail. This cyber-lore process is similar to one of Mattel's marketing strategies, as seen in collections such as the Dolls of the World series, wherein Mattel generates a narrative solely devoted to a Barbie and prints it on the back of each doll's box. The parodic folklore inverts and critiques Mattel's use of the structures of consumerism, such as serialization, by employing similar structures but different content, causing an ironic effect. In an article about the serialization of folktale collections, Kimberly J. Lau rightly points to some of the problems of serialization (1999, 71).[13]

Cyber-lore that relies on serialization for structure and uses it to critique Barbie presents a counterpoint to the downside of serialization that Lau highlights. Barbie cyber-lore provides an example of the positive function—critical analysis—to which serialization can be put. In the form of a satirical critique of some ways in which Mattel employs serialization to market Barbie, the e-lore demonstrates the manner in which serialization can provide a structure conducive to folk play.

At the beginning of the twenty-first century Mattel had not yet produced a Computer Geek Barbie, but cyber-lore filled the void with "Hacker Barbie":

These new dolls will be released next month. The aim of these dolls is to negate the stereotype that women are numerophobic, computer-illiterate, and academically challenged.

This new line of Barbie dolls comes equipped with Barbie's very own X-terminal and UNIX documentation as well as ORA's "In a Nutshell" series. The Barbie clothing includes a dirty button-up shirt and a pair of well-worn jeans. Accessories include a Casio all-purpose watch, and glasses with lenses thick enough to set ants on fire. (Pocket protectors and HP calculators optional). . . .

"We are very excited about this product," said Ken Olsen, Marketing Executive, "and we hope that the Hacker Barbie will offset the damage incurred by the mathophobic Barbie." (A year ago, Mattel released Barbie dolls that say, "Math is hard," with a condescending companion Ken.) The Hacker Barbie's Ken is an incompetent management consultant who frequently asks Barbie for help.

The leading feminists are equally excited about this new line of Barbie dolls. Naomi Falodji says, "I believe that these new dolls will finally terminate the notion that womyn are inherently inferior when it comes to mathematics and the sciences. However, I feel that Ken's hierarchical superiority would simply reinforce the patriarchy and oppress the masses." Mattel made no comment. . . .

"Over Forty Barbies," "Barbies We'd Like to See," and "Hacker Barbie" all exhibit humor generally rooted in incongruity and superiority. That is, audience perception of incongruity (Mattel's Barbie when compared to the Barbies in the list) and of superiority (Mattel's artificial construction of Barbie versus the list's more realistic versions) may prompt laughter. In addition, the text of "Over Forty Barbies," being heavily based in bodily processes that include such taboos as menopause, could generate laughter that signifies a perceived release from convention that a folk presentation of these taboo physical processes entails (Oring 1992; Thomas 1997b). For those who find humor in darker items such as Barbie Brown Simpson in the "Barbies We'd Like to See" list, mirth may also be triggered by release from normal and polite conventions.

The elements that cause an individual response of "That's funny!" vary from person to person and context to context. In general, however, the mechanisms of incongruity and superiority—which can trigger laughter—are present in the "Over Forty Barbies" and "Barbies We'd Like to See" lists. The incongruity generated in pairing an actual Barbie doll with more realistic and extreme depictions of her in folk parodies may cause laughter. A feeling of intellectual superiority generated by such pairings could produce laughter, and mechanisms of superiority and incongruity might also work together to prompt laughter (Thomas 1997b, 42–43).

The text, and therefore the humor, of "Hacker Barbie" is more open to divergent readings than the texts of "Over Forty Barbies" and "Barbies We'd Like to See." Audiences could find it funny for two almost diametrically opposed reasons: its feminist critique of Barbie or its critique of feminists. "Hacker Barbie" could be seen as satirizing Mattel's version, especially because it refers to the Barbie who said "math is hard" and generated much criticism about gender stereotypes. "Hacker Barbie" could also be read as a critique of the excesses of feminism. That interpretation could be supported by the paragraph quoting "leading" feminist Naomi Falodji, a parodic merging of the names of two well-known media feminists, Naomi Wolf and Susan Faludi. The parody relies on irony, and, as Stanley Fish argues, one characteristic of irony is that its inclusive nature can encompass divergent readings by different audiences, as is the case here (Fish 1989, 180–82, 194–96).

In e-lore, Barbie's usual glamour incongruously gives way to geekiness. "Hacker Barbie" and its possible critiques of Mattel's bimbo Barbie or criticism of feminists could trigger the humor mechanism of superiority. Those two reversals could touch on incongruity and thereby generate the perception of humor—and, again, combining both could also contribute to the material being seen as funny. Adults can playfully and linguistically manipulate Barbie's form to generate a text that is funny due to its incongruous images and uses humor to convey social critique.

Like "Hacker Barbie," there are other examples of esoteric cyber-lore. Unlike "Hacker Barbie," however, they do not limit themselves to a single figure but involve a culture or folk group. This type of e-lore also employs the list form demonstrated in "Over Forty Barbies" and "Barbies We'd Like to See." Like Mattel's Barbies and like those presented in previous lists, the two e-lists that follow generalize and present stock figures. If the figures are recognized as "true" enough or as types actually found in the culture, they can potentially generate a perception of humor among readers (Thomas 1997a, 307). In many cases "FWD" (forward) prefacing the title of a list signifies that the sender either found it funny or thought the recipient would.

The recipient often has to know something of the culture to understand a list. One e-list, for example, is called "Mormon Barbie" and includes esoteric types such as RM (Returned Missionary) Barbie. In order to appreciate humor, it is essential to know enough about a group to be able to interpret references to it. A similar example is the cyber-lore known as "Indian Barbie Dolls" or "NDN [Indian] Barbies":

> Commod Barbie: comes with, can opener and cheese slicer added bonus, she comes with pliers and thread to make a jingle dress out of commod lids (available at cree reservations, only!). . . .
>
> "49" Barbie: sits in her pick-up til her beer is gone, then closes in on next snag, come sunlight she's gone
>
> Chorus Girl Barbie: sits in her lawn chair, making fun of all the dancers, but when her drum gets the song, she stands up to sing and all the men really dance their best. . . .
>
> Wannabee Barbie: jet black (Clairol) hair, brown cordoury dress, made in japan mocs and beadwork, turkey feather fan and an attitude that is intolerable.
>
> Non Indian Man Married to an Indian Barbie: attends every meeting and ceremony and uses terms like "we" and "us", often times feels compelled to speak out, as in, "what mr. so and so really means is, blah, blah, blah. . . . . ". . . .
>
> New Age Barbie: comes with her own crystals, beads and "sacred" smudge shell. . . .
>
> "My Great Grandmother Was Cherokee" Barbie: exact replica of regular Barbie, no distinction from every other Barbie in the store.

Appreciating the humor in this list requires awareness of government distribution of surplus commodities on reservations, what a jingle dress is and how they are traditionally made, customs such as powwows and 49s, and whites' continual lack of knowledge about, and encroachment upon, tribal cultures. The list is most likely to circulate among Indians and those familiar with their cultures. Readers would be reminded that understanding requires some insider knowledge of a group and its culture. In contrast, Mattel's numerous Indian Barbies sometimes present Hollywood-style stereotypes and have generally been unsuccessful in conveying cultural complexity (Thomas 2000a, 73–74). The texts that Mattel prints on boxes for Dolls of the World usually do not indicate the esoteric complexity of the cultures the dolls represent—nor are they intended to.

In addition to looking at religious and ethnic groups through a "Barbie lens," the Internet contributes to campus folklore through a description of Barbie as a graduate student:

Graduate School Barbie comes in two forms:
Delusional Master's Barbie (tm) and Ph.D. Masochist Barbie (tm). Every Graduate School Barbie comes with these fun filled features guaranteed to delight and entertain for hours. . . .
—Comes with two outfits: a grubby pair of blue jeans and five year old gap T-shirt, and a floppy pair of gray sweatpants with a matching "Go Screw Yourself" T-shirt.
—Grad School Barbie talks! Just press the button on her left hand and hear her say such upbeat grad school phrases like, "Yes, Professor, It'll be done by tomorrow" "I'd love to write it all over again" and "Why didn't I just get a job, I could have been making $40,000 a year by now if I had just started working with a Bachelor's. But noooooo, I thought I wanted a masters degree, I wish somebody would drop a bomb on the school so that I'd have an excuse to stop working on my degree that's sucking every last drop of life force out of my withered and degraded excuse for a soul" (9 V lithium batteries sold separately). . . .
Other accessories include:
—Grad School Barbie's Fun Fridge (tm) Well stocked with microwave popcorn, Coca-Cola, Healthy Choice Bologna (99 percent fat free!), and several bottles of Mattel Brand Beer (tm).
—Grad School Barbie's Medicine Cabinet. Comes in Fabulous pink and contains Barbie sized bottles of Advil, St. Johns Wort, Zantac, and your choice of three fun anti-anxiety drugs. . . .
And Grad School Barbie is not alone. . . . GRADUATE ADVISOR KEN: Barbie's mentor and advisor in her quest for increased education and decreased self esteem. Grad Advisor Ken (tm) comes with a supply of red pens and a permanent frown. . . . Buy three or more dolls, and you can have Barbie's Thesis Committee! (Palm Pilot and tenure sold separately.). . . .

The lists satirize specific cultures represented by drawing on more esoteric knowledge than such e-lore lists as "Barbies We'd Like to See." "Graduate School Barbie," for example, emphasizes the difficulties of graduate school.

"Hacker Barbie" plays with computer culture and feminists and also parodies Mattel's Barbie and makes specific references to problematic Barbies. These lists parody the cultures they depict—Indian, non-Indian, and academic—even more than they satirize Barbie.

Like the other forms of cyber-lore, "Hacker Barbie" and "Graduate School Barbie" are evidence of adults at play with Barbie in a fashion that parallels children's play with her. The Barbie that children create, to paraphrase Shelley's comments, does everything they do and many things they dream of doing. Whether they love or hate the actual doll, the Barbie that adults create experiences many things they do and many things they imagine other adults doing, especially those who are part of selected groups. It is significant that Barbie invites both adults and children to mirror and extend personal worldviews and life experiences. The process is important because it allows them to address key issues in their lives—topics that range, for example, from sexuality to sexism. In contrast, folk narratives about G.I. Joe are much narrower, which perhaps indicates that the cultural texts associated with him are dominated and limited by a stereotypical, aggressive male script and thus do not allow for exploration of a range of life issues.

Not all e-lore about Barbie is in list form. Epistolary folklore is also popular. Because Barbie is often mentioned in letters to Santa, it seems appropriate that cyber-lore provides a chance for her to write a letter of her own:

Dear Santa:

Listen you fat little troll, I've been helping you out every year, playing at being the perfect Christmas present, wearing skimpy bathing suits in frigid weather, and drowning in fake tea from one too many tea parties, and I hate to break it to ya Santa, but IT'S DEFINITELY PAYBACK TIME! There had better be some changes around here this Christmas. . . . So, here's my holiday wish list, Santa:

1. A nice, comfy pair of sweat pants and a frumpy, oversized sweatshirt. I'm sick of looking like a hooker. How much smaller are these bathing suits gonna get? Do you have any idea what it feels like to have nylon and velcro crawling up your butt?

2. Real underwear that can be pulled on and off. . . .

3. A REAL man . . . maybe GI Joe. Hell, I'd take Tickle-Me Elmo over that wimped-out excuse for a boyfriend Ken. And what's with that earring anyway? If I'm gonna have to suffer with him, at least make him (and me) anatomically correct.

4. Arms that actually bend so I can push the aforementioned Ken-wimp away once he is anatomically correct.

5. Breast reduction surgery. I don't care whose arm you have to twist, just get it done.

6. A sports bra. To wear until I get the surgery.

7. A new career. Pet doctor and school teacher just don't cut it. How about a

systems analyst? Or better yet, an advertising account exec. Or even an accoun-
tant for goodness sake!

8. A new, more '90s persona. Maybe "PMS Barbie," complete with a miniature
container of chocolate chip cookie dough ice cream and a bag of chips; "Animal
Rights Barbie," with my very own paint gun, outfitted with a fake fur coat and
handcuffs . . .

9. No more McDonald's endorsements. The grease is wrecking my vinyl.

10. Mattel stock options. It's been thirty-seven years—I think I deserve it.

Ok, Santa, that's it. Considering my valuable contribution to society, I don't think
these requests are out of line. If you disagree, then you can find yourself a new
bimbo doll for next Christmas. It's that simple.

I received copies of Barbie's letter more frequently, but Ken was not to be
outdone. Versions of his letter to Santa, a response to Barbie's, circulate on
the Internet or via fax machine:

Dear Santa,

I understand that one of my colleagues has petitioned you for changes in her
contract, specifically asking for anatomical and career changes. In addition, it is
my understanding that disparaging remarks were made about me, my ability to
please, and some of my fashion choices.

I would like to take this opportunity to inform you of some of issues concerning Ms. Barbie, and some of my own needs and desires. First of all, I along with
several other colleagues feel Barbie DOES NOT deserve preferential treatment—the
bitch has everything. I, along with Joe, Jem, Raggedy Ann & Andy DO NOT have
a dream house, corvette, evening gowns, and in some cases, the ability to change
our hair style . . . My decision to accessorize my outfits with an earring . . . reflects
my lifestyle choice.

I too would like a change in career. Have you ever considered "Decorator Ken",
"Beauty Salon Ken", or "Out of work Actor Ken"? In addition, there are several
other avenues which could be considered such as: "S & M Ken" . . . And as for
Barbie needing bendable arms so she can "push me away," I need bendable knees
so I can kick the bitch to the curb. Bendable knees would also be helpful for me
in other situations—we've talked about this issue before.

In closing, I would like to point out that any further concessions to the blonde
bimbo from hell will result in action being taken by myself and others. And Barbie
can forget about having Joe—he's mine. . . .

In her cyber-lore letter Barbie assumes the letter-writing role of a child but
addresses Santa in a very adult tone of voice. She reverses the usual suppli-
catory tone of the letter and turns it into a demanding one ("Listen you fat
little troll"). Much of the letter lambastes Barbie's physical appearance. She
wants comfortable clothes, breast reduction surgery, a different boyfriend,
more anatomical accuracy, a better career, and stock options. "Barbie's

Letter to Santa," then, is very similar in theme to "Over Forty Barbies" and "Barbies We'd Like to See" in its emphasis on reality. As someone who e-mailed a copy of "Over Forty Barbies" to me said, "Barbie's world is getting realistic!" In this e-lore she is making sure Santa gets that message.

"Ken's Letter to Santa" is one of the few pieces of e-lore in which Ken has a starring role. To present Ken as gay may be a subtle signal of the interest in Barbie and Ken dolls among some parts of gay culture.[14] It also points to Mattel's much-lampooned Earring Magic Ken (1993) who wore an earring, a lavender vest, and a ring pendant, causing many, straight as well as gay, to wonder if the doll represented a gay Ken. Mattel, however, denied that was the case. In Mattel's world Ken is not gay, but in cyber-lore, just as in real life, he can be gay. The issue speaks of Ken's ambiguous nature and the ease with which he can be adapted to suit the expressive needs of a variety of groups.

"Ken's Letter to Santa" also evinces some hostility to Barbie on Ken's part, and tension between Barbie and Ken is found in other jokes about the two that circulate orally and on the Internet. One has a man stopping at a store to buy a Barbie for his daughter's birthday, and he discovers a Divorced Barbie that costs $265. He asks why this Barbie is so expensive, and the clerk replies, "Divorced Barbie comes with Ken's house, Ken's car, Ken's furniture."

Other bits of lore that circulate on the Internet have a similar focus on the difficulties of Barbie and Ken's relationship: "After a twenty-year marriage, Barbie and Ken (they have no last name) have finally called it quits. A spokesman for Mattel says Ken was distraught over Barbie's recent redesign, which included a reduction in the size of her chest. However, close friend Chatty Cathy claims the marriage had been on the rocks since Ken began a clandestine affair with GI Joe in 1989." Like many other forms of cyber-lore, the jokes about a rocky relationship satirize the rosy, static, and unrealistic world Mattel has created for the dolls.

In one case of consumerism imitating folklore, the Get Real Girl, Inc. company has internalized the folk message that Barbie needs more reality and is marketing that notion in the form of well-executed Get Real Girl dolls. Created by Julz Chavez, a former Mattel employee and the daughter of a migrant farmworker, the line includes dolls who have been given various ethnic backgrounds and are bound for various "adventures" that include scuba diving in Mexico, backpacking in Africa, and snowboarding in France. The back of the box for Skylar the snowboarder (figure 33) reads:

Birthday: March 12th—Pisces
Hometown: Whistler, Canada
Favorite Sport: Snowboarding

Figure 33. Get Real Girl.

Best Friend: Corey "SurfGirl"
Ambition: Studying to become a veterinarian
Passions: Snowboarding and animal rescue
Want to Explore: Mount Everest, Europe and Japan
Pets: Mixed breed puppy named, "Snowball"
Favorite pastime: "Designing my homepage online"
E-mail Address: skylar@getrealgirl.com

Skylar's Got Gear! Skylar takes you on a snowboarding adventure
in Europe! "I've perfected my boarding skills in my own backyard
on the slopes of Whistler. My X-treme personality takes me
around the world competing and having a blast with my other
Get Real Girl friends. Travel with me to collect all the adventure
stamps for my Passport Journal! Someday I want to be a veterinarian and I'm on my way to reaching that goal by having my own
Pet Rescue site online. I'm going for it!"

The dolls are "teen girls in real sports with the hottest gear and awesome
attitudes," and their athletic bodies can be posed "like a real action girl." Girls
can log onto the Get Real Girl Web-site and read the dolls' journals as they
"share their deepest secrets about friendship and how to follow your dreams."

When I showed Skylar to the six- and eight-year-old girls I interviewed,
their responses were identical: "COOOOOL!" The six-year-old wanted to log
onto the Web-site immediately. Not only have the dolls' marketers embodied the get-real message that is so dominant in e-lore, but they have also
taken a page from the G.I. Joe handbook by emphasizing adventure and
positioning the doll as an "action figure." The dolls are centered primarily
on sports and do not emphasize other creative or intellectual realms as
strongly for little girls. The world of girls' toys, however, would benefit from
more action figures, and Get Real Girl addresses that need. Little girls have
long been interested in active play, and a doll that furthers such activities
is a good idea (Calvert 1992; Formanek-Burnell 1993).

Despite the fact that Skylar has an "awesome attitude" and is "going for it,"
however, it is clear that Barbie rules in dolldom as well as cyber-lore. G.I. Joe
and Ken play distant seconds to her lead, but Barbie gets the most attention.
It is the late-twentieth-century parallel to what happens with nineteenth-
century cemetery statuary: The bodies of women get more notice (in the folk
tradition in the form of legends) than the statues of soldiers and other men.

Barbie also draws more fire, more cultural critique, than G.I. Joe. Because
G.I. Joe is a war toy, he has the potential to be even more controversial than
Barbie although he lacks her ubiquity and attendant visibility. He also does
not face a gender double standard. Unlike Barbie, he does not have the

negative historical baggage that accompanies the female gender—in Barbie's case, an association with the corrupting influence of fashion, the evils of witchcraft, and the seductive quality sometimes attributed to women's long tresses. A soldier, a warrior, although he can be fearsome, has a long historical tradition of being admired, respected, and even becoming the subject of public monuments and memorials. Even when a children's male doll is made in the image of a particularly villainous soldier, such as a Nazi, little is said. G.I. Joe can associate with Nazis and few notice, but Barbie's every hairstyle and hemline receives attention.

The great Barbie divide—that is, the two opposing views of Barbie—continues to exist. One has it that she is a bad influence on children, the other that she is merely a doll or even that she is a positive influence on kids. Because her form allows her to be put to such a range of uses, some positive and others negative, the answer to the question of who is right is situational. Parents need to decide whether to buy a Barbie doll on the basis of specific situations and children. The critique of Barbie, especially concerning gender roles and body image, that comes from parents, scholars, feminists, and folklore is helpful, however, because it pressures Mattel to keep improving and refining this very influential doll.

Barbie has deconstructed dolldom, an idea that perhaps can be considered further in a theoretical sense. Jacques Derrida presents deconstruction as undoing, decomposing, and desedimenting existing forms (1991, 272). Both adults (through wordplay) and children (through play behaviors) often employ Barbie in a manner that deconstructs stereotypes. Although Derrida Barbie would likely not be a big-seller, a Barbie doll does have the capacity to be played with in a positive and deconstructive (not destructive) fashion. She can also be played with in a stereotypical and negative manner as well. This Barbie could be called Binary Barbie because she presents binaries to those who encounter her. She is often viewed as either good or bad. Folk play with her can encompass these binaries and demonstrate how they blend; ultimately, it can collapse the binaries as well. Like flesh-and-blood adults who exist in the "real world," Barbie embodies radical contradictions and differences. She is both "good" and "bad" at the same time.

Barbie's ability as a form to encompass binaries makes her a complex and interesting cultural object. Her dominance in the toy market is more troubling, however. Other dolls of adult females that have as much or even more potential to invite a wide range of varied and creative play are locked out by Barbie, who remains toyland's high priestess of hegemony. The Get Real Girls will have to get real tough to compete successfully.

Moreover, the G.I. Joe doll that emerges from the oral narratives and folk play could most accurately be called Reify Joe. I am using the term *reify* because the narrow soldier script is made concrete and material—that is, reified—through its embodiment in Joe dolls. In the accounts I studied, G.I. Joe generally did not foster the same level of multivalent play and narratives that Barbie did, and Joe lore was less likely to open up or critique gender roles than Barbie lore. Joe is a monolithic figure, and despite some creative play (Joe as camera man, fashion critic, or game show contestant) most play I encountered with G.I. Joe centered on war or aggression. Such activity easily tends to reify and sell stereotypical machismo. Although descriptions of play with G.I. Joe show some of the promise that an adult doll holds for little boys in terms of imaginative and creative play, his official story line is still over-determined and dominant.

The G.I. Joe doll did not stimulate the imaginative range that children seem to want and appreciate, so perhaps it is not surprising that he disappeared from the toy market for several years and *Star Wars* toys, which had a greater variety of figures and stories, took over children's imaginations. Female figures such as Princess Leia, although she may have encouraged some fairly stereotypical save-the-princess type of play, are at least present in the play world of boys and not immediately rejected, as was the female nurse of G.I. Joe's world (Cross 1997, 176). Although *Star Wars* toys can be critiqued as encouraging violent play or a distorted male body image (Pope, Olivardia, and Gruber 1999, 69), there is opportunity for variety in the types of play the figures inspire. As Nick, a twenty-four-year-old white male said, "Everyone played G.I. Joe; this [*Star Wars* figures] was the first thing that was creative and unfamiliar . . . [from] the norm." Nick said that a lot of his friends liked to be the two male heroes: Luke Skywalker or Han Solo. Nick, however, preferred to be the small, old-looking character, Yoda, who "already knew everything."

In the twenty-first century, action figures/dolls like the Get Real Girls that blend action, adventure, and sports may be a move in the right direction, but there is also need for Get Less Violent Guys and Get Real Boys that more closely reflect boys' lives and offer varied storylines, including intellectual and creative scripts. That such themes appeal to boys is attested to by the success of the Harry Potter books.

In the 1960s, and in a generally homophobic society that endorsed rigid gender roles, Joe broke new ground for boys by being a doll—albeit one redefined as an "action figure." During the early 1980s, *Star Wars* toys introduced even more figures onto the playing field, and not every one of them was a macho soldier. At the beginning of the twenty-first century— still limited by American culture's gender stereotypes—society will, ironically, likely continue to go to other worlds and other galaxies for boys' dolls that begin to get real and break down the most rigid of gender stereotypes.

4

Bodies Beautiful and Violent: Virgins, Barbies, and Joes

As soon as each hour of one's life has died, it embodies itself in some
material object. . . . There it remains captive . . . unless we should
happen upon the object, recognize what lies within, call it by its
name and so set it free.

—Marcel Proust

I live in a valley that is tucked high among the western slopes of the
Rocky Mountains. Surrounding my town on all sides are blue mountains that are tempered year-round by the green of conifers, the
translucent yellows of aspens and the orange-reds of scrub oaks in
the fall, the moving shadows of whites and iced indigos that are the
snows of winter, and the mantle of spring green that later blooms
into summer wildflowers. Despite the distinctiveness of this setting,
much of what I see when I look closer to home, especially the sculptural presentations of women, can be seen anywhere in America.
Just as in many other houses across the country, for example, a walk
through my family room could easily reveal naked, tangled-haired,

and broken-limbed Barbies lying on the floor. Even if there were no children in my house, Barbie could easily access my home via television advertisements and the brightly colored ad inserts that are always falling out of the Sunday newspaper.

If I step outside of my house and look up the street, I will see a classically inspired statue of a woman gracing my neighbor's lawn. If I get into the older-model Jeep that is parked in my driveway and drive down the street, I do not have to go far before I pass a cemetery where I can see a statue of the Virgin that is the subject of legends. If I continue toward the retail section of town, I will pass much yard art—including frogs holding hands, more classically attired women, peeing boys, and cut-outs of little girls in dresses and on swings.

Once I turn onto Main Street, which is clogged with the overflowing traffic of a mountain college town that is home to twenty thousand students, I will pass the same chain retail stores found anywhere in rural or urban America, Wal-Marts, Kmarts, and the like. If I stop at one of these stores to buy anything from yard supplies to groceries to children's clothes, my search for consumer goods could easily take me past an arresting wall of pink packaging signifying Barbie territory. Among the brown, black, and green packaging of a nearby aisle, I will find G.I. Joe and other action figures. If I were to forego the stop at the store and instead drive on to the university campus where I work, I would pass the larger cemetery where the statue of the Weeping Woman supposedly cries her tears.

So, like many other people, not far from wherever I am there will be culturally visible, gendered images. In addition, I found and heard much lore about these figures. Thus, this book has focused on the most noticeable gendered forms I have seen that also generated folklore.[1] The ubiquity and ease in finding these images suggest that they are significant cultural objects. The fact that folklore and folk behaviors appear in relation to them is additional indication of their ability to embody noteworthy cultural currents. When taken together, these sculptural forms reveal a consistent and influential way of constructing gender over the last two centuries.

Pattern and Gendered Forms

An emphasis on looks is a dominant pattern in culturally visible forms that are gendered female. From cemeteries to front yards, there are similar, classically draped concrete statues of women. The statues do not represent anyone in particular, but they embody a cultural idea that has come from fine-arts renderings of the female figure in a manner signifying ideal beauty rather than individual identity or personality.

The female as an aesthetic ideal is a gendered stock pattern discernible in cemetery statuary, yard art, and the perennially popular Barbie doll. Stock figures of females often fall into one of two camps, sometimes both: the lovely, comforting, motherly figure or the sexualized, erotic woman. The Virgin Mary represents the comforting but beautiful mother figure who appears in both cemeteries and yards. She stands alongside sexier female counterparts, such as the surrogate mourners in cemeteries. Like the mourners, Barbie's form is perpetually youthful, perfect, and sexually provocative, as many recollections of Barbie play involving anatomical or sexual exploration attest.

Much feminist theory has focused on how the female body is constructed in language and culture—and how that has an impact on the lives of women.[2] This theory often grapples, directly or indirectly, with essentialism, that is, the notion that particular characteristics are inherent because of gender. The gendered objects discussed in this book appear to make material some views of women that could be classed as essentialistic— woman as nurturer, for example. When the body of folklore that surrounds these forms is studied, however, it becomes apparent that gender essentialism does not escape folk critique. Many people of both genders quietly but persistently undo essentialistic messages in their everyday lives through the creative and idiosyncratic deployment of gendered objects. The folklore about these figures provides a kind of folk meditation on gender essentialism and reveals that meanings associated with everyday, sculptural forms of females are at present more fluid that those connected to males.

Along with gender, ethnicity figures in all three types of material culture. A lack of visible ethnic indicators is a characteristic of the stock, idealized female figure. Although ethnic bodies appear in all these kinds of material culture, they are usually not the norm; in some cases, especially yard art, they are more likely to be male than female. Nineteenth-century gravemarkers provided few, if any, images of the idealized beauty of African American women. Neither do yard art images of African Americans usually represent widespread cultural beauty ideals. Barbie is the most progressive gendered form when it comes to ethnicity, but Anglo Barbie still dominates the market and some ethnic Barbies have anglicized features.

The ideal female as rendered in cemetery statuary shares with yard art and Barbie dolls a history of being constructed passively rather than actively. In a cemetery, she is the quiet mourner. In a yard, she appears in frilly dresses and confines herself to swinging or bending over, unlike male counterparts who engage in a wider range of activities. Lilli—a doll meant to be the object of the male gaze—inspired the creation of Barbie. The teenaged Barbie was at first a "fashion doll," a plastic form intended to be aesthetically pleasing. Unlike a Get Real Girl, Barbie is not seen primarily as an action doll; indeed, emphasis on action is a marketing tactic that sets Get Real Girls apart from Barbies.

In cemeteries, statues often portray their male subjects as active and engaged in business, battle, or sports. They are specific men, usually not stock figures, and their reason for being is not to represent idealized beauty. Male figures on lawns are often engaged in active and even mischievous behaviors, and dolls of males also emphasize the active over the passive. They are marketed specifically as "action figures."

Figures of males, although usually more individualized than those of females, also assume stereotypical roles. Yard art is replete with stock figures of females *and* males. Whether idiosyncratic or stock, men generally appear in traditionally masculine roles, whether in the toy world, the cemetery, or on front lawns. They are less frequently sexualized than their female counterparts and rarely associated with the domestic or intimate. In addition, they are less routinely depicted as a parent than are figures of women. Instead, they are often limited to certain masculinized realms, including battle or business. An examination of the differences between the forms of males and those of females indicates that gender is a significant factor in determining (consciously or not) how a culturally visible form will be designed.

A consideration of the three kinds of gendered images provides a reminder of elite culture's influence, which has shaped all the types of material culture I have discussed. Despite America's democratic values, the relative prosperity of its citizens has allowed them economic access to smaller-scale versions of the forms, such as yard statuary, that emerged from elite culture. The use of elite culture's images and themes in non-elite forms such as yard art is pervasive, and so yard art kitsch—in some aspects—is not as removed from fine art as is commonly thought.

The three venues I have studied—homes, yards, and cemeteries—also share gendered forms. For example, yard art gnomes, flamingos, and even Barbies appear in cemeteries (figures 34, 35). In addition, the same masculine images, such as soldiers, appear on lawns, in graveyards, and in playrooms. Figures from each venue are used in the same roles. There are angel Barbies, for example, as well as angels in cemeteries and angels on front lawns. Other ethereal, beautiful female figures, such as Virgins or fairies, are embodied in yard art, cemetery statuary, and Barbie dolls (figures 36, 37, 38, 39). These forms are iterable, mutable, and sometimes interchangeable among various venues or within roles because they are available and thus able to fit into traditional gender patterns. Sculptural figures are part of a familiar tide of images; they are also an influential component in the visual signification of gender.

Figure 34. Yard art gravemarker, West Norwood Cemetery, London.

Figure 35. Yard art gnome on gravemarker, Smithfield, Utah.

Figure 36. Yard art Virgin
Mary statue in cemetery,
Ogden, Utah.

Figure 37. An angel Barbie.

Figure 38. Yard art fairies on tree trunk, Logan, Utah.

Figure 39. Cemetery statue of fairy or angel, Lexington, Kentucky.

Even in these stereotypical forms, women have access to more roles than do men. Males are often rigidly essentialized—but presented as more powerful—in both the visual and verbal traditions. Perhaps it is the cultural power that has been granted to these masculine roles that accounts for their tenacity even though their negative qualities are widely recognized. Unfortunately, American culture still grants less power to women's positions than men's. Public meanings of the objects, however, do not foreclose on their ability to allow for idiosyncratic meanings and messages, which is part of the value and appeal of the forms. Whether in the home and its environs or beyond its boundaries, a surfeit of representations of the human form has been sculptured into shapes that range from bathtub virgins to Barbies to warrior Joes. The ubiquity of the human figure in these venues (and others as well) speaks to its relevance as a symbolic form and its utility in expressing cultural attitudes.

Gendered Sculptural Forms in Historical Context

One factor that links the three forms of material culture I discuss is the manner in which they are grounded in the nineteenth century. They all manifest the era's emphasis on the individual, the increase in the production of material culture, and the greater affordability of mass-produced objects. Although the forms—cemetery statues, yard statuary, and dolls—became even less expensive and more varied in the twentieth century, in many respects, they continued to follow nineteenth-century patterns. A rise in production, for example, promoted the use of goods as a means of conspicuous consumption and a way to express individual personality and aesthetic views, behaviors that continued into the twentieth century.

Developments in technology helped fuel increases in the production and availability of goods during the nineteenth century, and technology continued to mark twentieth-century responses to material culture. Technological advances or shifts affected yard statuary, gravemarkers, and Barbie dolls. Technology also allowed for a noticeably larger range of variation in form. There were more and different kinds of Barbies, more diverse and idiosyncratic images on gravemarkers, and a larger variety of yard statuary. Similar dramatic changes in gendered patterns, however, did not take place. All of the objects employ significant elements of gender imagery that date from the nineteenth century.

Art historians have identified the nineteenth century as the era in which the female nude became the dominant vision of nudity. The practice of linking the female with nudity in order to embody abstract notions of ideal beauty was a strong cultural current of the time. Because the century allowed for greater access to goods, more and more people could own less expensive depictions of this romanticized image of beauty and in forms ranging from cemetery statuary to yard art. The nineteenth century, which, Michael Kimmel argues, saw the rise of the self-made man, continued to link images of men to active, powerful roles, whether in fine-art depictions or in more mundane aesthetic forms. Kimmel notes that men who sought to cast themselves in this masculine role avoided characteristics seen as feminine. They did not, for example, overtly embrace passive or eroticized designs of masculine imagery, which fell into the realm of feminized signifiers.

The nineteenth century gave birth to a ubiquity of forms—for example, cemetery angels or surrogate mourners—that visually gendered intimacy as a female trait. As Kimmel describes contemporary views of intimacy, "The very definitions of emotional intimacy bear the mark of gender" (2000b, 311). The association again indicates the impact of the 1800s. Francesca Cancian (2000) argues that notions of love have been linked to the female, particularly since the nineteenth century. The cultural linkage of the female and intimacy is manifest in the sculptural forms examined in this book, and it is pervasive, persistent, influential, and exclusionary of the masculine.

During the twentieth century the types of three-dimensional objects under examination were still seen and presented in a stock fashion. Nineteenth-century patterns remained evident in much gravemarker imagery, yard art, and even in the Barbie doll. Gender typing remained despite the fact that many people, inspired by the women's movement, questioned and critiqued stereotypical gender roles and patterns during the latter half of the twentieth century. The gendered figures that are the focus of this book illustrate the significant gap between what we say about gender equality and what we do in everyday practice in everything from the toys we buy to the art we choose for private and public spaces.

The discussion of men's gender roles began to change by late in the twentieth century. More attention was given to the idea of men as nurturing, care-giving partners and parents. The sculptural presentation of woman as the subject of the male gaze continued, however. Very few visible, everyday images were created of men as pleasing, eroticized objects of the female gaze. Men were most frequently portrayed in similar active and powerful roles as those imagined for them in the nineteenth century. Indeed, throughout the twentieth century renderings of the self-made man were apparent in the numerous visual references to male occupations on gravemarkers (although very few references to women's careers appeared), the active and mischievous male figures that graced lawns, and male dolls that literally were rechristened "action figures."

In her study of the male body, Susan Bordo says, "Mostly men's bodies are presented like action-hero toys—wind them up and watch them perform" (1999, 191). Yet she cites 1995 as the year when she finally saw a male form constructed for the female (or homosexual male) gaze. This male body was in a Calvin Klein photo advertisement. Bordo describes the man, dressed only in his underwear: "He offers himself nonaggressively to the gaze of another. Hip cocked in the snaky S-curve usually reserved for depictions of women's bodies, eyes downcast but not closed, he gives off a sultry, moody, subtle but undeniably seductive consciousness of his erotic allure. . . . Such an attitude of male sexual supplication, although it has . . . classical antecedents, is very new to contemporary mainstream representation" (1999, 171).

Bordo is correct in noting the visual change in the presentation of male bodies that some Calvin Klein advertising signaled, although there is yet to be a wholesale cultural shift. Male images in advertising are less conservative than those in the material culture that I study. Bordo, however, is cautious about reading too much into the advertisements: "In this 'postmodern' age, it's more of a free-for-all, and images are often more reactive to each other than to social change" (1999, 192–93).

Bordo admits to being both attracted to and ambivalent about the male image (1999, 168, 215). I understand her ambivalence. Even in this advertisement the man is still encased in a well-muscled and powerful physique, a construction of the male form that follows a fine-art tradition designed to avoid a feminized reading of the male figure. Indeed, the body of the model is not the softer, more flowing figure of the fine-art ephebe. The 1995 Calvin Klein image blends and masculinizes two old art traditions. The first is the use of a body (although usually a female one) to represent idealized beauty, and the second is the tradition of using a muscled (armored) male body to communicate power. The advertisement merges these two ideas into a male form that signifies that ideal male attractiveness is embodied in the powerful but available armored physique—not a particularly radical or even realistic view of maleness. In fact, the image continues to communicate some nineteenth-century views of men.

Although gender roles and images may have changed, we still encounter ubiquitous gendered images that speak of nineteenth-century ways of seeing women and men. In considering the three forms of material culture collectively, it is apparent that there is still a long way to go when it comes to creating gendered, culturally visible sculptural forms that reflect contemporary discussions about gender. The United States may be at least a hundred, perhaps nearly two hundred, years behind on this score. The culturally ubiquitous forms offer a picture of the gendered past.

The Folkloric Revising and Revisiting of Gendered Forms

All of these forms of gendered material culture have symbolic potential, and, like many symbols, all three are multivocal and polyvalent (Turner 1967, 43–46). Their symbolic capacity is enhanced by the folklore and folk customs that surround them. I have tried to be sensitive to this range when writing about these forms, and I have worked to identify some of the different and even contradictory meanings associated with them. A look at the folklore related to all three also reveals that the objects are used in ways far beyond the original intent of their creators.

These three types of material culture—cemetery statuary, Barbie and Ken, and yard art—together constitute the most common gendered sculptural forms apparent both inside and outside the home. The three also share the capacity to negotiate between public and private space, and they all prompt human physical interaction with them. Even though most cemetery statues I examined are in public cemeteries, their forms, especially if of a female, often create a sense of intimacy. They can generate some feeling for the deceased because the sculptor, through a public display of an intimate body, allows the viewer into a private realm.

The other two objects examined in this book also function in some fashion to mediate between the public and the private. Barbie is a public figure with an image carefully honed by Mattel, but folk play and folklore about her demonstrate what an effective tool she is in creating private worlds and idiosyncratic statements (figure 40). Yard art appears on lawns, a semiprivate, semipublic area in America, and communicates a homeowner's private sense of aesthetics or humor to a larger public without the owner having to leave the privacy of home.

Whether their meaning is private or easily discernible and public, another commonality shared by the forms is the manner in which they reach out to and engage a viewing audience. This is exemplified by the audience response that all three evoke. Barbie, of course, prompts folk play behaviors, which makes sense given that play is her reason for being. Physical interaction occurs in relation to the other figures as well, even though, unlike Barbie, they were not primarily created to generate such activities. Adolescents, for example, engage in "legend-tripping" in relation to the cemetery statues. Yard art statuary prompts pranking, such as the activities

Figure 40. Barbie on the Fence of Shoes, Parker, Colorado.

of the French Gnome Liberation Front or when members of a Utah State University fraternity stole the animals from Bernice's lawn and set them up in the yard of one of their professors.

Even stock forms can, on occasion, produce imaginative responses and critiques of the stereotypes. The folklore, the oral narratives, can revise the patterns apparent in the objects themselves, thus opening the door to creative, subversive, and idiosyncratic reconstructions of the forms. Oral narratives and folk behaviors are capable of lending dynamism to the more conservative nature of an object. Although folklore can perpetuate the same stereotypical views of gender as a form does, it also has the potential to critique stereotypical views of gender and create different gender roles in response to an object. Perhaps the best illustration of this process is the Barbie e-lore that comments on the stereotypical aspects of Barbie and revises her in more realistic ways (as, for example, Blue Collar Barbie or Post-Menopausal Barbie).

The mere presence of a capacity for dynamism and rethinking in the folk process does not necessarily mean all troubling, culturally visible, and stereotypical objects are redeemed through folklore, especially since folklore is equally capable of merely revisiting and perpetuating the stereotypes the forms may embody. Even when folklore does revise a stereotypical figure, it is also not at all clear whether the folklore provides enough of a visible reworking to truly vitiate the visual impact of the form.

Moreover, some types of gendered material culture do not seem to invite the same wide range of dynamic responses as do others. Images of actual men in cemeteries, for example, whether merely portraits or depictions of individuals engaged in work, sports, or a hobby, do not tend to inspire the same amount of folk response as do statues of women. Unlike those generated in relation to the statues of surrogate mourners, there are very few legends about gravemarkers bearing portraits of men. There are legends about statues of male soldiers, but these accounts provide few individuating details. They tend to revolve around the role of the soldier and present him in an active, aggressive role consistent with his occupation.

The folklore and folk play that emerge in relation to G.I. Joe dolls are similar to the soldier legends in their limited construction of male roles. Barbie play, although it can be conservative, can depart wildly from convention. The G.I. Joe play that I studied, however, did not reflect such a wide range of play behaviors. It generated much less folklore and e-lore, let alone folklore that critiqued the doll, even though Joe, being a war toy, is ripe for criticism. Yard art figures also followed similar patterns. The presentations of active, assertive males ranged from hunters shooting guns to soldiers firing cannons.

This pervasive folkloric gender pattern is at least suggestive. Perhaps it indicates that stereotypical male roles and their cultural scripts are more rigid and less open to revision within the culture than are women's roles that have been seen as stereotypically feminine. I find the pervasive association of aggression with masculinity particularly disturbing, as is the lack of a significant folk critique of this linkage. Although there is folk criticism of Barbie's unrealistic "body beautiful," I did not see a parallel folk critique of the association between G.I. Joe and the "body violent."

Perhaps the research of some anthropologists and sociologists may account for the folkloric pattern that I saw. Considering that research in relation to the lack of a greater folk critique of culturally visible, violent, and aggressive male images leads me to wonder if the lack is not due in some part to the fact that American culture, at some level, accepts images of aggressive masculinity. As context and as an indication of the degree of cultural tolerance of the association of maleness with even violent aggression, consider some statistics on gender and violence: *"Young American men are the most violent group of people in the industrialized world.* Our homicide rate is between five and twenty times higher than that of any other industrial democracy, and we imprison five to twenty times more people than does any other country on earth except Russia" (Kimmel 2000a, 246, emphasis in the original). Near the millennium, the U.S. Department of Justice reported that men constituted 99 percent of all persons arrested for rape, 88 percent of those arrested for murder, 92 percent of those arrested for robbery, 87 percent of those arrested for aggravated assault, 85 percent arrested for other assaults, 83 percent arrested for all family violence, and 82 percent arrested for disorderly conduct. Finally, it is men who kill nearly 90 percent of all murder victims (Kimmel, ed. 2000b, 361). According to the National Academy of Sciences, the "most consistent pattern with respect to gender is the extent to which male criminal participation in serious crimes at any age greatly exceeds that of females" (Kimmel, ed. 2000b, 361). If women's crime constituted these same percentages there would be much more attention to this as a gender issue, a "woman's problem."

Kimmel notes that long-term historical evidence indicates that female criminality has actually decreased since the eighteenth century (2000a, 248). Some types of women's crime have increased, however, especially property crime and petty theft such as credit card fraud, writing bad checks, and shoplifting or "stealing beauty" (Kimmel 2000a, 248). Because I am concerned with notions of female beauty in this book, I was intrigued to find it mentioned in the writing of criminologists. In discussing young women who engage in shoplifting, for example, Jack Katz, a criminologist, notes, "Females take symbols of adult female identity—cosmetics, jewelry and sexy underwear" (1988, 71). Crime is gendered. It is also likely, in a significant number of cases, that cultural gender ideals and behaviors help shape what types of crimes are committed by whom.

My intent in citing these statistics is not to brand all men as violent—indeed, most men are not—but to indicate the presence of a striking and sobering gender pattern. My point is to provide a societal context for the material cultural patterns and folklore I have analyzed, especially the lack of extensive folk critique of male dolls and the seemingly wide acceptance of violence in relation to them.

> Of course, to argue that men are more prone to violence than women are does not resolve the political question of what to do about it. It would be foolish to resignedly throw up our hands in despair that "boys will be boys." Whether you believe this gender difference in violence derives from different biological predispositions (which I regard as dubious because these biological impulses do not seem to be culturally universal) or because male violence is socially sanctioned and legitimated as an expression of masculine control and domination (a far more convincing explanation), the policy question remains open. Do we organize as a society so as to maximize this male propensity toward violence, or do we organize as a society so as to minimize and constrain it? (Kimmel, ed. 2000b, 362)

Society's norms are both reflected in and shaped by its expressive cultural forms. When the three most pervasive types of sculptural presentations of males are analyzed, it is apparent that we still are not minimizing the propensity toward violence in culturally visible images of men. Some progress has been made in critiquing the linkage of women with the body beautiful, but, as examination of these three types of material culture indicates, there is still far to go in undoing the association of the male with the body violent.

Kimmel, who discusses aggression, cites the work of social anthropologists Singe Howell and Roy Willis, who studied societies in which very little violence occurred. They found that constructions of masculinity had a significant impact on violence: "In societies in which men were permitted to acknowledge fear, levels of violence were low. But in societies where masculine bravado—the posture of strength and the repression and denial of fear—was a defining feature of masculinity, violence was likely to be high. It turns out that those societies in which bravado is prescribed for men are also those in which the definitions of masculinity and femininity are very highly differentiated" (Kimmel 2000a, 245).

Summing up the work of several anthropologists, Kimmel lists characteristics that they associate with facilitating a climate of violence. The factors include societies that idealize warriors; associate public leadership with male dominance; prohibit women from public and political participation; systematically separate boys from girls; focus the initiation of boys on a lengthy constraint wherein they are separated from women and taught male solidarity and bellicosity; engage men in emotional and elaborated displays of male virility, ferocity, and sexuality; hold ritual celebrations of fertility that focus on male generative ability; and prize male economic activities over female ones (Kimmel 2000a, 245).

Many of these characteristics are present in American culture, and some—such as the warrior as a masculine ideal, public leadership as a male domain, and the privileging of male economic activities—are reflected in the sculptural forms discussed in this book. Cemetery statuary, for example, provides patterns that illustrate the three characteristics. In addition, it seems highly likely that children could easily learn bravado (as Kimmel defines it, the "posture of strength and the repression and denial of fear") through playing with action figures such as G.I. Joe, which are primarily warriors.[3] Many play situations that boys described to me used the backdrop of battle—surely one of the most fearsome of human activities—in a manner that denies the real fear it can evoke and instead emphasizes the pleasures to be found in war play.

Regarding the rigid gender roles that boys face in American culture, William Pollack, a psychologist, observes, "Many years ago, when I began my research into boys, I had assumed that since America was revising its ideas about girls and women, it must have also been reevaluating its traditional ideas about boys, men, and masculinity. But over the years my research findings have shown that as far as boys today are concerned, the old Boy Code—the outdated and constricting assumptions, models, and rules about boys that our society has used since the nineteenth century—is still operating in force" (1999, 6).

It is instructive to remember the comments of the informants in chapter 3, which indicate that some children hunger for options other than war toys—which can reinforce the outdated "Boy Code"—when it comes to boys' toys. I am not arguing that children should never be aggressive in their play or that they should not "play with their fears." Sometimes doing so may be a helpful process. Children who choose to costume as frightening Halloween figures, for example, may be playing with, addressing, and overcoming fears. Yet play formats that consistently repress fear about real-life situations such as war and turn it into bravado could have problematic ramifications.

In some circumstances the general public's attention is undeniably drawn to violence, and some parents do express concerns about violent toys. In a story that appeared shortly after the horrifically violent terrorist attacks on the World Trade Center and the Pentagon on September 11, 2001, for example, the Associated Press reported:

> Parents are trying to rid their children's lives of violent toys.
>
> "We just need a break," said Lisa Eastman, a thirty-eight-year-old New Yorker who bought Lego blocks and puzzles for her six-year-old girl and three-year-old boy. "My kids now have nightmares about fires and about all those bad guys."
>
> The industry also has been doing some soul-searching, pulling toys off shelves, rethinking products and putting off the release of items that might be seen as too violent.
>
> Chris Byrne, an independent toy analyst predicted that heroes who restore order . . . would replace "nasty toys that destroy enemies for the sake of unspecified violent play." Mattel the world's largest toy manufacturer, has withdrawn its Heli-Jet vehicle, which contains a mission card with a specific goal: save New York from a villain called Vitriol, who stands atop the World Trade Center, ready to blast the city with deadly energy waves. (2001, 1)

The tragedy of September 11, 2001, brought the realities of violence and training in violence into sharp, undeniable, and painful relief and caused some Americans to feel that violent toys were "just too much" (Associated Press 2001, 1). Ironically, however, according to reports on CNN television, G.I. Joe sales increased after the terrorist attacks. He was considered an American hero who could help restore order.[4]

In terms of folk processes that relate to culturally visible, sculptural objects that are gendered male, it is likely that such forms reflect expectation of aggression as being a male characteristic, and that is part of a masculine cultural script that is still too rigid. Given the statistics on violence in America, it is certainly a script that, at the very least, is limiting and even dangerous for some little boys and for society as a whole.

At (almost literally) the grass-roots level, yard art provides an alternative to these narrow and stereotypical constructions of the masculine. Although due to its limited nature, the alternative has not likely had much impact on changing them. The different view of the masculine can be found in the form of the concrete geese costumed as males. Although some can be dressed in stereotypical male costumes, often the very "gooseness" of a form undercuts its machismo. Many geese dressed as males project kind, gentle, and even nurturing images, as does some yard art of males associated with holidays (e.g., Santa Claus and the Easter Bunny). Women construct many of these masculine images, and none of the figures sport hard, muscled bodies. Their forms communicate humorous playfulness and nurturing comfort. Moreover, the male images, which are visible, are more expansive than other culturally ubiquitous presentations of stereotypical machismo.

A goose costumed as a woman may also, depending upon context and viewer, be a means of poking fun at notions of idealized female beauty. A goose wearing a bikini is neither sexy nor erotic, but it is a humorous take on the notion of the body beautiful. Such yard art establishes some cultural space for a kind of play with, and variation upon, traditional gender characteristics, something to which much more visible cultural space could and should be devoted at all levels of culture.

All three types of forms discussed in this book evince patterns that downplay male sexuality but emphasize female sensuality. In cemeteries, statutes of males lack erotic features to the point of the omission of genitals. At the opposite end of the spectrum, the erotic female body is often accentuated through nudity, partial nudity, or form-revealing drapery. As Alison Smith, an art historian, notes, "Drapes (semi-transparent, or *draperie mouillée*) were often added to offset the form and contours of the figure" (1996, 4). Classical yard art statuary, whether of males or females, exemplifies the same patterns as cemetery statues. An exception might be the urinating boy, whose buttocks are revealed and penis indirectly referenced through his activity. It is not a depiction of an adult male and likely to convey mischief or even innocence rather than eroticism. Finally, Barbie usually cuts a more sensual figure than either Ken or G.I. Joe. As they are on cemetery statues of women, her breasts are particularly prominent. (The Get Real Girl dolls minimize the eroticism of breasts; theirs are smaller than Barbie's and covered by a formed, painted-on plastic sports bra that cannot be removed.)

Folklore, in relation to sexuality, does not always follow patterns set by form, however. Much folklore concerning objects that portray females does follow the same pattern established by the figure and links the female with sexuality. Some, however, does not make direct connections. Although numerous narratives exist about Barbie play and sexuality, for example, legends concerning cemetery statues of females may emphasize stereotypical gender roles. They often do not overtly sexualize a female protagonist. The customs and narratives surrounding stock images of yard art figures of women do not usually blatantly eroticize them. Still, sexuality is an aspect of many images. One student told me, for example, about his mother-in-law, an art student in Indiana who, as an ironic comment on the sexual imagery found in yard art, created Sadomasochistic Goose, dressed in black leather and sporting a pierced bill along with a small whip.

Even though cemetery statues of males are more individualized than are those of women, they often receive less attention and less response. Armored in the suits and trappings of self-made men, many statues hide their subject's body. The sculptors did not intend to communicate vulnerability and emotion, which an exposed, eroticized form, whether male or female, can signify. Because the sculptors of surrogate mourner figures of women employed the body to communicate these qualities—which were not acceptable for masculine sculptural forms—statues of females, which are evocative, are often more noticeable, memorable, and compelling than those of males. By using figures of females, sculptors can frequently elicit emotional response on the part of viewers, whether male or female.

Artistic renderings of nude and vulnerable bodies can humanize a work of sculpture and create a sense of connection and intimacy. The body is revealed to indicate the tenderness and sublimity of flesh in some form, generally that of a female, in folk, popular, and elite cultures. Whether stereotypical in execution or not, those forms of material culture may also attract viewers in that they use the powers of the body to evoke emotion and perhaps even the fleeting pleasures of human intimacy, whether sexual, parental, nurturing, or based on friendship. A significant element of the sculptural forms' lasting appeal is that, for a time, they make the emotive and transitory verities of human flesh appear to be material and lasting, whether in the hard, plastic bodies of dolls, the unweathered concrete of yard art, or the enduring stone of cemetery statues.

Notes

Introduction

1. My approach is meant to be folkloristic rather than sociological. That is, I present a slice of life—often as it is seen through narratives and folklore—and analyze it. Although I sometimes draw on the work of sociologists for contextual support, it is not my intention to present any kind of a statistical view of my subject matter.

2. I borrow the term *culturescape* from Santino, who uses it to refer "not simply to the ways people have shaped the land, but to the many markings left on the environment, both built and natural" (1999, 517).

3. The European use of the phrase *popular culture* often includes what I separate into two categories—the folk and the popular levels of culture. I delineate three levels of culture: folk, popular and mass, and elite. "Folk culture" encompasses those things that are informally learned via word-of-mouth communication, watching and doing, or through other nonformal conduits (Thomas and Enders 2000, 43). "Elite culture" refers to the "fine arts" that require formal schooling and training, such as opera, ballet, literature, and some types of visual arts. By "popular and mass culture" I am referring to television, films, and the print media in addition to those objects that are mass produced and marketed.

Chapter 1: Cemetery Statues

1. This legend shares motifs with the Latino La Llorona legend body.

2. An ellipsis in legend texts or oral interviews indicates that material has been omitted. In addition to the legends from oral tradition to which I refer in this chapter, I consulted more than eighty legends set in various cemeteries in the United States and abroad. Thanks to my students and to the Indiana State University Folklore Archives, Terre Haute; Utah State University, Fife Folklore Archives, Logan; the University of California–Berkeley Folklore Archives; the clerk in Bobby's Bothy in Edinburgh, Scotland; and Brian McConnell in London for making some of the leg-

ends available to me. In contrast to the weeping woman legends, I found only seven versions of the cemetery soldier legend in the Fife Folklore Archives.

3. While researching and writing this chapter I drew on visits to well over fifty cemeteries and burial sites, particularly the following: Sailor Pioneer Cemetery, Elmira, Oregon; Glen Abbey Memorial Park, San Diego, California; Westwood Memorial Park, Los Angeles, California; the Smithfield, Logan, Ogden, and Salt Lake City cemeteries, all in Utah; the Mount Olivet Cemetery, Salt Lake City; Tiffany Mack Memorial Pet Cemetery, Ogden, Utah; the Cody, Wyoming, cemetery; Aspen Cemetery, Jackson, Wyoming; the Elizabeth, Colorado, cemetery; Fairmount Cemetery, Denver, Colorado; the Vermilion cemetery, Vermilion, Illinois; the Madison, Wisconsin, cemetery; the Bloomington, St. Omer, and Bedford, Indiana, cemeteries; Highland Lawn Cemetery, Terre Haute, Indiana; Crown Hill Cemetery, Indianapolis, Indiana; Spring Grove Cemetery, Cincinnati, Ohio; the Lexington, Kentucky, cemetery; Cave Hill Cemetery, Louisville, Kentucky; the Ashville, North Carolina, cemetery; Victoria Cemetery, British Columbia, Canada; the Anglican cemetery and the Catholic cemetery, both in St. John's, Newfoundland, Canada; Highgate Cemetery, West Norwood Cemetery, Nunhead Cemetery, and Westminster Abbey, all in London; Greyfriar's Kirkyard, Edinburgh, Scotland; St. Kevin's Monastery cemetery, Glendalough, Co. Wicklow, St. Ciaran's Cemetery, Co. Meath, Drogheda Protestant Cemetery, Co. Lough, and Fore Churchyard, Co. Westmeath, all in Ireland; numerous other small churchyard cemeteries throughout the Midlands of Ireland; and Père Lachaise Cemetery, Montparnasse Cemetery, The Catacombs, Notre Dame Cathedral, and Fontaine des Innocents, the former location of Cemetery of the Innocents, all in Paris, France.

4. The decree, however, was not always uniformly followed.

5. After all, political rights such as the vote were often slow in coming to women. French women, for example, did not get the vote until 1944.

6. While a discussion of ethnicity and burial customs is beyond the scope of this project, a few cemeteries did evince a slight interest in having Native Americans interred there. In these cases, the literary vision of the "noble savage" influenced their inclusion in the cemetery's pantheon of historical figures (Sloane 1991, 82).

7. See Thomas (2000b) for a fuller discussion of this component of supernatural legends.

8. For an analysis of these Virgin legends, see Thomas (2000b).

9. See Thomas (2000b) for a more detailed discussion of this subject.

10. Because of the biblical emphasis on male angels, it is often assumed that angels are men, but such is not the case. As Gustav Davidson explains, "True, angels are pure spirits and so should be presumed to be bodiless and, hence, sexless. But the authors of our sacred texts . . . pictured angels in their own image (i.e., in the guise of men). . . . Angels in Scripture, as a consequence, were conceived of as male. However, it was not long before the female of the species began putting in an appearance. In early rabbinic as well as in occult lore, there are quite a number of them" (1967, xxi).

11. That is, woman is the other in patriarchal cultures. Among women, man could be the other, but the masculine is the rule and the feminine is the exception in patriarchal cultures.

12. Thanks to Jack Santino for pointing out that the illustrations on romance

novel covers attempt to address women's "erotic needs" (Nochlin 1972, 14). These renderings of men often employ the kind of armored Chippendales masculinity that Bordo discusses (1999, 30).

13. See Bordo (1999, 196–97, 208–9) on this subject. Although she agrees with Berger on many points, she also demonstrates how contemporary ethnic imagery can present a counterpoint to Berger.

14. For a visual example of the ephebe, see Charles Meyneir's painting *Adolescent Eros Weeping over the Portrait of the Lost Psyche* (Solomon-Godeau 1997, 6).

15. It is also possible that a paucity of images of male intimacy has contributed to some heterosexuals' discomfort with male homosexuality.

Chapter 2: Yard Art

1. This is a similar, focused approach to that taken by Simon Bronner in his study of chain carvers (Bronner 1996, ix).

2. In writing this chapter, I drew on my photographic documentation of 122 yard art sites in Oregon, Colorado, Utah, Wyoming, Idaho, Illinois, Wisconsin, Indiana, Kentucky, Tennessee, and North Carolina. In these states and several others I have observed many times the number of sites I actually documented. In addition, I documented or observed yard art sites in Ireland, France, England, Scotland, British Columbia, and Newfoundland.

3. In the early 1900s Dutch children were used to represent cleanliness in American culture, and Dutch-He and Dutch-She dolls were manufactured and described as "the perfect picture of Holland Health." Dutch dolls were also modeled after the Old Dutch Cleanser images (Formanek-Brunell 1993, 108, 212). It is likely that these male and female dolls, in addition to the use of Dutch figures as product logos, influenced the yard art adoption of the images.

4. Statues of white women devouring watermelon are probably descended from earlier depictions of black women doing the same.

5. The name of this band, Nains Porte-Quel (gnomes carry something), is a pun on the phrase *n'importe quel* (whatever or whichever).

6. Sheehy notes the importance of whimsy in yard art and says that officials and formally trained artists often overlook the need for "humor, spectacle, and whimsy" in public art, which could benefit from heeding yard art's emphasis on "seasonal changes, ephemeral elements, and accretion" (1998, 60, 59). See Doss (1995) for a discussion of official public art.

7. This critique is limited and does not address, for example, gender stereotypes.

Chapter 3: Barbie and Her Consorts

1. For examples of fax lore, see Dundes and Pagter (1975).

2. Mattel not only created Barbie but it also produced a flock of friends and family dolls with whom Barbie could associate.

3. Handler was as interesting and complicated as her creation. One of the earliest women in a leadership position at a major company, in 1978 she was indicted for conspiring to violate federal securities, mail, and banking laws by preparing false financial statements for Mattel (Lord 1994, 95). In addition, she was a breast cancer

survivor and established a firm that designed and marketed mastectomy prostheses. As she described her career from Barbie to the creation of prostheses, "My life has been spent going from breasts to breasts" (Lord 1994, 8; see also Handler 1994).

4. This doll came out in the same year that Mattel created the short-lived Growing Up Skipper, whose breasts grew when her arm was twisted.

5. For specific instructions on how to accomplish this surgery, see Santelmo (1997, 148).

6. See Lord (1994, 264) for a description of the work of Julia Mandle, for example.

7. In 1918 Victoria Ross and Evelyn Berry, residents of Harlem, were the first African Americans to engage in the large-scale manufacture of black dolls (Formanek-Burnell 1993, 150). The first black friends of Barbie, Christie and Julia, arrived in 1969. Black Barbie was marketed in 1980 (Lord 1994, 108, 62). Hasbro created a black G.I. Joe in the mid-1960s but timidly marketed him in the North for the first few years of his existence (Michlig 1998, 111).

8. The Barbie and G.I. Joe interviews in this chapter are drawn from 180 interviews with 76 male informants and 104 female informants; 80 of the interviews discuss G.I. Joe or action figures. I and my undergraduate students at Indiana State University or Utah State University conducted the interviews. In addition, I drew on notes made from numerous casual comments and conversations about Barbie or G.I. Joe. In general, demographic information indicating class background of informants was not usually available, but most were from either working-class or middle-class backgrounds. Several were college students, but none were college professors. The six-year-old girl and the two-year-old boy interviewed are, however, the children of a college professor. The other informants came from a range of professional and blue-collar backgrounds. Ethnicity and age, when available, are noted in the chapter.

9. *Thelma and Louise* (1991) is a female buddy movie in which two women take a road trip and embark on an inadvertent crime spree. At the end of the film, they drive their car, suicidally, over the rim of a canyon. The film generated much debate due to its depiction of women.

10. See Hohmann (1985) for another account of a child's play with Barbie. Further discussion of Barbie appears in Inness (1999), Motz (1983), and Yocom (1993).

11. In 1991 Hasbro introduced a short-run, twelve-inch G.I. Joe. More recently Hasbro created different G.I. figures but marketed them to adults and collectors rather than primarily to children (Michlig 1998, 196, 194).

12. In order to make the e-lore, which had been forwarded many times, consistent and clear in my text, I made a minor format change. I put in a colon or period where a hard return appeared in the original. Otherwise, grammatical and punctuation errors have been left in the texts.

13. In her article, Lau references Santino's work (1996) on serialization and says Santino "touches briefly on serialization as it relates to comic books and popular romances" and emphasizes the ways "in which acts of serialization structure the year cycle" (1999, 71). Santino's argument about serialization runs throughout his book, and in its entirety is focused on an issue that is different from Lau's brief reference and characterization. Santino argues that serialization is critical to consumer culture and the marketing of consumer goods. Traditional forms such as holidays are used to imbue many consumer products—which are not temporally sequential in

nature—with the novelty (and serialization) they so rely upon to generate sales (1996, 151, 69).

14. For example, in her film *Barbie Nation* (1998) Susan Stern documents how gay men use Barbie and Ken dolls in elaborate dioramas.

Chapter 4: Bodies Beautiful and Violent

1. Store mannequins, another culturally visible gendered image, are not included in this discussion because I heard very little folklore about them.

2. For examples of this kind of scholarship, see Butler (1990), Cixous (1980), Irigaray (1977), Jagger and Bordo (1989), Kristeva (1982, 1984), Martin (1987), and Peiss (1998). For examples of folkloric takes on women's bodies, see also Young, ed. (1993) and Thomas (1997b).

3. For more on the figure of the warrior and children, see Jordan and Cowan's "Warrior Narratives in the Kindergarten Classroom" (1998).

4. For discussions of violence and play, see Carlsson-Paige and Levin (1987, 1990), Miedzian (1991), and Sutton-Smith in Padus (1986).

References Cited

Abbott, Marion. 2000. "Do Not Steal This Article, Please!" *San Francisco Chronicle*, 8 Oct., n.p.

Alexander, Sidney, trans. 1991. *The Complete Poetry of Michelangelo*. Athens: Ohio University Press.

Ariès, Philippe. 1962. *Centuries of Childhood: A Social History of Family Life*. New York: Vintage.

———. 1974. *Western Attitudes toward Death: From the Middle Ages to the Present*. Baltimore: Johns Hopkins University Press.

———. 1981. *The Hour of Our Death*. New York: Oxford University Press.

Associated Press. 2001. "Toy Makers Move away from Violence." Logan, Utah, *Herald Journal*, 28 Sept., A1.

Berger, John. 1977. *Ways of Seeing*. New York: Penguin.

Bogart, Michele H. 1985. *Fauns and Fountains: American Garden Statuary, 1890–1930*. Southampton: The Parrish Museum.

Bordo, Susan. 1999. *The Male Body: A New Look at Men in Public and in Private*. New York: Farrar, Straus, and Giroux.

Bourdieu, Pierre. 1984. *Distinction: A Social Critique of the Judgment of Taste*. Cambridge: Harvard University Press.

"Boys' Toys Warp Body Images: Study." 1999. Toronto *Globe and Mail*, 22 May, A7.

Briggs, Katharine. 1976. *An Encyclopedia of Fairies, Hobgoblins, Brownies, Bogies and Other Supernatural Creatures*. New York: Pantheon Books.

———. 1978. *The Vanishing People: Fairy Lore and Legends*. New York: Pantheon Books.

Bronner, Simon, ed. 1989. *Consuming Visions: Accumulation and Display of Goods in America, 1880–1920*. New York: W. W. Norton.

———. 1995. *Piled Higher and Deeper: The Folklore of Student Life*. Little Rock: August House Publishers.

———. 1996. *The Carver's Art: Crafting Meaning from Wood*. Lexington: University Press of Kentucky.

Brown, John Gary. 1994. *Soul in Stone: Cemetery Art from America's Heartland.* Lawrence: University Press of Kansas.

Brunvand, Jan. 1989. *Curses, Broiled Again! The Hottest Urban Legends Going.* New York: W. W. Norton.

Burl, Aubrey. 1985. *Megalithic Brittany.* London: Thames and Hudson.

Butler, Judith. 1990. *Gender Trouble.* London: Routledge.

Calvert, Karin, 1992. *Children in the House: The Material Culture of Early Childhood, 1600–1900.* Boston: Northeastern University Press.

Cameron, Deborah. 1992. "Naming the Parts: Gender, Culture, and Terms for the Penis among American College Students." *American Speech* 67(4): 367–82.

Cancian, Francesca. 2000. "The Feminization of Love." In *The Gendered Society Reader.* Ed. Michael Kimmel, 312–23. New York: Oxford University Press.

Carlsson-Paige, Nancy, and Diane E. Levin. 1987. *The War Play Dilemma: Balancing Needs and Values in the Early Childhood Classroom.* New York: Teachers College Press.

———. 1990. *Who's Calling the Shots? How to Respond Effectively to Children's Fascination with War Play and War Toys.* Philadelphia: New Society Publishers.

Cavendish, Richard. 1970. *Visions of Heaven and Hell.* London: Orbis Publishing.

Cerf, Delphine, and David Babinet. 1994. *Les Catacombs de Paris.* Meudon: Éditions Moulenq.

Chase, Dan. 2000. "Church Members Suffer Pink Flamingo Plague." Logan, Utah, *Herald Journal,* 6 Feb., n.p.

Cixous, Helene. 1980. "The Laugh of the Medusa." In *New French Feminisms.* Ed. Elaine Marks and Isabelle Courtivron, 245–64. Brighton, Eng.: Harvester.

Clark, Kenneth. 1976. *The Nude.* Harmondsworth: Penguin Books.

Cleveland-Peck, Patricia. 2000. "Agenda 1: Gnome Truths." *The Observer,* 9 April, 7.

Clifford, Derek. 1967. *A History of Garden Design.* New York: Frederick A. Praeger.

Cochrane, Lynn. 1997. "Suburban Kings of Kitsch Defy the Mockery in the Rockery." *The Scotsman,* 21 Nov., 12.

Combs, Diana Williams. 1986. *Early Gravestone Art in Georgia and South Carolina.* Athens: University of Georgia Press.

Cross, Gary. 1997. *Kids' Stuff: Toys and the Changing World of American Childhood.* Cambridge: Harvard University Press.

Csikszentmihalyi, Mihaly, and Eugene Rochberg-Halton. 1981. *The Meaning of Things: Domestic Symbols and the Self.* Cambridge: Cambridge University Press.

Culbertson, Judi, and Tom Randall. 1986. *Permanent Parisians: An Illustrated Guide to the Cemeteries of Paris.* Chelsea, Vt.: Chelsea Green Publishing.

———. 1991. *Permanent Londoners: An Illustrated, Biographical Guide to the Cemeteries of London.* New York: Walker and Company.

Curl, James. 1972. *The Victorian Celebration of Death.* Detroit: Partridge Press.

da Costa Nunes, Jadviga. 1987. "The Naughty Child in Nineteenth-Century American Art." *Journal of American Studies* 21(2): 225–47.

Dahlburg, John-Thor. 2000. "France's Littlest Victims: Stolen Garden Gnomes." *Los Angeles Times,* 15 April, A1–A2.

Davidson, Gustav. 1967. *A Dictionary of Angels: Including the Fallen Angels.* New York: Free Press.

de Beauvoir, Simone. 1971. *The Second Sex.* New York: Alfred A. Knopf.

Deetz, James. 1996. *In Small Things Forgotten: An Archaeology of Early American Life.* New York: Anchor Books.

Derrida, Jacques. 1991. "Letter to a Japanese Friend." In *A Derrida Reader: Between the Blinds.* Ed. Peggy Kamuf, 269–76. New York: Columbia University Press.

DiMaggio, Paul. 1991. "Cultural Entrepreneurship in Nineteenth-Century Boston: The Creation of an Organizational Base for High Culture in America." In *Rethinking Popular Culture: Contemporary Perspectives in Cultural Studies.* Ed. Chanda Mukerji and Michael Schudson, 374–97. Berkeley: University of California Press.

Dinkelacker, Horst. 1996. "The Renaissance of the German Garden Gnome." *Journal of Popular Culture* 30(3): 27–33.

Doss, Erika. 1995. *Spirit Poles and Flying Pigs: Public Art and Cultural Democracy in American Communities.* Washington: Smithsonian Institution Press.

Dowle, Jayne. 1996. "Sitting Tenants." London *Daily Telegraph,* 10 Aug., 36.

Dubin, Steven C. 1999. "Who's That Girl?" In *The Barbie Chronicles: A Living Doll Turns Forty.* Ed. Yona Zeldis McDonough, 19–38. New York: Touchstone.

duCille, Ann. 1994. "Dyes and Dolls: Multicultural Barbie and the Merchandising of Difference." *Differences* 6(1): 48–68.

———. 1999. "Barbie in Black and White." In *The Barbie Chronicles: A Living Doll Turns Forty.* Ed. Yona Zeldis McDonough, 127–42. New York: Touchstone.

Duncan, Carol. 1982. "Virility and Domination in Early Twentieth-Century Vanguard Painting." In *Feminism and Art History: Questioning the Litany.* Ed. Norma Broude and Mary D. Garrard, 293–313. New York: Harper and Row.

Dundes, Alan, and Carl R. Pagter. 1975. *Work Hard and You Shall Be Rewarded: Urban Folklore from the Paperwork Empire.* Bloomington: Indiana University Press.

Edison, Carol. 1985. "Motorcycles, Guitars, and Bucking Broncos: Twentieth-Century Gravesites in Southeastern Idaho." In *Idaho Folklife: Homesteads to Headstones.* Ed. Louie W. Attebury, 184–89. Salt Lake City: University of Utah Press.

Ellis, Bill. 1996. "Legend Trip." In *American Folklore: An Encyclopedia.* Ed. Jan Harold Brunvand, 439–40. New York: Garland Publishing.

———. 2000. *Raising the Devil: Satanism, New Religions, and the Media.* Lexington: University Press of Kentucky.

Evans-Wentz, W. Y. 1990. *The Fairy Faith in Celtic Countries.* New York: Carol Publishing.

Fish, Stanley. 1989. *Doing What Comes Naturally: Change, Rhetoric, and the Practice of Theory in Literary and Legal Studies.* Durham: Duke University Press.

Formanek-Brunell, Miriam. 1993. *Made to Play House: Dolls and the Commercialization of American Girlhood, 1830–1930.* New Haven: Yale University Press.

Fraser, Antonia. 1966. *A History of Toys.* New York: Delacorte Press.

"Garden Gnomes Stolen." 1998. *Glasgow Herald,* 25 July, 4.

Geddes, Diana. 1997. "Hi Ho, Hi Ho, Off to Court for Gnome Liberation." *Scotland on Sunday,* 16 Nov., 18.

Glassie, Henry. 1975. *Folk Housing in Middle Virginia.* Knoxville: University of Tennessee Press.

———. 1999. *Material Culture.* Bloomington: Indiana University Press.

"Gnome Alone." 1998. *Financial Times,* 6 July, 15.

"Gnome Assault Case Fails." 1999. *Glasgow Herald,* 12 Nov., 4.

"Gnome Place Like Home." 1997. *The* (London) *Guardian,* 14 Jan., 10.

Guiley, Rosemary. 1996. *Encyclopedia of Angels.* New York: Facts on File.

Handler, Ruth, with Jacqueline Shannon. 1994. *Dream Doll: The Ruth Handler Story.* Stamford: Longmeadow Press.

Harvey, John. 1981. *Mediaeval Gardens.* Beaverton: Timber Press.

Havelock, Christine Mitchell. 1982. "Mourners on Greek Vases: Remarks on the Social History of Women." In *Feminism and Art History: Questioning the Litany.* Ed. Norma Broude and Mary D. Garrard, 45–61. New York: Harper and Row.

Hebdige, Dick. 1989. *Subculture: The Meaning of Style.* New York: Routledge.

Helphand, Kenneth. 1999. "'Leaping the Property Line': Observations on Recent American Garden History." In *Perspectives on Garden Histories.* Ed. Michel Conan, 137–59. Washington: Dumbarton Oaks Research Library and Collection.

Hohmann, Delf Maria. 1985. "'Jennifer and Her Barbies': A Contextual Analysis of the Child Playing Barbie Dolls." *Canadian Folklore Canadien* 7(1–2): 111–20.

Hollander, Anne. 1994. *Sex and Suits: The Evolution of Modern Dress.* New York: Kodansha Press.

Houlbrooke, Ralph. 1998. *Death, Religion, and the Family in England, 1480–1750.* New York: Oxford University Press.

Hughes, Diane Owens. 1992. "Regulating Women's Fashion." In *A History of Women in the West: Silences of the Middle Ages.* Ed. Christiane Klapisch-Zuber, 136–58. Cambridge: Harvard University Press.

Hult, David. 1988. "Roaming Gnomes." *Australian Folklore,* March (2): 87–92.

Hunt, John Dixon. 1999. "Approaches (New and Old) to Garden History." In *Perspectives on Garden Histories.* Ed. Michel Conan, 77–90. Washington: Dumbarton Oaks Research Library and Collection.

Huxley, Anthony. 1998. *An Illustrated History of Gardening.* New York: Lyons Press.

Inness, Sherrie A. 1999. "Barbie Gets a Bum Rap." In *The Barbie Chronicles: A Living Doll Turns Forty.* Ed. Yona Zeldis McDonough, 177–81. New York: Touchstone.

Irigaray, Luce. 1977. *This Sex Which Is Not One.* Ithaca: Cornell University Press.

Jackson, John Brinckerhoff. 1980. *The Necessity for Ruins and Other Topics.* Amherst: University of Massachusetts Press.

Jackson, Kenneth T. 1985. *Crabgrass Frontier: The Suburbanization of the United States.* New York: Oxford University Press.

Jagger, Alison M., and Susan R. Bordo. 1989. *Gender/Body/Knowledge: Feminist Reconstructions of Being and Knowing.* New Brunswick: Rutgers University Press.

Jekyll, Gertrude. 1982 (1918). *Garden Ornament.* Woodbridge, Suffolk: Antique Collectors' Club Ltd.

Jenkins, Virginia Scott. 1994. *The Lawn: A History of an American Obsession.* Washington: Smithsonian Institution Press.

Jones, Michael Owen. 1987. *Exploring Folk Art: Twenty Years of Thought on Craft, Work, and Aesthetics.* Logan: Utah State University Press.

———. 1994. "How Do You Get Inside the Art of Outsiders?" In *The Artist Outsider: Creativity and the Boundaries of Culture.* Ed. Michael D. Hall and Eugene W. Metcalf, Jr., 313–30. Washington: Smithsonian Institution Press.

Jones, Wendy Singer. 1999. "Barbie's Body Project." In *The Barbie Chronicles: A Living Doll Turns Forty.* Ed. Yona Zeldis McDonough, 91–107. New York: Touchstone.

Jordan, Ellen, and Angela Cowan. 1998. "Warrior Narratives in the Kindergarten Classroom: Renegotiating the Social Contract?" In *Men's Lives.* Ed. Michael S. Kimmel and Michael A. Messner, 127–40. Boston: Allyn and Bacon.

Jordan, Terry G., Jon T. Kilpinen, and Charles F. Gritzner. 1997. *The Mountain West: Interpreting the Folk Landscape.* Baltimore: Johns Hopkins University Press.

Katz, Jack. 1988. *Seductions of Crime: Moral and Sensual Attractions in Doing Evil.* New York: Basic Books.

Kimmel, Michael. 1996. *Manhood in America: A Cultural History.* New York: Free Press.

———. 2000a. *The Gendered Society.* New York: Oxford University Press.

———, ed. 2000b. *The Gendered Society Reader.* New York: Oxford University Press.

Kristeva, Julia. 1982. *Powers of Horror.* New York: Columbia University Press.

———. 1984. *Revolution in Poetic Language.* New York: Columbia University Press.

Kselman, Thomas A. 1993. *Death and the Afterlife in Modern France.* Princeton: Princeton University Press.

Lamb, Sharon. 2001. *The Secret Lives of Girls: What Good Girls Really Do—Sex Play, Aggression, and Their Guilt.* New York: Free Press.

Lang, Kristy. 1997. "Garden Guerrillas Go to War on the Gnome Front." London *Sunday Times,* 2 Nov., n.p.

Langley, William. 2000. "Gnome Kidnappers Strip French Gardens." London *Sunday Telegraph,* 21 May, 28.

Lau, Kimberly J. 1999. "Serial Logic: Folklore and Difference in the Age of Feel-Good Multiculturalism." *Journal of American Folklore* 113(447): 70–82.

Leighton, Ann. 1976. *American Gardens in the Eighteenth Century: "For Use or for Delight."* Boston: Houghton Mifflin.

Levinas, Emmanuel. 1996. "Reality and Its Shadow." In *The Levinas Reader.* Ed. Séan Hand, 129–43. Oxford: Blackwell.

Levine, Lawrence W. 1988. *Highbrow/Lowbrow: The Emergence of Cultural Hierarchy in America.* Cambridge: Harvard University Press.

Lord, M. G. 1994. *Forever Barbie.* New York: Avon Books.

Lynch, Kenneth. 1979. *Garden Ornaments.* Wilton: Canterbury Publishing.

Marsden, Michael T. 1995. "Dressing the Goose: Anthropomorphizing Yard Art of Northwest Ohio." *Popular Culture Review* 6(1): 53–60.

Martin, Emily. 1987. *The Woman in the Body: A Cultural Analysis of Reproduction.* Boston: Beacon Press.

McClary, Andrew. 1997. *Toys with Nine Lives: A Social History of American Toys.* North Haven: Linnet Books.

McManners, John. 1981. *Death and the Enlightenment: Changing Attitudes toward Death among Christians and Unbelievers in Eighteenth-Century France.* New York: Oxford University Press.

Michlig, John. 1998. *G.I. Joe: The Complete Story of America's Favorite Man of Action.* San Francisco: Chronicle Books.

Miedzian, Myriam. 1991. *Boys Will Be Boys: Breaking the Link between Masculinity and Violence.* New York: Doubleday.

Mitchell, Claudia, and Jacquelin Reid-Walsh. 1995. "And I Want to Thank You, Barbie: Barbie as a Site for Cultural Interrogation." Review of *Mondo Barbie* (Ebersole and Peabody). *Review of Education/Pedagogy/Cultural Studies* 17(2): 143–55.

Modra, Ronald C., and M. B. Roberts. 1998. *Garish Gardens, Outlandish Lawns.* Minocqua, Wis.: Willow Creek Press.

Motz, Marilyn Ferris. 1983. "'I Want to Be a Barbie Doll When I Grow Up': The Cultural Significance of the Barbie Doll." In *Popular Culture Reader.* Ed. Christopher

D. Geist and John G. Nachbar, 122–36. Bowling Green: Bowling Green University Press.

Mukerji, Chandra. 1997. *Territorial Ambitions and the Gardens of Versailles*. New York: Cambridge University Press.

Murphy, Peter F. 2001. *Studs, Tools, and the Family Jewels: Metaphors Men Live By*. Madison: University of Wisconsin Press.

Nahoum-Grappe, Véronique. 1993. "The Beautiful Woman." In *A History of Women: Renaissance and Enlightenment Paradoxes*. Ed. Natalie Zemon Davis and Arlette Farge, 85–100. Cambridge: Harvard University Press.

Nilsen, Alleen Pace. 1991. "Sexism in English: A 1990s Update." In *The Shape of Reason*. Ed. John T. Gage, 228–37. New York: Macmillan.

Nochlin, Linda. 1972. "Eroticism and Female Imagery in Nineteenth-Century Art." In *Woman as Sex Object: Studies in Erotic Art, 1730–1970*. Ed. Thomas B. Hess and Linda Nochlin, 8–15. New York: Newsweek.

Norton, Kevin I., Timothy S. Olds, Scott Olive, and Stephen Dank. 1996. "Ken and Barbie at Life Size." *Sex Roles* 34: 287–94.

O'Brien, Richard. 1990. *The Story of American Toys: From Puritans to the Present*. New York: Abbeville Press.

Ockman, Carol. 1999. "Barbie Meets Bougereau." In *The Barbie Chronicles: A Living Doll Turns Forty*. Ed. Yona Zeldis McDonough, 75–88. New York: Touchstone.

Oring, Elliott. 1992. *Jokes and Their Relations*. Lexington: University Press of Kentucky.

Ots, Angela, and Paul Doherty. 1996. "Victim Finds Healing Gnomes." Wellington, N.Z., *Evening Post*, 14 Dec., 17.

Padus, Emrika. 1986. "Do War Toys Make Sense? Two Top Experts Debate." *Good Toys*, Fall, 26–28.

Paradkar, Bageshree. 2000. "Stuff Gnome Sweet." *Toronto Star*, 20 May, n.p.

Peiss, Kathy. 1998. *Hope in a Jar: The Making of America's Beauty Culture*. New York: Metropolitan Books.

P.H.S. 1996. "All Ungnome." *The* (London) *Times*, 9 Aug., n.p.

Plumptre, George. 1989. *Garden Ornament: Five Hundred Years of History and Practice*. London: Thames and Hudson.

Pocius, Gerald L. 1995. "Art." *Journal of American Folklore* 108(430): 413–31.

Pollack, William. 1999. *Real Boys: Rescuing Our Sons from the Myths of Boyhood*. New York: Henry Holt.

Pollan, Michael. 1991. *Second Nature: A Gardener's Education*. New York: Dell Publishing.

Pope, Harrison G., Jr., Roberto Olivardia, and Amanda Gruber. 1999. "Evolving Ideals of Male Body Image as Seen through Action Toys." *International Journal of Eating Disorders* 26(1): 65–72.

Preston, Cathy. 1996. "Cultural Politics: Angel Trees in Boulder and Panty Trees in Beaver Creek." Unpublished paper presented at the annual meeting of the American Folklore Society, Pittsburgh.

Price, Jennifer. 1999. *Flight Maps: Adventures with Nature in Modern America*. New York: Basic Books.

Proust, Marcel. 1982. *Remembrance of Things Past*. New York: Knopf.

Ragon, Michel. 1983. *The Space of Death*. Charlottesville: University Press of Virginia.

Rand, Erica. 1995. *Barbie's Queer Accessories*. Durham: Duke University Press.

Richardson, Paul. 1997. "Keep the Gnome Fires Burning." *The* (London) *Times,* 18 Oct., n.p.

Ringle, Ken. 2000. "Glue That Works." *Washington Post,* 30 Dec., C1.

Robinson, David. 1995. *Saving Graces: Images of Women in European Cemeteries*. New York: W. W. Norton.

———. 1996. *Beautiful Death: Art of the Cemetery*. New York: W. W. Norton.

Rose, Carol. 1996. *Spirits, Fairies, Leprechauns, and Goblins: An Encyclopedia*. New York: Penguin Studio.

Rosenzweig, David. 2001. "Open Season on Barbie." *International Herald Tribune,* 15 Aug., n.p.

Ross, Marty. 2000. "Gnomes Loom Large in the History of Gardens." *San Diego Union-Tribune,* 22 Oct., I26.

Ryden, Kent C. 2001. *Landscape with Figures: Nature and Culture in New England*. Iowa City: University of Iowa Press.

Sage, Adam. 2000. "Parisians Discover Discreet Charm of Bourgeois Gnomes." *The* (Montreal) *Gazette,* 28 March, B5.

Sanders, Scott Russell. 1991. *Secrets of the Universe: Scenes from the Journey Home*. Boston: Beacon Press.

Santelmo, Vincent. 1997. *The Complete Encyclopedia to G.I. Joe*. St. Iola, Wis.: Krause Publications.

Santino, Jack. 1992a. "The Folk Assemblage of Autumn: Tradition and Creativity in Halloween Folk Art." In *Folk Art and Art Worlds*. Ed. John Michael Vlach and Simon J. Bronner, 151–69. Logan: Utah State University Press.

———. 1992b. "Yellow Ribbons and Seasonal Flags: The Folk *Assemblage* of War." *Journal of American Folklore* 105(415): 19–33.

———. 1994. *All around the Year: Holidays and Celebrations in American Life*. Urbana: University of Illinois Press.

———. 1996. *New Old-Fashioned Ways: Holidays and Popular Culture*. Knoxville: University of Tennessee Press.

———. 1999. "Public Protest and Popular Style: Resistance from the Right in Northern Ireland and South Boston." *American Anthropologist* 101(3): 515–28.

———. 2001. *Signs of War and Peace: Social Conflict and the Use of Public Symbols in Northern Ireland*. New York: Palgrave.

Schellmann, Jörg, and Joséphine Benecke. 1988. *Christo Prints and Objects, 1963–1987*. New York: Abbeville Press.

Schroeder, Fred E. H. 1993. *Front Yard America: The Evolution and Meanings of a Vernacular Domestic Landscape*. Bowling Green: Bowling Green State University Popular Press.

Shapiro, Sam, Edward R. Schlesinger, and Robert E. L. Nesbitt, Jr. 1968. *Infant, Perinatal, Maternal, and Childhood Mortality in the United States*. Cambridge: Harvard University Press.

Shapiro, Susan. 1999. "My Mentor, Barbie." In *The Barbie Chronicles: A Living Doll Turns Forty*. Ed. Yona Zeldis McDonough, 121–24. New York: Touchstone.

Sheehy, Colleen J. 1998. *The Flamingo in the Garden: American Yard Art and the Vernacular Landscape*. New York: Garland Publishing.

Singleton, Esther. 1927. *Dolls*. New York: Payson and Clarke.

Sloane, David Charles. 1991. *The Last Great Necessity: Cemeteries in American History.* Baltimore: Johns Hopkins University Press.

Smith, Alison. 1996. *The Victorian Nude: Sexuality, Morality, and Art.* New York: Manchester University Press.

Smith, Mary Riley. 1991. *The Front Garden: New Approaches to Landscape Design.* Boston: Houghton Mifflin.

Snyder, Ellen Marie. 1992. "Innocents in a Worldly World: Victorian Children's Gravemarkers." In *Cemeteries and Gravemarkers: Voices of American Culture.* Ed. Richard E. Meyer, 11–29. Logan: Utah State University Press.

Solomon-Godeau, Abigail. 1997. *Male Trouble: A Crisis in Representation.* New York: Thames and Hudson.

Spirago, Francis. 1921. *The Catechism Explained.* Rockford: Tan Books and Publishers.

Stahl, Sandra K. Dolby. 1977. "The Personal Narrative as Folklore." *Journal of the Folklore Institute* 14(1–2): 9–30.

Stern, Susan. 1998. *Barbie Nation: An Unauthorized Tour.* 54 min. New Day Films. Videocassette.

Stern, Sydney Ladensohn, and Ted Schoenhaus. 1990. *Toyland: The Highstakes Game of the Toy Industry.* Chicago: Contemporary Books.

Storey, John. 1998. *An Introduction to Cultural Theory and Popular Culture.* Athens: University of Georgia Press.

Swain, Pauline. 1997. "Who Killed Good Taste? Gnome Lore." *The* (Wellington, N.Z.) *Dominion,* 18 Sept., 11.

Terwilliger, Cate. 2000. "Saints, Gnomes Grow on You." *Denver Post,* 22 July, F1.

Thacker, Christopher. 1979. *The History of Gardens.* Berkeley: University of California Press.

Thomas, Dana. 1997. "Gnome Is Where the Heart Is; In France, a Mania for Elfin Ornaments." *Washington Post,* 12 July, C5.

Thomas, Jeannie B. 1997a. "Dumb Blondes, Dan Quayle, and Hillary Clinton: Gender, Sexuality, and Stupidity in Jokes." *Journal of American Folklore* 110(437): 277–313.

———. 1997b. *Featherless Chickens, Laughing Women, and Serious Stories.* Charlottesville: University Press of Virginia.

———. 2000a. "Ride 'Em, Barbie Girl: Commodifying Folklore, Place and the Exotic." In *Worldviews and the American West: The Life of the Place Itself.* Ed. Polly Stewart, Steve Siporin, C. W. Sullivan III, and Suzi Jones, 65–86. Logan: Utah State University Press.

———. 2000b. "Stone Angels, Naked Mourners, and Various Virgins: Statues, Legends, and the Gendering of Intimacy." *Contemporary Legend* 3: 127–60.

Thomas, Jeannie B., and Doug Enders. 2000. "'Bluegrass and White Trash': A Case Study Concerning the Name 'Folklore' and Class Bias." *Journal of Folklore Research* 37(1): 23–52.

Thompson, Stith. 1955–58. *Motif-Index of Folk-Literature.* Copenhagen: Rosenkilde and Bagger.

Tosa, Marco. 1998. *Barbie: Four Decades of Fashion, Fantasy, and Fun.* New York: Harry N. Abrams.

"Twin Fates (and Dates) for Barbie and Kato." 1999. *Time* magazine, 22 March, 121.

Turner, Victor. 1967. *The Forest of Symbols: Aspects of Ndembu Ritual.* Ithaca: Cornell University Press.

Uhlenhuth, Karen. 1997. "New and Improved, Not-So-Busty Barbie." *Kansas City Star,* 18 Nov., A1.

Urla, Jacqueline, and Alan Swedlund. 1995. "The Anthropometry of Barbie: Unsettling Ideas of the Feminine in Popular Culture." In *Deviant Bodies: Critical Perspectives in Science and Popular Culture.* Ed. Jennifer Terry and Jacqueline Urla, 277–313. Bloomington: Indiana University Press.

Warner, Marina. 1983. *Alone of All Her Sex: The Myth and Cult of the Virgin Mary.* New York: Vintage Books.

Wesmacott, Richard. 1992. *African-American Gardens and Yards.* Knoxville: University of Tennessee Press.

Wilson, Peter Lamborn. 1994. *Angels: Messengers of the Gods.* London: Thames and Hudson.

Yocom, Margaret R. 1993. "'Awful Real': Dolls and Development in Rangeley, Maine." In *Feminist Messages: Coding in Women's Folk Culture.* Ed. Joan Newlon Radner, 126–54. Urbana: University of Illinois Press.

Yoe, Craig. 1994. *The Art of Barbie: Artists Celebrate the World's Favorite Doll.* New York: Workman Publishing.

Young, Katharine A., ed. 1993. *Bodylore.* Knoxville: University of Tennessee Press.

Index

Jeannie Banks Thomas is an associate professor in the English department and Folklore Program at Utah State University. She is the author of *Featherless Chickens, Laughing Women, and Serious Stories,* which received the Köngäs-Miranda Prize for outstanding work in gender studies.

The University of Illinois Press
is a founding member of the
Association of American University Presses.

Composed in 9.5/13 Stone Serif
with Stone Sans and Modula Tall display
by Jim Proefrock
at the University of Illinois Press
Designed by Dennis Roberts
Manufactured by Thomson-Shore, Inc.

University of Illinois Press
1325 South Oak Street
Champaign, IL 61820-6903
www.press.uillinois.edu